NORTH AND SOUTH

Marek A. Cichocki

NORTH AND SOUTH

On Polish Politics, History, and Culture

Translated from the Polish by Charles S. Kraszewski

Angelicum University Press
Fundacja Świętego Mikołaja
Rome—Warsaw 2024

Angelicum University Press
Fundacja Świętego Mikołaja
Rome—Warsaw 2024

Published by the St. John Paul II Institute of Culture at the Pontifical University of St. Thomas Aquinas in Rome—Angelicum.
Founded at the Angelicum, the St. John Paul II Institute of Culture is run in cooperation with the Saint Nicholas Foundation.
www.angelicum.it/institutes/st-john-paul-ii-institute-of-culture

Angelicum University Press
Largo Angelicum, 1—00184 Rome, Italy

Fundacja Świętego Mikołaja
Koszykowa 24/7—00553 Warsaw, Poland
redakcja@teologiapolityczna.pl—www.teologiapolityczna.pl
www.mikolaj.org.pl

ISBN: 978-83-67065-62-7
Managing editor: Adam Talarowski
Copy edited by Małgorzata Broniewska, Agnieszka Maria Gernand
Designed and typeset by Katarzyna Solecka
Cover design by Michał Strachowski, Dariusz Karłowicz

This book has been published with the support of the ©POLAND Translation Program

TABLE OF CONTENTS

THE SECRET MAP OF EUROPE

Excess of unity may be due to barbarism and may lead to tyranny.
—T.S. Eliot, *Notes Toward the Definition of Culture.*[1]

North and South

Does there exist some secret map of Europe? Such a one that, should we be able to decipher it, would lead us along the hidden paths of our continent, overgrown with the ages? And tell us who we are? Or who we cannot be?

When one speaks of Europe today, one's attention is focused, primarily, on the unification of the continent. We busy ourselves chiefly with the question: to what extent does our continent constitute a unity, or in other words, under what conditions might we constitute such a thing, how much is still lacking us to at last unify completely—for such is the goal that indicates a horizon full of historical happiness—and what are the obstacles that stand in our way thereto? This political and intellectual compulsion of unity, which, it cannot be denied, possesses a certain amount of practical logic, but which draws its strength from a terror of divisions, has, in effect, killed off in contemporary Europe our ability to notice and understand differences, and along with that, the potential for a critical recognition of ourselves and the complicated character of our own identity. This compulsion, or duress, of unity has not only become a sort of placebo, but also a comfortable rationalisation for our flight from our own selves. It permits, and even demands, that we turn our eyes away from ourselves. It is for this reason that contemporary Europe has become, politically and intellectually, boring and empty; there are some who will even compare her to an old, decrepit woman. Meanwhile, from a cognitive perspective, division and differences are more interesting. And these constitute another, and, as far as culture is concerned, a more important, side of the question concerning the essence of Europe.

The lines of division which crisscross our continent determine our present consciousness. They are the basis for varied behaviors and different understandings of the world. They coalesce into something of a secret map of Europe. For the inhabitants of East-Central Europe, the chief division, which still imposes itself as something obvious and all-important, is the division into East and West. But more and more it seems to me that its gravity arises, above all, from the fact that we are still constantly lacking in strength sufficient to consider the experiences of the last two hundred years from a distance. It is for this very reason that this division forms so fundamentally the present consciousness of Europeans, our imagination and aspirations, our way of looking at as well as our place in Europe. The unjust post-Yalta order, our geographical location, so disastrous in effect, between German and Russian Imperialism in the nineteenth and twentieth centuries; on the one hand aspirations toward modernity, and on the other, a critique of modernisation—the lion's share of these questions, which so engage the contemporary imagination (and Poland is no exception to the rule here; perhaps it is to be found most vividly here) all have their justification in the continuing division of Europe into East and West. We constantly feel ourselves constrained to self-definition and explanation according to these two basic tendencies, in reference or in opposition to one or the other of them. Now we are closer to the West, and now again to the East: "I ought to go and hang, I'll / in the gentle breezes dangle / now toward the West and now the East / *das ewig Polnische*,"[2] as Gałczyński once wrote with his characteristic gallows humour.

Actually, this division has been decisive for European identity for over three hundred years—especially as far as the fate of the nations in our part of the continent is concerned. It has created the impression of a fixed, unchanging framework of history and geography; the framework in which our eternal Polish destiny is played out.

Yet besides the division into East and West there exists an even deeper division, one much more important for the European identity, for an understanding of what Europe is and how it came about, and simultaneously, one that is key to an understanding of Polishness and its indissoluble links to the formation of European culture. This is the division between North and South. Our Europe was born from this clash of North and South, a division that for centuries determined the spiritual, cultural, and political development of the Old Continent. The demarcation line between North and South, geographically speaking, is more or less consistent with the lines traced by Rhine and Danube, and thus, the historical border reached, in a political sense, by the ancient civilisation of Christianised *romanitas*. This border will both divide and unite the continent throughout history. From Arminius, the chief of the Germanic Cherusci, who in the Teutoburg forest destroyed twenty thousand legionnaires under Varus, through Charlemagne, who had been king of the Franks, but became the first emperor of reborn Latin, Western Europe, to the subsequent Germanic emperors who strove to obtain leadership over the Western world as a new Rome. Moving forward, the division into North and South can be noted in many historical events of key significance to Europe. The various renaissances, the Reformation, the Napoleonic wars waged against Alexander I, that great antagonist of the Emperor of the French, and at last, the two world wars understood as a conflict between the Latin civilization of Europe and new barbarisms. Even the present crisis of the project of European integration, the European Union, once more uncovers to our eyes the vitality of this ancient division of the continent as the chief fissure of the Eurozone runs between the countries of the North and those of the South.

Where, in this division, is Poland to be found? Right in the very middle.

From her very beginnings, Poland found herself in the orbit of the basic division between North and South, which created both Europe and European culture. Polishness springs from this division and the constant attempts at overcoming it. It is for this reason, among others, that today we on the banks of the Wisła (Vistula) may gaze in wonder at authentic exemplars of the architecture of the Italian Renaissance without having to take the trouble of travelling to Florence or Rome. As a matter of fact, as I see it, Polishness cannot be understood at all if one abstracts it from this question. Indeed, something definitely has changed over the course of the centuries. In the eighteenth century, on the Old Continent, there occurred a violent shift of direction, and the division between North and South was questioned to a great degree by the Enlightenment (the anti-Christian attitude of which is not without significance here). The West became reorganized according to the new secularized virtues of rationalism, while at the same time it became fashionable to speak of "Eastern Europe" as a sort of orientalism opposed to rational Western Europe. This overturning of vectors coincided with a deep crisis in Polishness, which led to the partitioning of the First Republic. At this historical moment, due to a new division between West and East, Poland ceased to be a country of the North and was cut off from its Southern roots, becoming instead a region subject to the imperial politics of Berlin and Petersburg. In this way, it disappeared as a European entity. It was with undisguised satisfaction that the Prussian King Frederick II, whose grandfather still spoke fluent Polish, summed up the new situation by calling the Poles the "Iroquois of Europe"—i.e., a people who found themselves beyond the pale of Western European civilization.

The examples and arguments I adduce here allow us to formulate the thesis that Poland is capable of greatness; that she has a consciousness of her own being and her basic role in the culture and civilization of Europe (and thus may be, simply put, herself), above all when she is able to write herself into the basic, ancient division between North and South. On the other hand, she falls into non-being, becoming a victim and subject of pressure exerted by outside forces, when she finds herself set on the line dividing East and West.

Barbarians at the Gates

Since the division of Europe into North and South is so decisive, indeed crucial to our understanding of Europeanness and Polishness as well, it would be worthwhile to give ourselves the trouble of finding an answer to the question—*what exactly is it?* What, in the history and culture of Europe, constitutes the geographical differentiation between North and South? For, as it seems, this has a deep and very concrete significance. Above all, it touches upon the problem of form. It has to do with one's relationship to form; more precisely, with the acquisition of the ability that would allow one, through form, to endow human life—and along with this, the world in which man lives—with a concrete character. At the intersection of North and South different ways of dealing with this problem begin to take shape, through varied forms of life and activity. The most various manners of adapting form appear, as well as different symptoms of rebellion against said form. The entirety of European culture is constituted of just such attempts, and it is they that provide the secret map of Europe with its contours—on the basis of which map we are still able to uncover the path toward the emergence of the spiritual and material sense of Europe as a special place in the world. They also determine the continent's historical, and contemporary, inner similarities and differences.

Without the collision of North and South, the capability of forming different aspects of life in general would not exist. The grand process of collision and permeation of North and South that created Europe got underway with a gigantic earthquake: the great migration of the peoples: the migration of the barbarian tribes, above all the Huns and the Germans, who rolled through the continent over the space of several centuries. This was a world in decline, the civilisation of *romanitas* breaking down, and yet what a splendid world it was! A world ordered by functioning laws and institutions, which provided a sense of comprehensibility, of justice, and peace; a world in which people could live comfortably in their villas or homesteads surrounded by open farms and orchards; a world traversed by a network of roads, aqueducts, and other irrigation systems; a world of domesticated evil held in check by the paragraphs of the law, and a world in which people were guided in their life by the precepts of ethics.

From the point of view of *romanitas*, real evil was located on the other side of the dividing line, in the North, in the barbarian world—beyond the *limes*, that is, beyond the chief boundary guarded by the Roman legions who kept watch lest elementary chaos intrude upon the area of peace. The barbarians were not evil by law, nor an ethical evil. They constituted an ontological evil—a vacuum, decomposition, darkness, an un-world. Even their language, in contrast to Latin, seemed an empty gibberish. And yet, the perforation of that ontological frontier between civilization and the barbarian un-world did not so much determine the final decline of the world of *romanitas*, as rather its rebirth in a new form. For although the barbarians brought with them destruction, they represented above all strength and power lacking in the form that characterized the civilization of *romanitas*.

They were in essence an empty might, a dynamic element, however lacking in any capabilities of creating a reasonable, just order, peace, or security. Although theirs was a blind strength, unchannelled, potentially capable of destroying everything it met upon its way, still history turned out completely otherwise. The destructive power of the barbarians, encroaching upon the Roman world between the fourth and sixth centuries, did not sweep *romanitas* away from the face of the earth; it did not destroy the world of Roman form, but rested upon it, allowed itself to be in a certain sense seduced by its beauty and grandeur, to accept, in the end, the heritage of Rome as its own. It did not destroy it, it adapted it. This came to be because in the depths of that ontological vacuum of barbarity there was hidden the natural ability to convert, the instinctive directioning toward that which is essential and valuable, proper to each and every human person.

The assumption of the form of Roman civilization was of epochal significance for the barbarians themselves, as it transformed them into people conscious of their ontological vacuum and their search of a new shape. This had a bearing on the character of European culture as a whole. From this perspective, one may look upon contemporary Europe as a world inhabited by those who were once barbarians, but who constructed their culture by overcoming ontological evil thanks to the Southern form which they adopted and adapted. This means that still, continually, somewhere in the depths of the consciousness and activities of contemporary Europeans lays that barbarism, that blind power capable of destroying everything it comes across in its path. The heritage of the Roman form is indispensable to the success of the historical process of barbarian inculturalization. Thanks to it, blind force could be transformed into a new European civilization with its enduring forms of existence—varied societies, states, traditions. The heritage of Rome also provided the barbarians with the possibility of acquiring wisdom, self-knowledge, and at last—what is arguably the most important thing—the opportunity of ethical self-consideration and transformation into fully formed persons.

However, all of this, which must be kept unconditionally in mind, would most likely not have been possible without Christianity. And not only because *romanitas* had been Christianized earlier, long before the barbarians broke through the Northern *limes*, but also because Christianity awoke the barbarians to the significance and real power of conversion. Thanks to Christianity they understood what conversion is, upon what it is based, and why their inner transformation is necessary. Christianity opened the barbarians to the Roman form and provided them with the opportunity of self-knowledge, and further, of salvation.

The Barbarian Converted

What makes Europeans is the ability of dealing with the problem of form. However, this is not at all a manifestation of practical power or human might, but rather of an ethical ability upon which depends the choosing of the Good. So in essence we are speaking here of the capability for *metanoia*, conversion.

Such indeed was the fate of the barbarians who came into contact with the Roman form of *romanitas*, thanks to which, through the offices of Christianity, they underwent a transformation to become contemporary Europeans. We are speaking here of a phenomenon which must have very deep theological bases: what exactly is that capability for transformation? What is the ability to convert, which continually endures, present in our European culture and identity, without which we would not be in a position to accept any concrete form or build any sort of civilization, but would remain alone with our destructive, blind power that in effect always leads to the void?

In order to answer that question, it is worth reaching for the example of St. Augustine, the bishop of Hippo. He was given to live during the ages of decline of *romanitas* and he himself experienced the destructive power of the barbarians, too. He died in a Hippo under siege by the Vandals, who, possessed by a frenzy of destruction, had been devastating the western coast of North Africa.

According to Augustine, creation is nothing other than an act of formation, a certain capability to bestow upon matter some sort of form. Of course, the very essence of that formation is found in the divine act of the creation of the world. In it we may recognize certain directives as to how we are to understand human activity, that is, our acts of creation—how man forms and creates the reality that surrounds him, and also why it is that in doing so that he must struggle all the while against recalcitrant matter. As is well known, St. Augustine was vitally interested in the problem of matter, especially in the context of his quarrel with the Manicheans in which he was involved for most of his life. He strove to eradicate the view, so harmful in his opinion—and in the opinion of all of Christianity as well—according to which matter is something in opposition to human creation, and divine creation as well, due to which it acquires some sort of wondrous autonomy, indeed is raised to the rank of an anti-deity—by which means the Manicheans strove to explain the phenomenon of evil.

And so St. Augustine poses the question to himself: what is matter, and why is it that it puts up such resistance? In Book XII of his *Confessions*[3] he cites a beautiful passage from Genesis (which in Jakub Wujek's translation has a very apt and engaging ring): we read there that before creation, before the act of creation, the earth was empty and void. The Bishop of Hippo comes to the conclusion that, despite what the Manicheans assert, there is nothing demonic to matter at all; it possesses no autonomous, destructive strength. The problem rests in that an autonomous destructive strength, which is recalcitrant and does not allow us to encompass reality in an ordered, rational manner, does not allow us to form it—it is empty, void, because it gives us nothing and is incapable of creating anything itself. This, actually, is that void of blind power, which we see in violent death and destruction, that fills us with the greatest horror.

According to St. Augustine, evil is a void, nothing, a lack—to put it in other words: a vacuum, or chaos—un-being. Now, if we consider the acts of God's creation from this perspective, His creation of our world, as well as when we consider the acts of creation that each of us takes in hand—every single person who has ever lived—we see the true sense of what we are doing. In creating the world from nothing, God transformed evil into good. Through His act of creation, we have received a clue as to how we are to proceed in our own activity. Human action possesses, each and every time, a deeply ethical dimension, because man is not capable of creating anything enduring, meaningful, or comprehensible if at the bases of his act the ethical decision is not found, which constitutes a choice of the good and a turning away from evil, that is, from the void. Only with this provided for can people shape reality, create a world, order it, and set it in motion—or also make it into a historical reality. St. Augustine says quite plainly that only through formation, shaping, does our world live in time and is a historical world; it is due to this alone that some sort of yesterday, today, and tomorrow exist. But at the foundations of it all lies the ethical decision of man—choosing good and rejecting evil.

Let us now return to the division of Europe into North and South. If we continue to follow St. Augustine's thought, we can plainly see that this division refers to the acquisition of a capability for positive orientation to form, which becomes possible only thanks to this basic ethical decision taken by man when he turns toward the good. This choice allows us to have a positive effect on reality. And so one might say that form is nothing other than human acts of creation, which in practice signify the ability to approach reality in a positive way. Here we are not speaking of any strength or efficacy of those acts, but above all, of their ethical dimension, something that we—in our contemporary culture—quite frequently neglect. I am pointing out the ethical dimension because such is the effect of inner conversion. The struggle with form as well as the division of North and South, fundamental to this issue, will be for this reason especially straitly bound to Christianity, which showed us the sense of conversion. In the history of Europe, this means the conversion of the barbarians from the North who, coming into contact with the order of the South, come to recognize their inner void. They recognize their evil, thanks to which they are able to turn away from it and obtain the capability to positively shape reality.

Poland as a Form of Being

It is this very capability of conversion to the good, its positive recognition and acceptance—something that we shall find even at the very bottom depths of the barbarian void—which constitutes the foundation and essence of European culture; the foundation, without which said culture cannot even be imagined. At the same time, this capability constitutes the essence of Polishness. This special characteristic enabled the European communities and nations to shape their own, unique manners of being. The sense of the significance of form, and respect for form, lead to the bestowal of form upon matter that is anything but homogeneous; all too concrete, but for that very reason multisignificative and chaotic—historical reality. It allows us to tame it, and to separate out from this mass the nations and cultures of Europe, our own, which have their own "style and beauty." And that's how it's been from age to age.

The only thing is that we, Poles, met with catastrophe as we went along our particular road. According to Gombrowicz, in the eighteenth century Poland "fell out" of its own form. The Saxon years are a symbol of that horrid Polish fall, which for the author of *Trans-Atlantyk* were an event so poignant and extreme, that—as he put it—never before had Poland brushed up so close against Hell. There is something important to be found in this remark—a warning that chaos, terse, earthy realism, and disdain for the autonomy of form always bring us near that terrible yawning void described by St. Augustine. "Any thought about Poland and the Poles is not worth much if it bypasses the period of Saxon scurrility," says Gombrowicz, because it was in that very eighteenth century that the greatest "crisis of Polish beauty, which put us face-to-face with our Ugliness, our Profligacy... a century of sclerotic, senile old stiffening and at the same time, a dull unruliness, when the armistice between form and instinct had created a chasm."[4] We need to study that fall carefully, fully, in order to understand the Polish problem with form, the curse of weak Polish form. Very significant in this regard is the observation made of Poles by *Monsieur* Bernardin de Saint-Pierre, who arrived in Warsaw in 1764: "The ease with which they move from place to place imbues their acts with the stamp of impermanence, and in this very thing nearly all of their freedom finds its expression. There is no other people who so quickly forget an insult, but benefaction as well. The Pole is motivated by the matter at hand, with no regard paid to the future, and deriving no advantage from the lessons of the past."[5] Formless matter is deprived of beauty, of charm, and of the form of life. And therefore it seems that however much in the sixteenth century Poland possessed its own form and was capable of working at it, demonstrating an unwavering power of shaping it, following the experiences of the eighteenth century, it lost the same and has ever since been in search of how to regain it.

At the same time when Poles lost the most obvious instrument for the shaping of their own life—their state, another great transformation occurred in Europe herself. Above, we term this a complete overturning of vectors. The new definition of the West, proposed by the Enlightenment, as well as the discovery of orientalism (a mirror into which Western culture has been gazing ever since then, now with relish, and now with dread), made it so that the old division into North and South lost its instrumental power in favor of that of West and East. Along with this the very understanding of form and our attitude toward it changed completely as well. Instead of a conversion toward the good, which earlier constituted the *sine qua non* for the shaping of various forms of life in Europe, there appeared the desire of universal self-redemption, the self-perfection of humanity, comprehended as a type of mastery fulfilling itself in the promises of modernization. It is that which now provides the tools indispensable for the construction of the civilization of modernity, which will signify the final obliteration of Rome not only in the literal significance of the role of the Papacy but also Rome as a cultural point of orientation for barbarians, as well as the European axis of division into North and South. Christianity ceases to be redemptive, becoming instead a burden and a scandal. And *romanitas*, Roman form, becomes transformed into a dead history and an archeological site.

The division into West and East is, therefore, a symbol of modernization and the mastery in Europe of the barbarians, for whom form had ceased to be a method of conversion and became instead a tool for unconditional domination in the name of their own might. By deracinating themselves from their cultural sources, the paramount significance of which is uncovered only on the North-South line, the inhabitants of the Old Continent returned to the state of ignorant, though modern, barbarians, who wish to be a pattern and goal for their own selves. More powerful than all the gods of Olympus, and even the all-powerful and severe Yahweh of the Old Testament, the Europeans have constructed their barbarian empire in which no one will need conversion because everyone can be himself—a barbarian liberated from the rule of form. In this new European empire in which naïveté and optimism were so omnipresent during the nineteenth century, the Poles not only lost the certainty of their own form and their own state but also the source which constituted the distinctiveness and peculiarity of their form—the South. From then on, they could only choose and describe themselves in reference to two competing, contemporary, barbarian modernizations of West and East. Will they ever free themselves of this curse? Will they ever find the road back to their true roots, which lie in the South, in order once more to beautifully and surely work at their own form?

Endnotes

1. T.S. Eliot, *Notes Toward the Definition of Culture* (New York: Harcourt, Brace and Co., 1949), p. 49.
2. Konstanty Ildefons Gałczyński, "Das ewig Polnische." *Dzieła* (Works) Vol 1, *Poezje* (Warsaw: 1979), p. 433. The citation in Polish reads: "Najlepiej się powieszę, / wietrzyk mnie pokołysze, / raz na Wschód, raz na Zachód, / *das ewig Polnische.*"
3. Saint Augustine, *Confessions*, trans. T. Williams, Indianapolis/Cambridge 2019, Book XII, chapter 3, p. 235. *Translator's note*: the reference is to Genesis I:1–2 in the translation of Fr. Jakub Wujek, SJ (Kraków: 1599) which reads "Na początku stworzył Bóg niebo i ziemię. A ziemia była pusta i próżna i ciemności były nad głębokością, a Duch Boży unaszał się nad wodami" (In the beginning God created heaven, and earth. And the earth was void and empty, and darkness was upon the face of the deep; and the spirit of God moved over the waters). For an English translation of the salient text by St. Augustine, see: Saint Augustine, *Confessions* (London: Penguin, 1969), p. 282. Among other things, Augustine says here that "'the earth was invisible and without form' [...] a kind of deep abyss over which there was no light [...] it had no form."
4. W. Gombrowicz, *Diary*, trans. L. Vallee, Yale 2007, p. 276.
5. W. Zawadzki, ed., *Polska stanisławowska w oczach cudzoziemców* (Stanislavian Poland Through the Eyes of Foreigners), Warsaw 1963, p. 207.

WINCENTY

What sense is there to reading Kadłubek these days? What is the sense of even posing the question? The text of Master Wincenty (known as Kadłubek)—his *Kronika polska* (Polish Chronicle)—as well as the views it contains, have aroused extremely opposite reactions and evaluations for many ages now. These range from uncritical adoration, certainly at least partly motivated by the respect one has for the authority of the author, who was beatified in 1764 and is an object of veneration for pious Catholics, to complete scornful disdain or even jolly mockery, as we find in the *Myszeidos* (Mouseiad) of Bishop Ignacy Krasicki. The conflict flamed forth again, attaining perhaps its apogee at the beginning of the twentieth century when, in his 1904 book *Szkice historyczne XI wieku* (Historical Sketches of the Eleventh Century),[1] the Lwów art historian Tadeusz Wojciechowski cast into question Master Wincenty's account of the conflict between King Bolesław Śmiały (the Bold) and the Bishop of Kraków, St. Stanisław Szczepanowski. In reference to the martyrdom of St. Stanisław, one of the patron saints of Poland, Wojciechowski states, straight from the shoulder: "We now know that Kadłubek, as unable as he was to provide his reader with a single soberly formulated account of anything concerning the fatherland's history, was more than capable of perfectly creating, and inventing, the most various stories. What is more, one might point out several dozen examples of bald lies, made consciously and with aforethought." In his criticism of the glorification of the figure of St. Stanisław, which Master Wincenty carries out consistently in the text of his *Chronicle*, refusing the monarch any sort of excuse for his conduct in the quarrel with the bishop, Wojciechowski asserts that the only credible and reliable historical source for the matter is the chronicle written by Gallus Anonymous. Wojciechowski's book was awarded a prize by the Academy of Arts and Sciences (Akademia Umiejętności) in Kraków, but it also called down upon his head a veritable hurricane of criticism from the camp of "conservative" historians and journalists. In the exceptionally sharp debate that ensued, the weightiest, and stupidest, arguments were put forward, not excepting anti-Semitic brickbats and accusations of his "befouling the sanctities of the nation."[2] What we find interesting here is not so much the intensity of the quarrel—nor the character or weight of the arguments that erupted—but rather the line of division that appeared concerning Master Wincenty. Above all, the whole affair touched upon a patron saint of Poland, St. Stanisław, and chiefly the question of whether or not Bolesław Śmiały had any good reason to punish the bishop with death; whether or not the great martyr had been, perhaps, entangled in a conspiracy aimed at the king (as Wojciechowski asserts). This was not a novel question at the time, for Tadeusz Czacki put forth the very same thesis one hundred years before. And he was a very respected figure, a co-founder of the Society of the Friends of Science (Towarzystwo Przyjaciół Nauk) in Warsaw, who established the legendary lyceum at Krzemieniec.[3] And yet in the Wojciechowski case, Wincenty was wounded by such a ricochet as denied his work any value whatsoever. By the same token, his supporters were recognized to be representatives of some antagonistic opposite party, and Wojciechowski, under the pressure of a wave of often lavatorial criticism, prepared in answer thereto an article bearing the very suggestive title "Plemię Kadłubka" (The Tribe of Kadłubek).[4] In this manner, the author of the *Chronicle* became hostage to two opposing camps, which for some two hundred fifty years now have effectively organized public games in the Polish agora on such topics as: modernity, Europe, tradition, culture, history, and politics. Thus, for some, Master Wincenty will be an example of Polish anachronism, mythomania, and backwardness, while for the others—a representative of the sacred traditions of Polishness. Now, if we wish to move even a step forward in the question that interests us, we must first, quite simply, leave this quarrel behind us. Naturally, there are eminently good reasons for us to treat the text of Master Wincenty with a certain distance. These will be a historian's reasons, not at all in their boring, Positivist edition: the sort which has us repeat again and again the mantra of the objectivism of facts and the author's lack thereof. As a matter of fact, from this perspective, the most convincing critical arguments have been put forth by Paweł Jasienica, who is no run-of-the-mill historian, but someone quite exceptional in the Polish scholarly tradition. In the text of his "Antykronika" (Anti-Chronicle), which he had first intended to title even more pithily "Stracona szansa literatury polskiej" (Polish Literature's Lost Opportunity),[5] he rolls out the heavy artillery against Master Wincenty. First of all, he accuses him of: a lack of historical passion (his incomprehensible motives for not finishing the work), cheap showiness, a monstrously convoluted style (which among other things kills the authenticity of the narrative), and finally, something that betrays his provinciality, that is, his desire "at all costs to bring his work in line with the literary conventions accepted in the wider world."[6] Some of Jasienica's arguments are simply irrefutable. Master Wincenty does not seem to be a conscientious chronicler when set against a background both of earlier practitioners of the genre as well as those of his own day and age. He was rather a combination of the mediaeval *litteratus*, a "man of books," and the *homme de lettre*, the "man of the pen": in other words, a phenomenon characteristic of the twelfth century European "renaissance." As Jasienica incisively notes, the sort of early humanism we find in Master Wincenty sins by imitation. For he was conditioned by the essential circumstance of having become very familiar with the western center of mediaeval Europe, while later condemned to function on its periphery: "Wincenty, the son of Kadłub, studying in Bologna or Paris, in other words Roman Lutetia, must have been quite pained at the retardation of his fatherland," which resulted in "the West bedazzling Wincenty, and Wincenty bedazzling Wisłaland"[7] with varied literary and historical effect.

However, it is not my intent to establish the value of the *Chronicle* as history or chronicle-writing. I do not wish to argue the matter of—to what degree, or if at all—Master Wincenty was a historian or what value his text possesses for our knowledge of history. I would rather most like to "take this text away" from the historians. And since, in practice, this is impossible, I at least want (following Oswald Balzer) to draw a clear dividing line between the *Chronicle* as the *Chronica de gestis illustrium principum ac regum Poloniae*[8]—and thus a typical collection of stories concerning the deeds of the princes and kings of Poland (their activities in which the history of the nation is contained)—from the layer of political reflection found in the text and its general meditations on the essence of politics since I consider this matter to be something quite unjustly overlooked, indeed snubbed. To a certain degree following in the footsteps of Kazimierz Tymieniecki,[9] and independent of all doubts touching upon the historical layers, I would like to treat the *Chronicle* as the first text in the Polish tradition devoted to politics. Such a definition of the work, certainly a tempting one, as the first tract of political philosophy in the Polish tradition, would of course be something of an exaggeration. For indeed the layer of political reflection has no fully autonomous character; it is not a disquisition in the full sense of the word. His reflections on politics appear only as generalities, or as references to the classical tradition of concrete events. On the other hand, we do come across fragments in the *Chronicle* that clearly separate themselves from the historical layer to such an extent as seems to obtain for them the status of independently enunciated political thought. This can be seen, for example, in the significant fragment of the second book devoted to the treason of Zbigniew, and in the fourth and final book, which takes in hand the key question of royal succession and governmental continuity. As is well known, Master Wincenty did not hold himself aloof from politics. It is possible that he was entirely emotionally dependent upon it. He was, in short, a politically engaged man of the pen, whether or not, as a man of the book, educated abroad and fluent in Latin, he functioned as a "legal expert" in the circles of the prince's chancellery. And so, beyond his probable chancellery and notarial offices, he was a participant in the life of the court, which provided him with a close familiarity with the arcane ropes of Piast dynasty politics. It was such experiences as well as his entire baggage of classical literature, which accompany Wincenty during his writing of the *Chronicle* and make it so that in engaging with the work, we have to deal with a rich vein of political reflection of varying intensity. For this reason it is neither a coincidence nor a formality that the text of the *Chronicle* proper begins with a travesty of Cicero's *Oratio in Catilinam*.[10]

Myth as Foundation of Political Identity

There is no way of approaching the presence of political philosophy in the work of Master Wincenty without a proper consideration of the first book of said work. Traditionally, it is the very initial fragments of the *Chronicle*, as "fairy-story history," which have provided his critics with a pretext to attack the historical value of his writing. Indeed, we find here the most fantastic and indeed incredible narrative threads here: the Wawel dragon, the victorious struggles of the Poles against the Romans, Gauls, and the Greeks, the letter written to Aristotle by Alexander the Great concerning Krak, and the stories of Piast Kołodziej (the Wheelwright) as well as prince Popiel devoured by mice. Now, my task will be to prove that, although from the point of view of the contemporary historian, the text of the first book must seem a complete fantasy —and consequently, criticism thereof as a historical source is entirely well-deserved—still an analysis of the first ten chapters of the book from the perspective of political philosophy leads us to entirely different conclusions.

At the outset of the book we come across a phrase that is key to the text. In the dialogue between the worthy Archbishop Jan and Bishop Mateusz there falls a question, around which the entire conversation that follows will be formed: "At which period are we to think that the infancy of our legislation (*constitutiones*) had its beginning?"[11] The question brings in its wake various implications, and Master Wincenty will address them in various ways. At the outset, Jan also notes that "We [...] are moderns and are not possessed of the hoary knowledge of yesterday,"[12] for which reason—as we quickly come to know from the conversation as it develops—the concern is not with the determination of historical facts strictly understood, such as uncovering the circumstances of the rise of Polish statehood or the Piast government. Authentic, factual knowledge concerning these things is perhaps impossible to reconstruct—and there is much to indicate that this is the starting point chosen by author himself. So the question has a more general, speculative, reflective character. It is above all a fundamental question of beginnings and, in this sense, something that concerns the identity of the community—and as a question of *arche* it is of a strictly political nature, which fundamentally focusses our attention on the political subject. Of course, Jasienica is right when he suggests that Master Wincenty is not very much, or consistently, interested in searching out historical answers to the historical questions posed. This is never more evident than in this first book of the *Chronicle*. We find nothing here that would remind us of the characteristic tones of the introduction to Herodotus' *History*: "Herodotus, from Halicarnassus, here displays his enquiries."[13] There is no statement to be found such as "I, Master Wincenty from Kargów, here present the results of my studies into how the kingdom of the Piasts came about." It is, however, somewhat logical: we possess no "knowledge of yesterday," we are not in possession of such source material, we have no witnesses thereto. The very theme concerns mist-shrouded beginnings, sources, and this makes it so that the subject of our enquiry is rather a fairly broad field of matters associated with how we see ourselves, whence we derive who we are, how we understand the sense of our "birth" as a political community.

Since we are lacking in "historical" knowledge, the most proper answer to the question concerning our beginnings will be myth; a mythological comprehension of the wellsprings of our community. In reality, such a choice has more in common with an act of political establishment or political reflection than history, in other words, knowledge of the past. Some momentous consequences result from this. Because we are not in possession of the "hoary knowledge of yesterday," the answer to the question of our beginnings, which is a question concerning who we are, must be formed above all in the language of myth. (As we shall see, this is not, however, the only language at the author's disposal wherewith to describe us). That, which from the perspective of a Positivist historian seems absurd and crazy—and above all inadequate as far as the state of factual knowledge goes—from the point of view of the formation of European proto-nations and proto-states in the eleventh and twelfth centuries seems to place the *Chronicle* and the author's thought in the very center of the main processes then at work. In Wincenty's days, a mythological understanding of one's history was one of the chief phenomena that marked the inception of the process of the genesis of the nations of Europe. We see this expressly in examples from the Franco-English literature of the period. In 1136, Geoffrey of Monmouth published his *History of the Kings of Britain* (*Historia Regum Britanniae*)[14] which enjoyed great popularity on the continent. In his book, Monmouth constructs his own founding myth of Albion, full of magical figures like sorcerers, demons, and giants. But the ancient protoplast of the inhabitants of Albion was to be Brutus—a descendant of Aeneas. On account of this Trojan pedigree, in the middle ages the inhabitants of Britain frequently referred to London as "New Troy" (*Troynovante*).

In the French kingdom as well the story of their descent from the Trojans enjoyed great popularity. We find this in the *History of France*, written by Master Matthew at the beginning of the thirteenth century, as well as in the text *Quaestio in Utramque Partem* (A Matter from Both Sides), penned by an anonymous author in 1302, where the generation of the French from the Trojans as free people—"franks"—is described. They are "free," as they did not wish to subject themselves to the dictate of the Roman Empire. Most often, texts like this merely developed various versions of previously extant myths of the ancient generation of the peoples of mediaeval Europe. The conception of *translatio studii et imperii* was the common property of all, according to which description the peoples or kingdoms of mediaeval Europe "inherited" political power, wisdom, as well as noble virtues from the ancients. It is for this reason that, in the writings of Chrétien de Troyes, a French poet of the twelfth century, we find the following statement, so full of undisguised pride: "From such books which have been preserved we learn the deeds of men of old and of the times long since gone by. Our books have informed us that the pre-eminence in chivalry and learning once belonged to Greece. Then chivalry passed to Rome, together with that highest learning which now has come to France. God grant that it may be cherished here, and that it may be made so welcome here that the honour which has taken refuge with us may never depart from France."[15] Even if Master Wincenty was not familiar with all of these texts, certainly the whole debate concerning the *translatio studii et imperii* must have been well known to him from his studies in Bologna and Paris. One can also wager that he understood its political context quite well: the struggle of some mediaeval peoples and realms for autonomy in the face of the universalist conception of Empire, and also, to a degree, that of the papacy, through their own foundational myths and ancient sources. For this reason, one may propose the thesis that the language of myth employed by Master Wincenty in his first book, as well as the book's setting in the framework of ancient tradition—was not merely "cheap showiness," the desire to flaunt one's familiarity with fashionable, "western" intellectual currents, to say nothing of an inclination for mythomania—but a decision, to a great degree conscious and intentional, which reveals his familiarity with the political realities predominant in twelfth-century Europe. Above all, however, it was the author's own great, political plan.

This use of the language of myth in a description of beginnings, weaving the fates of the community into the tapestry of ancient history, was, therefore, an intellectual response to the challenges both geopolitical and internal with which the Piast state was confronted—just as in the case of the "state" myth of foundation of Bolesław Chrobry (the Brave) relating to the golden age of the realm, which was just forming in the twelfth century, or the myth of the unity of the state symbolized by the miraculous reunification of the quartered body of St. Stanisław, so creatively developed by Master Wincenty himself. An analysis of the first ten chapters of Book I indicates that his choice of the language of myth has, indeed, multifarious and more profound consequences, and in Master Wincenty's writing it is not just a question of utilitarian advantage assessed from the perspective of any immediate political goal (even if that goal be a great, or even visionary, one). For the question is also about an understanding of the nature of politics itself. So the author isn't just introducing twelfth century Polish thought into the arena of the political, but also presenting his own interpretation of the theological and philosophical bases of that thought.

The mythologising of one's own beginnings is not just an act of self-establishment, a response to the question: who am I? It is also a decisive separation of oneself from others. It is here indeed that the line of tension runs between Christianity and the national identities which had been forming in Europe over the ages. In Master Wincenty's writings we see the inception of that division in Polish political reflection. In this way, the history of Poland becomes woven into the most fundamental conflict that continues to constitute Europe to this very day. From the Christian perspective, the basic question is: following the Incarnation, the most perfect manifestation of God and His Creation, can any return to a national polytheism even be possible? Is it not so that in basing the Faith upon the Incarnation, Resurrection, and finally Parousia of Christ St. Paul has established finally and for all times the existence of only one, universal, all-embracing people—the people of God on Earth? And that being the case, how are we to understand the genesis of the variety of historical peoples, not excepting the people of Piast? By referring to myth, Master Wincenty wishes to give expression to that genesis in philosophical-theological categories, anchoring the source of the "birth" of the people at a much deeper level than historical fact or the usual geographical-ethnic categories. The division of mankind into different peoples, just like their division into different languages or different identities, has for him an aboriginal character, essential, and inexplicable by any one historically documented fact, geographical surroundings, or natural environment (area, rivers, mountain ranges). The effect he achieves in this way is extraordinary. The genesis of a people constitutes an expression of its identity (the inference being that the loss of identity indicates the actual disappearance of the people in question). Thanks to this, any local event, such as the emergence of the kingdom of the Piasts, and thus the act of establishment by

Mieszko I familiar to us from our schoolbooks, isn't really a beginning at all, but rather one element of a continuum, one part of the great narrative that describes the history of mankind. It is also one part of the great drama of human rule, which may only be described by the language of philosophical and theological reflection.

The act of establishment, which is basic to each and every political reality (as it is the source of everything that sets the public arena in order: the *auctoritas* of the government, the political community, the division into "enemy" and "fellow-citizen," the stratification of the aims of activities, the efficacy of agency), is at the same time an act of schism with the aboriginal unity, an act of violence perpetrated on its body, and against it. It is this that makes the political impulse two-sided in the context of Christianity. For on the one hand it is born, each and every time, from sin—violence, actualized by will, carried out against the original unity—while on the other hand, as an expression of human prudence, it also constitutes a manner of dealing with evil. Politicality introduces order: rules and norms, which make the world less evil—but this does not mean that it makes it automatically good (for the reestablishment of the original unity is impossible, since it has been torn apart). Master Wincenty must have realized this, perfectly, thanks to his university readings (at the very least, thanks to St. Augustine and Boethius),[16] as well as his observations and the experiences he amassed at the court of Kazimierz Sprawiedliwy (the Just).

In the fifth chapter of the first book, the development of events is laid out in a very significant manner. At the start, the author describes the act of establishing the community for which the constituting situation is a *wiec*, a gathering of the people, a moot, an assembly. Grakh, a princely warrior whose valiant nature makes him the natural leader of the Poles, summons all to the assembly—as Master Wincenty suggests—at a time of none too well-defined crisis that threatens the people with fragmentation: a striving toward particular goals or the advantages of individual rivals: “From that time forward, more than one began to have a hankering for partial rule. For this reason Grakh [...] summoned the entire community to an assembly.”[17] The intent is clear: the establishment of a unified royal power and the introduction of an enduring political order (“Just as the world without the sun, so is a state without a king”).[18] As has been said, Grakh was already in possession of *auctoritas* on account of his valor and his many victories in battle, against the Gauls and the Romans, among others. It is certainly for this reason that his summons to the assembly could not be ignored and that, when he spoke during the assembly, “the faces of all were turned unto him,”[19] as the center of events, the main point of reference, the source of authority for all the rest. This also happened because of his wisdom: “He had the gift of expressing deep thoughts.”[20] All of this leads to the constitution of the kingdom, and the election of Grakh as king—not a tyrant, a ruler whose will is law, but “a companion to the kingdom [...] which was born not to his sole advantage, but to that of the world entire.”[21] The vision of political community presented here by Master Wincenty as common weal, and that of government as service, echoes the tone of John of Salisbury’s *Policraticus*, with which he was familiar.

Valor, magnanimity, prudence, wisdom, and certainly also political cunning (the right moment for summoning the assembly had to be carefully anticipated—false starts or belatedness in such a matter generally end in total disaster), are proven to be indispensable characteristics that allow a person to “unify” others around himself. This is impossible to achieve by mere force, usurpation, subjection. The very act of “unification” is not conceived here as serving the might of its establishment or its broadening, nor is it for the satisfaction and ambitions of the governing person. Rather, it aims at goals found in a completely different, impersonal, unique area. That goal is the establishment of a new order ensuring liberty and justice: “And so arose the association of our civic rights and laws which then came into being.

For before this, liberty had to bow before slavery, and justice walked side by side with injustice," asserts Master Wincenty, immediately following which, clearly inspired by Plato's *Gorgias*, he adds: "From henceforth, however, liberty ceased to submit to naked violence, and justice was called that which most supports him who is least capable of doing things for himself."[22] Our attention is arrested by the fact that, according to the author, the chances for the formation of a community so conceived are not reduced to the simple choice of the right moment, nor the personal qualities of any capable politician. As we can clearly see on the basis of the earlier chapters (above all the second), the appearance of the community occurs before the process of the formation of proper virtues common to all, such as: bravery, measure, magnanimity. Amongst these Master Wincenty places the most emphasis on the significance of bravery, which in his description, in a thought-provoking manner, calls to mind vitality, courage, resourcefulness, as well as a readiness to search out new challenges to face—as did the ancient Athenians, which is so suggestively comprehended by Thucydides in his *Peloponnesian War*. Only then do these virtues constitute a foundation upon which proper *constitutiones* may be raised, which allow for the perpetuation of liberty and justice.

Wincenty Kadłubek doesn't restrain himself to a mere description of the situation of the community's formation in philosophical and political categories; he also strives to exhibit the dialectical character of the consequences it evokes. Let us remember: the act of establishment, as an act of ordering, is simultaneously an act of schism with an original unity, and so an act of destruction—and for this reason it always brushes up against the problem of sin and evil. The happy-end story of the brave Grakh, who thanks to his virtues and cleverness is able to unify others, and in this way establish a kingdom in service of liberty and justice, introduces us, in this very same chapter, into the murky regions of evil. These are symbolized by the dragon *holophagus*—an omnivore like no other, who has made his nest "in the crevasses of a certain cliff."[23] The monster, like evil itself, is characterized by an unheard of gluttony, consuming everything in his path, from cattle and flock to people themselves, sowing devastation everywhere. It is striking that the appearance of politicality here is not the solution of the problem of evil; rather, it casts a shaft of light upon it. (Before the constitution of Grakh's kingdom, warlike, but basically benevolent and magnanimous people were living in natural communities, in a state of so to speak moral infancy. They never came into contact with the problem of radical evil). The constituted political community must, therefore, grapple with this destructive force, which becomes incarnate in its immediate neighborhood, and is even manifestly present in its very foundations. One might even assume that the capability of effectively dealing with evil—that monstrous, destructive force that would swallow everything—becomes the condition for the continued existence of any political structure brought to life by people; it is its first and most basic touchstone. It is for this reason that, in Master Wincenty's narrative, we are not surprised at the fact that the king selects his two sons to overcome the beast: he is the founder, and they—as the next generation—must show themselves capable of sustaining his political work. For this reason, the moment of complete triumph arrives only after the slaying of the dragon, when "the famous city was immediately founded on the cliff of the omnivoracious dragon"[24] (a scene which viscerally recalls to mind Aeschylus' *Eumenides*). However, the nexus between politicality and evil is dialectical. The conquering of the beast is not a final solution to the problem, but just the ultimate grounding of the political community in its unsurmountable entanglement in evil. After the slaying of the dragon the sons of Grakh fall to quarrelling about which among them is first in glory, the result of which is a horrid act of fratricide and the banishment of the murderer from the kingdom.[25] Evil takes its vengeance upon the community, uncovering to the eyes of all its sinfulness, showing that, as an area of power, politics always has its source in the age-old sin of Cain.

Indeed, in light of this there is no way of considering the first book of the *Chronicle* as an example of "fairy story" writing or the prating of mythomanic nonsense on the banks of the Wisła. It is just the opposite of that. The text is a splendid example of its author's sense of the spirit of the times, during which the proto-nations of mediaeval Europe began to define themselves through a process of constructing their own, separate identities on the foundation of myth inscribed into the flow of universal history. In this sense, the text is not at all an example of intellectual obscurantism, but rather of contemporary thought: it introduces us into the circle of European political concepts. It also contains an attempt at a basic understanding of politicality and the mechanism of how political communities come to be—an attempt that simply cannot be ignored or batted away. Political beings arise here as a breach of aboriginal unity in the name of the establishment of a well-defined order that guarantees justice and good. They make over the world of man into one less penetrated by evil, but they do not divinify it. The ambiguity of politicality remains unremovable since each political unit rests upon some act of violence or crime. In the further sections of the *Chronicle* of Wincenty Kadłubek, the author will recall and develop these basic threads contained in the first chapters of his first book.

A Digression on Henryk Sandomierski

It is decidedly good to read Kadłubek's work along with two remarkable novels, separated from one another by just a few years, although one must admit that, for the history of Poland, those years—let us say the decade stretching between 1933 and 1943—are one great stretch of tragedy. I have in mind here Iwaszkiewicz's *Czerwone tarcze* (Red Shields) and Parnicki's *Srebrne orły* (Silver Eagles). I hasten to explain, or perhaps to attempt to convince the reader of why it is worthwhile to interrupt our analysis of Kadłubek's *Chronicle* at this point in order to draw attention to these two novels, which offer us a taste of the political history of Piast Poland during the first two centuries of our statehood. Iwaszkiewicz was, supposedly, tortured by the emptiness of his diplomatic work in the Polish consulate in Copenhagen during the 1930s. This torment turned out to be to the benefit of Polish literature. Somewhat in order to free himself from his hopeless situation, he began working on a historical novel dealing with Henryk Sandomierski, the younger, fourth son of Bolesław Krzywousty (the Wry-Mouthed) and Salomea von Berg. Such a situation gave rise to what is, in my opinion, one of the most interesting novels concerning the Piasts; one that sheds light on the geopolitical and ideological context in which Kadłubek's *Chronicle* came to be. Above all, this context is the unsuccessful expedition of the German King Konrad III Hohenstaufen against Poland in 1146, and later the reviving of the power of the German Empire by Frederick Barbarossa. The novel is set in an age to which Master Wincenty himself was an eyewitness, or knew of from the relations of those who had seen it at first hand. For when Henryk Sandomierski perished in the shameful circumstances of his elder brothers' senseless expedition against the treacherous Prussians in 1166, Wincenty was perhaps already a youth in his early teens. But history is not the point here—as Iwaszkiewicz himself said concerning his book in one of his letters to his wife—but politics. Politics on a grand scale, concerning Poland's place is mediaeval Europe, and the timeless problem, which stretches into our own day: where exactly in Europe is that Poland to be found, and what sort of place is she capable of winning for herself? We've already touched upon this in our analysis of the first book of the *Chronicle*, where, among other things, we state that all these political myths concerning the birth of Piast Poland worked up with an admirable cleverness by Wincenty are located in direct contact with and in contestation of the imperial German myth of the *translatio imperii*. There is therefore in these myths of Wincenty's a clearly visible attempt at the assumption of subjectivity by the young Poland of the Piasts. This is also to be found in the "tract on treason," at which we will arrive later, in which Wincenty makes use of the language of Roman republicanism in order to express the community of Poles in political-civic categories. Simultaneously, we are after all speaking here of the period of dramatic interior division of the Piast state between the sons of Bolesław Krzywousty and their subsequent internecine battling, and thus of a weak subjectivity lacking a clear political form. Iwaszkiewicz's Henryk dreams of the reestablishment of political subjectivity, of the bestowal of a strong and decisive form upon the vital political substance of the Poles—the existence of which we can, after all, read on many pages of Wincenty's *Chronicle*. This form is, of course, that of unity, symbolized by that crown of his great forefathers, as Henryk himself is to call his great antecedents, those political giants Bolesław Chrobry (the Brave) and Bolesław Szczodry (the Generous, later the Bold), who had been capable of turning Poland into a European kingdom. Taking into consideration all of the geopolitical circumstances of that mediaeval world, this was indeed an assumption of subjectivity (we shall return to this in a moment when we come to speak of *Silver Eagles*), which, however, along with the banishment of King Bolesław Szczodry, was to be forfeited for a long time. The establishment of the kingdom of the Piasts was therefore a violent and spectacular event, an explosion of a supernova in our part of Europe, but, just as quickly, that sudden flash of political form disappeared in the reflux of the political chaos of inner conflicts and dependency upon exterior powers. Still and all, despite that, it already determined a certain type of Polish thinking concerning political form, the crown, and the kingdom, from which path the Poles never were to turn. Henryk—as Iwaszkiewicz describes him (for actually, we know very little about Henryk except for the nimbus of glory that surrounds him as a knight crusader, a Polish prince who took part in the Second Crusade to the Holy Land and introduced the Knights of Malta to Poland)—stands head and shoulders above his brothers in his capability of profound perception of the political conditions of Poland in the Europe of his time. This includes both his eldest brother, the indolent Władysław Wygnaniec (the Exile), who was constantly living in hope of garnering the Emperor's aid for the reacquisition of his lost authority over Kraków, the intellectually sluggish, provincial Bolesław Kędzierzawy (the Curly-Haired), the timid and excessively prudent Mieszko Stary (Mieszko the Old) and, finally, the simple and practical Kazimierz Sprawiedliwy (the Just), whose feet were set just a bit too firmly on the ground. Sojourning in the German Empire, where Iwaszkiewicz locates him as a hostage guaranteeing peace between the Emperor and Bolesław Kędzierzawy, ruling in Kraków as the senior duke, Henryk engages in two conversations that are very instructive for him, and simultaneously interesting for the readers of the novel. They are of a political nature, and deal with the future of the Christian world. The first takes place in the gardens of the Benedictine cloister of Zwiefalten in Swabia with Agnes Babenberg, princess, granddaughter of an emperor, and wife of that unfortunate Władysław Wygnaniec, the eldest son of Krzywousty, who, following his conflict with the powerful Piotr Włostowic, lost the reins of government and was forced to flee Poland for Germany. Agnes, a woman of immense political ambitions, whom in his *Chronicle* Wincenty will call a "tigress" and to whom he will ascribe the most dangerous character traits, gives Henryk to understand that the reunification of Poland lies in the interests of the Empire, which is in need of a strong ally in the East. The return of power in Poland into the hands of her husband is the only way to achieve this goal, though several paths lead thereto. The main thing is for a unified and strong order to be established in Poland under the patronage and care of the Emperor so that the Emperor might be able to communicate there with a unique, strong ruler who, in the framework of Christian, feudal Europe, would help him to execute his supreme, universal rule over the entire Christian world. Henryk has his doubts. It seems to him that such a bestowal of kingship from above, from the Emperor's hands, completely overlooks the fact that following the death of Bolesław Krzywousty, Poland had become something entirely different than she was, let us say, one hundred fifty years earlier, when Bolesław Chrobry accepted that legendary spear from the hands of Otto III in Gniezno. At the present time, even if she has been split up into districts, even if she has been deprived of that unity, which the Emperor would wish for himself and his own advantage, she constitutes a rich, variegated, vital, and far-developed material possessed of its own political consciousness—which is borne out for us in those very pages of Wincenty's *Chronicle*. For this reason, any new form of a united, reborn kingdom might only arise from the interior of that same political material, through its own individual effort, and not by any such bestowal from the outside. Henry tells the German princess, the wife of his eldest brother, and above all the granddaughter of the Emperor that "One thing seems important to me: that times are changing and that no river can change its course to flow back to its wellsprings. It seems to me that we find ourselves in the grip of the current of just such a river. It toys with us, and frustrates all our efforts. As the Empire changes, so must Poland change. Your plans are doomed to failure, sister, because something else is hanging in the air. Wszebor, Wojsław, Świętopełk, Włostowic, all of them... they're also after something."[26] By this he means at least this much: that the Poland of Henryk's days, and those of Wincenty too, was already living its own, independent political life, independent even of the will of the powerful German Emperor. But one thing in Agnes' words intrigued Henryk greatly. It was her account of how, supposedly, on the day of her marriage in Kraków to Władysław, his father Bolesław Krzywousty led the married couple to some distant, dark chamber in Wawel castle to show them a crown, resting on a velvet cushion in the midst of a little chapel. At this recollection of Agnes' of the crown of Bolesław Śmiały (the Bold) preserved there by Krzywousty, "Henryk felt a shiver run down his spine. The sacred significance of the royal insignia, its golden rim full of mystical contents that reached back into the past, to the mysteries of the magic of anointing unknown and incomprehensible to them."[27] His interest reached its zenith when he heard that the crown preserved at Wawel was only a replica of the actual crown, which Bolesław Śmiały was to have taken with him when banished to Hungary following the death of St. Stanisław. This vision of the Polish crown will now never abandon Henryk. He leaves Zwiefalten in haste for the Benedictine cloister at Ossiach, in Carinthia, where it is said that Bolesław Śmiały was to have spent the last years of his life doing penance. He was supposed to have been buried there, too, and although that supposition has not been proven even to this very day, we can still visit his purported grave. It has even been beautifully restored recently, and attracts tourists and pilgrims. In Iwaszkiewicz's novel, when Henryk arrives at Ossiach, the king's grave is nothing but a worn hillock near the church wall: "some droopy grass on top, and a few leaves torn from branches and deposited there by the wind."[28] Henryk returns at night and excavates his grandfather's grave. He finds therein what remains of the crown—"Nothing but a gold band, certainly the base of the crown. It bore the marks of some violent blows, was broken in places, and the fittings which once held precious stones were black empty spaces, like the very sockets in the skull of Bolesław Szczodry."[29]

The other key conversation of Henryk's takes place upon his return from Ossiach. Konrad III Hohenstaufen, the German king, is expiring in Bamberg from a mortal illness contracted during the unsuccessful second crusade to the Holy Land. It was already common knowledge that his son wouldn't be the one to inherit the throne, but his nephew, his brother's son Frederick known as Barbarossa, a young, energetic man, with whom hopes for the rejuvenation of the Empire were associated. Henryk's meeting with him—an encounter of two young people—portends the appearance of a new European order in the none-too-distant future. Frederick unrolls before the eyes of the young Piast his vision of Christian Europe united under the Empire, which he desires to realize with the help of his allies. "There will be one shepherd and one fold,"[30] he says, pronouncing a sentence that will continually return in the conversation as a descriptor of the great matter of unification, which the future Emperor sees as his particular mission. "One can only create something, when one feels whole," says Barbarossa: "we cannot be divided and progress, as if everyone wanted to leave a city by all the gates at once. We must have one goal, for there is but one life, God is one, and the law is one."[31] And so Barbarossa wishes to found his unity on one law, for which the rule of the Emperor constitutes the greatest guarantee—the Empire. Only by subjecting all to that one universal and final form can one "create something"; only then will the liberating strength arise which will be capable of pulling the world free of "formless infirmity." Barbarossa's vision, inspired and grandiose, makes a huge impression on Henryk, but the question immediately arises within him—where, in this universal order of unity, will there be space for the objective existence of his own state, for the Piasts and their battered crown deprived of its jewels? On the other hand, in order to lift up that crown again, to have it regain its brilliance and its might, would it not be necessary to tread one's own paths, to proceed according to one's own will, and be the shepherd of one's own flock? Can Christian Europe, or any sort of European order in general, be created by only one liberating strength, which works from above according to one iron law, or is it that each must go his own way, in search of his own understanding of that unity? It is for this reason that, as he is listening to Barbarossa speaking of this one law, one shepherd, and one flock, "Henryk might well have wanted to add *one love*, or perhaps *one freedom*. Frederick said that everything that is scattered, pulverized, weak, and fallow, must unite, become whole, arise as one. But to Henryk it seemed that everything that lives must have its own roots, and push out its own leaves, blossoms, and flowers."[32] In this conversation with the future Emperor, the creator of the Holy Roman Empire, Henryk comes to the realization, at first murkily, of the insuperable difference which divides the strivings of the Piasts to objective being and their crown from the universalistic vision of Barbarossa. Some years later, this difference will work it so that when the Emperor invades the realm of the Piasts in order to punish them for the banishment of their eldest brother Władysław, the husband of Agnes Babenberg, and offers the Polish crown to Henryk with the words "You're one of us, born amongst us, you might say. And above all—you know what I'm after. And you can help me to it... You are brave, you are reasonable, you are certain—and beyond that I know that you're our man."[33] Henryk casts away the proposal thus formed, replying: "No, Your Imperial Highness, I won't be your sheep."[34]

Yet Henryk will not be successful in constructing his own new political unity. He dies a senseless death, ambushed during his brothers' crusade against the Prussians, somewhere in the marshy woods of the North—our eternal Polish fate. His dreams of the crown were to be set aside for another hundred and some years. For Iwaszkiewicz, the composition of this novel had a very important personal significance. For toward the end of the twenties, his own flirt with the idea of a greater Germany begins, given impetus by his contacts with the circle around Stefan George and his idea of a Ghibelline Europe, as well as with the conservative Intellectual Union of Karl von Rohan. This Union had a section in Poland as well, to which, among others, Tadeusz Zieliński and Oskar Halecki belonged. Iwaszkiewicz was to host Rohan in Stawisko; he was to take several trips to Austria and Germany to participate in Union gatherings—of which the meeting in Heidelberg would make the strongest impression on him. This went on for several years, not without the support of so-called "governmental elements," for it was also the moment when Warsaw was about to begin making tentative contacts with the nationalists and conservatives, who were growing in strength in Germany. Yet this fascination fades more and more, and Iwaszkiewicz comes to see that the enchanting idea of a European empire constructed on the domination of German culture and in reference to the times of the German Emperors, the Ottos and Fredericks, is nothing more than a smoke-screen to cover German ambitions that would lead to a new war and a new order in Europe. The book about Henryk, composed in Copenhagen, is an attempt at coming to terms with his illusions and delights with the vision of Ghibelline Europe, the political realization of the Biblical idea "There shall be one shepherd and one fold." This reckoning with the past was necessary, because as Iwaszkiewicz himself confesses, he wasn't concerned with history, but politics.

...and a Second Digression on Aron, Abbot of Tyniec

It's interesting that for this very reason—the politicizing of a historical novel—Teodor Parnicki, a young author living at the time in Lwów (Lviv), who had already written a popular novel on Aetius, the last Roman, supposedly made some serious reproaches to Iwaszkiewicz after having read *Czerwone tarcze.* For after all, no one but Parnicki himself could fully explain what Ghibellism in Europe actually was, how it arose and why its beginnings had such a significance for the political establishment of Poland. The world war, the omens of which Iwaszkiewicz sensed in the meetings of the Intellectual Union, arrived at its zenith when Parnicki, having extracted himself from Soviet Russia in 1943 along with the army of General Anders, began writing *Srebrne orły* (Silver Eagles) in Jerusalem.

I will not hide the fact that, for me, reading this novel was a true revelation. For that reason, I'm quite able to understand why it was so popular in the past. It describes the ancient division of Europe into North and South—the war waged between Saxon beer and Tusculan wine. The conflict of beer and wine—the Saxon warriors of the German Emperor and the inhabitants of Rome with the clan of the Crescentii leading them. If anyone should search for our place in this mediaeval quarrel of two worlds, he would certainly have to add a third, stronger drink to the mix: that brewed by our ancestors on a base of honey. There is something to this division of things. The Crescentii (Crescenzi) governed Rome in the tenth and eleventh centuries as Roman patricians, shielding themselves within the thick walls of their bastion raised on the banks of the Tiber, later to be known as Castel Sant'Angelo. They set their own people on the Papal throne. The title of patrician was to indicate that theirs was a self-reliant power, its rationalization directly derived from the authority the ancient Romans had over the Holy City of Rome. The solid base of their power was wine, the vineyards of Tusculum, which was a symbol not only of the European culture of the South, Mediterranean culture, but what is more important, of Christianity as a whole—above all, the sacrament of transformation. Each time a German king yearned for the Imperial crown, he had to take himself to that Rome ruled by the Crescenzi—and then there began those murderous bouts of the North with the South over primacy in the Eternal City. If the German King or Emperor was unable to come to terms with the self-reliant people and patricians of Rome and their popes, he had to come down from the North along with his margraves and Saxon army, lay siege to the walls, break their resistance, punish the rebels horribly, and at last, seat popes more inclined to his side on the throne of Peter. All that was in agreement with the imperial idea, that as the Vicar of Christ on the earth, he rules the entire world in order to fulfill the golden rule: "There shall be one shepherd and one flock."

The chief protagonist of Parnicki's novel is the Irish monk Aron, who later became abbot of the Benedictine monastery at Tyniec, founded, according to one version, by Rycheza, the German wife of Mieszko II, mother of Kazimierz Odnowiciel (the Restorer), and also by his friend Timotheus, a scion of the Roman Colonna clan, related to the Crescenzi and the counts of Tusculum, later legendary bishop of Poznań. Both these men are witnesses to what happened in Rome at the turn of the eleventh century, when Otto III, known also as the Eerie, wished to realize his dreams of revivifying, eternally, the Roman Empire of many nations, to which he also desired to unite the Slavs. He must however first break the resistance of the Crescenzi and their supporters, bring Rome under his control, establish his in-law Bruno of Carynthia (related to the German imperial family of the Ludolfings) as the new pope, who in turn, as Gregory V, will crown him Emperor. Following Gregory's death, he will raise to the see of Peter the famous Gerbert as Sylvester II, who was himself to be a great advocate of the resuscitation of the Empire of many nations. It is in these very circumstances that the state of Bolesław Chrobry (the Bold) appears as one element of the great, geopolitical and ideological puzzle of Europe at the turn of the century. It would be impossible to reconstruct, even in a general sketch, the complicated plot of the novel, so characteristic of Parnicki. The essence of the problem lays in Romanity, or rather in the creation of one's own autonomous relationship thereto. Otto III is of the opinion that he may become a new Roman Emperor, ruler of the world and the universal order, and make his Saxons or Germans into new Romans. This dream was the idea that fired his short life. It was Christianity that provided the necessary framework for that "unification." However, Otto wished to buttress his great project on the new Polish state and its ruler, Bolesław Chrobry. And here appears the legend, not only of the diadem, which he was supposed to place upon the brow of Chrobry during their encounter in Gniezno, but also of the title of Roman patrician, and the bestowal of the symbol of the silver eagles. This legend was even more fully developed in Parnicki's novel as well. According to it, Bolesław was to be taken under consideration as the Emperor's successor. Whether or not that was true, we do not know. At any rate, for the German margraves, who stood at the head of the Imperial armies and, if necessary, burst open the walls before them with battering ram, both the thought of Germans becoming new Romans, and what is more, thanks to the Slavs of Chrobry, was ludicrous. They wanted to be who they were—Germans, with a German king, who would allow them to rule and pillage both the rich lands of Italy, and those of the nearby Slavs. To put it plainly: they preferred to drink their Saxon beer over Tusculan wine.

However, unfortunately for them, Otto treated his Romanity with deadly seriousness. He wanted to be the real Emperor and renovator of Rome. The more he desired this, however, the more his doubts grew. In Parnicki's novel, Otto is a person torn in two. He doesn't know who he really is: a Roman, the real Roman Emperor, or only a German, and perhaps—thanks to his mother, the Byzantine princess Theophanu, a Greek. Which is closer to the truth? This is something that Otto will never be able to resolve to his satisfaction, although it is certainly true that his greatest desire was to be considered a Roman. And for this reason he drank a lot of wine, which supposedly did not agree with him.

As we've already said, this novel is about Romanity—not only that of the Germans, but that of the West entire, and the Romanity of the Poles and their own road to Roman form. Aron, whom Parnicki makes our chief guide through this history, having arrived in Poland already, meets a Greek on the road to Poznań. This is a mysterious traveler: a merchant, an emissary, maybe quite simply a spy. During a long conversation, Aron learns some things from him which allow him to understand what he'd surmised during his years in Rome, where he was able to observe Gregory V, Sylvester II and Otto III from up close. At the time, he was only guessing at things, but now, thanks to the information received from the Greek, he comes to the firm conclusion that Bolesław Chrobry's new state is an essential element in the game that is being played in Europe concerning the great plan of creating an Empire of the West, which would govern many nations from its capital in Rome. From this conversation it turns out that one great actor in this series of events—an actor behind the scenes, but always present and masterfully realizing his plans to shatter the dream of Rome's resurrection—is Byzantium, which after all is the one Empire still in existence, that of the Basileuses of Constantinople. Byzantium was waging effective war against the ecclesiastical politics of Sylvester II. Above all, however, it was fomenting conflicts between Otto and his Saxon margraves. For the crux of the matter was, as the well-informed Greek explains to Aron, to tear the Germans away from Rome once and for all; to divide, with some impenetrable wall of enmity, the South from the North, Roman form from the peoples of the North, thanks to which the crazy and harmful dream of a reconstruction of a Roman Empire of many peoples in Europe would vanish. For, after all, the one and only legitimate Empire is that ruled by the Byzantine Emperors from Constantinople. And here, in this context, arises the significance of Chrobry's new state. Emperor Otto, "the Wonder of the World," wished not only to insure a safe and friendly border for his Empire in the East (especially during times when he had some important matters to settle for himself in Rome), but more: he wanted to transform the Slavs into his vassals and, when necessary, set them shoulder to shoulder with his Saxon warriors at the walls of the recalcitrant Italian cities. As has already been mentioned, this was an unheard-of idea for the German margraves. First of all, it struck directly at their interests and desires of new conquests, to say nothing of their pride. After all, they liked to boast that the Slavs were like children, whom you need only present with a stick for them to believe that they're astraddle a real horse. So, how was one to stand with them now, shoulder to shoulder, as equals, in battle-ranks, in defense of the Empire? Was the next step—Heavens help us!—that they should also participate in the election of the German candidate to the Imperial throne? The plans of Otto, supported by Sylvester, were also for the German Church something like a heresy. It was one thing to Christianize the Slavs, and quite another to see in them one's Christian neighbors. And when you got right down to it, was it not that both Rome and the pope recouped their splendor and power thanks to Saxon lances? Who was it that breathed new life into old Rome? It was for this reason that Dietmar, the Bishop of Merseburg, would pronounce those pregnant words in the novel, which we would be well to remember: "In order to become a Roman, the Slav must first become a German."[35] I believe that this thought, set on Dietmar's lips by Parnicki, has not yet lost its currency even today. All you need do is give it a little twist: In order to become a European, the Slav must first become a German. As Parnicki sees it, it is this very danger that Chrobry senses and perfectly understands as he makes his appearance in the novel from time to time, at the very end. Just like Iwaszkiewicz's Henryk in relation to Barbarossa, Chrobry, faced with Otto III's successor, knows quite well that if a Slav were to become a German, he would certainly never become any sort of Roman, but more than certainly he would lose his powers of self-determination. It is for this reason that he asserts: "We want to be Rome. But how much we'd need to slog through before we accomplish that!"[36] Lots of slogging would be needed for a Pole to become a Roman. I reckon that a person would need to toil at it for quite a long time. In our case, it took over a thousand years, but in the end, a Pole did become lord of Rome. The only regret we can have about that difficult road is that we think about it so rarely and remind ourselves of it so reluctantly.

The Tract on Treason

These two novels, Iwaszkiewicz's and Parnicki's, are well worth remembering, as it is worthwhile to return to them during a consideration of Wincenty's *Chronicle* as the first Polish political tract. I reckon that Wincenty was perfectly aware of the fact that Poland's stakes were Romanity, its adherence to Roman form, which it could only attain by following its own path, laboring to construct said path by the erection of an independent state, and political unity. And so no "German" shortcut might help us here—on the contrary: that would shortly reveal itself to be nothing more than a trap. Essentially, then, he was concerned with the question of the subjectivity of Poland, which he will describe both in the language of myth, as in the first book of the *Chronicle*, and also in other portions of his work, in the language of politics and Roman republicanism. In order for us to follow the creation of the political language of the Poles on the basis of the *Chronicle,* we may avail ourselves of two excellent examples—the tract on treason, and the discussion of the succession of power.

There are such places to be found in the *Chronicle* where, alongside the historical layer, there appears with great intensity a layer of political reflection. Above all, the final chapters of the second book (22–32) should be taken into account. These are devoted to the war being waged among the sons of Władysław Herman—Zbigniew and Bolesław Krzywousty (the Wry-Mouthed)—which ended in the tragic death of the former. This conflict belongs among those of the deepest resonance in the history of the Piasts, around which many stories and legends have gathered. The dramatic possibilities here are so great that some might be tempted to see in it the prefiguration of a typical Shakespearean drama centering on a power-struggle. Indeed, under the pen of Master Wincenty (who of course draws upon the earlier account of the Anonymous Gall—but how different in form and expression!) the history of the fratricidal war rises to a story of imposing dimensions and becomes the occasion for the development of interesting considerations on the theme of the nature of political community and political treason, the character of patriotism, and civic solidarity in the face of a threat—all of which significantly extend beyond the simple flow of the concrete events). Naturally, the manner of describing the history of the conflict of Zbigniew and Bolesław has, for Master Wincenty, an added dimension of utility in light of the facts that he was directly commissioned to compose his *Chronicle* by Kazimierz Sprawiedliwy (the Just), Krzywousty's youngest son. For this reason, Bolesław must be described as the noble "lion of the North," the founder of a new constellation of power alluding in its aims to the ambitious accomplishments of the first Bolesławs to wear the crown—Chrobry (the Brave) and Śmiały (the Bold). In consequence, Zbigniew must incarnate in this account everything that is bad, wrongheaded, and destructive. He is irrevocably cast in the role of the *Schwarzcharakter*. Certainly, the manner in which the conflict is described can also be explained as an assertion of the rights of the younger sons of Krzywousty set against the eldest, Władysław Wygnaniec (the Exile), in that civil war of later which went on for several years. But we will not busy ourselves here with historical questions. It is enough for us to say that, most probably, the role of Zbigniew was neither so unequivocally evil, nor was the character of Bolesław so crystal-pure. The decisive thing is that, in making reference to one of the most significant—and pregnant in its results—events in the history of the Piasts, Master Wincenty does not restrain himself to the role of court chronicler, but makes use of it for a broader development of his own views on political questions, while leaving the solution of the political conflict open, as a philosophical and political problem.

Certainly, the pressing necessity of sharpening the description of the conflict between the brothers, presenting Zbigniew as the incarnation of evil—a bastard prince, Ahitophel, Cain (in one of the fragments, Master Wincenty makes a clear allusion to the Biblical

Satan)—necessarily cleared the path to more profound considerations of the problematics of human nature. In the portrait of Zbigniew that we find in the *Chronicle*, we have a walking catalogue of anti-virtues: pride, conceit, jealousy, recalcitrance, disobedience, mendacity, and finally: patricide, fratricide, and treason of the fatherland. It's hard to even imagine a character more vile. Yet this gives rise to the justified question which cannot be left unanswered: How is it possible? Where do such monstrous people come from? What is the hidden spring of their criminal activity? And so the act of treason committed by Zbigniew becomes the basis of meditations on human intentions and results, of political activity in the context of loyalty to the political community as a community of citizens. The story in question is brought to a close with a monumental judgment scene, during which the rationale of Zbigniew's accusers is laid out, as well as his defense. The entirety of these ten chapters from Book II may also be understood as the development of the above-described considerations of the foundational myth contained at the beginning of Book I. For here we witness the return of some initial threads and figures: the essence of the community's establishment, the conditions for its continued existence, acts of fratricide and patricide, the problem of absolute evil, the omnivore.

At first the conflict between Zbigniew and Bolesław (with their father Władysław Herman in the background) is a typical family-dynastic conflict. The drama plays out in the family circle and touches upon the question of obedience to the father-ruler, as a pattern of order in the political community. Indeed, the author, citing the *Codex Justinianeus*, states that censure or even punishment (imprisonment) by the father does not deprive the penalized son of honor; it is not a form of infamy, and yet "it hampers the good opinion of the person in question among worthy and grave persons, on account of the displeasure he caused his father."[37] And so the conflict of son with father—especially in the ambit of dynastic power—is to some degree inevitable, and the requirement of obedience can be taken as a yoke of filial dutifulness. However, despite that, the recognition of the primacy of the father's authority remains a virtue. "So speak as if your father were always listening to you; so act as if always under your father's gaze. For it is a foul thing to do anything vile in your father's sight, or to speak foolishly in his hearing."[38] Zbigniew is an absolutely negative character not only because he fell into conflict with his father Herman—he might have had weighty personal motives for that (the historical Zbigniew had good reasons for hating his father, who put away his mother, his first wife, in order to marry another woman), but also, as Master Wincenty plainly puts it, because he set himself to harm his father, wishing to deprive him of his throne, and even his life. He rated his own desire to reign, to acquire independence, to liberate himself from the yoke of dutifulness, above the virtue of obedience. In this aspect, Wincenty lays out an unequivocal view supported by many examples from ancient literature. It is impossible to construct any enduring political order on a foundation of patricide, as such an act, as an act constitutive of a new governmental order, unerringly brings more crime in its wake. And so patricide is only the illusion of liberation from the yoke of obedience. As an infraction of a taboo it becomes a curse for the society, since now it renders one unable to extract himself from the charmed circle of further crimes, repeated in consequence of the horrid first pattern of evil. Such people will never experience peace again. The same thing is true of the relationship between the brothers. Here, of course, it is no longer a question of liberating oneself from the yoke of the father's authority, of obtaining full governance over oneself and others, but of jealousy and the necessity of one's recognition in circumstances of rivalry with one's younger brother. And so the drama that is playing out in the family circle is likewise a dynastic drama, that is, a drama of government, and in consequence, of the state, which soon founders in civil war. From the start, then, Master Wincenty evidently moves in the framework of feudal monarchy (which is after all the actual reality of the Piast state of the time), where the private interests of the royal family are entirely identical with the interests of the state, or community, as the private *dominium* of the dynasty. What is more, the author seeks to respond to the question: *How did such a terrible black sheep as Zbigniew come to be found in the family?* in a traditional manner. He suggests (against all factual evidence) that he was Władysław Herman's bastard son. And the bastard must necessarily be a pariah and a degenerate.

However, the sense of the entire story changes radically in chapter twenty-seven, as it is now set in a completely different, new context. The dynastic, private-familial language of the argumentation cedes to a vocabulary arising from a completely different world. In describing the extraordinary, sacrificial devotion of the young Bolesław and his entourage in the struggle against the Pomeranians (here appears the story of the sacrifice of Skarbimir, a palace *comes*, who dies from his wounds), which so vividly differs from the constant intrigues and vacillations of the elder Zbigniew, Master Wincenty formulates a paean in praise of "love of the fatherland," which "is love, not insanity, courage, not brashness; for love is as strong as death."[39] Along with this concept we see how in the story as well as in the argumentation there is effected a transition from the world of feudal-private loyalty toward a stern father to political-legal loyalty to the political community as fatherland; the common weal, and finally the republic to which one owes one's love and devotion.

Here the Republic is not just some private property of the ruling family, but a "common wealth," which is accounted for by obligations of a public, general character. Since love of the fatherland can be seen—as Master Wincenty shows on the basis of the Old Testament Maccabees—in the fact that "forgetting oneself, one thinks rather of one's countrymen rather than one's own life" (also: "It is not [...] foreign to virtue to bring an end to public misfortunes through one's own personal harm"),[40] this is a virtue which fundamentally exceeds the obligations enjoined by blood relations (father–son, brother–brother) and becomes a higher duty, of a more general rank, in reference to one's fellow citizens. The problem of treason and the traitor's motives of action become simultaneously less visible and understandable than in the case of a drama that portrays the breaking of obligations of blood in the dynastic family circle. The question becomes more "subtle," multi-dimensional, complex, and for this reason demands another, more general, conceptualization via notions such as: the republic, citizenship, the common good, patriotism. Nor can it be simply solved thanks to the decision of the *pater familias*, on the strength of his natural *auctoritas*, but it is recognized, established, and at last decided via a judicial process in the full presence of all members of the community, that is, all the citizens.

It is beside the point how far afield this picture is from the factual relationships of the rulers reigning over Polish territories in the twelfth century. It is enough to say that the disproportion is surely a significant one. And yet, what does that matter? Certainly from his own historical twelfth-century perspective, as a person associated with the court of the youngest son of the main protagonist of the quarrel, Master Wincenty is exploiting one of the most important dynastic events in the history of the Piasts in order to describe the concept of a political community as a common good, and this he does using the language of legal concepts, and terms from political philosophy, taken indeed not only from his readings in ancient authors, but also the contemporary political reflections of the great John of Salisbury.

All this just increases the pressure on some obvious questions posed by the history of Zbigniew. Why this man "set himself to harm his father"[41] and later his brother is of course a horrid and disgusting thing, especially if he had no real reasons to do so. However, on grounds of human experience, it is something that can indeed be grasped. But whence comes the fierce rancor of Zbigniew toward his fellow-citizens? Why does he labor for their destruction? Zbigniew commits a crime against his fatherland (i.e. his fellow-citizens), because he "feigns love,"[42] and thus, in the key political question, he acts in a manner entirely contrary to his declared intentions. In a situation of war, disguised, he pretends to be someone he is not. By deceit, he introduces to the camp of his fellow-citizens their enemies (the Pomeranians), who—of course—quite simply want to kill them. However, his plan is foiled, he himself is caught, and (after a short tussle and the effective thwarting of a lynching) he is set before a tribunal of his fellow-citizens, on an open expanse in the middle of the camp, *sub Jove*—and thus directly before the eyes of the people and God. It is a significant fact—Zbigniew is accused of lèse-majesté (*crimine laesae maiestatis*) because: "he struck at the camp of his fellow-citizens in league with their enemies." And, as the author underscores, this act filled all present with horror. Naturally, the modern category of state treason was unknown to Master Wincenty; majesty appertains to the Republic as community of citizens to which we belong and which we guarantee, with our lives as token of our faith, that we shall not admit evil into the ambit of its walls, but we shall rather defend it therefrom. Most likely, the universal horror arises from the fact that, through this act of Zbigniew's, evil in its purest form sought to triumph in the very center of the community (despite all the names hurled at him, Zbigniew is, after all, the first-born prince). As we learn, the trial of the treasonous prince is not held in order to establish the facts. These seem indisputable and bear unambiguous testimony against him. Rather, it serves to explain the nature and motives of his act. And so, the matter at hand is an answer to the question: what are the sources of such horrid an evil as we find in the acts of Zbigniew? Are their roots to be found in some natural causes, or have these monstrous traits been acquired by him somehow? Finally, did

Zbigniew consciously wish to harm his fellow-citizens and give aid to their enemies?

Zbigniew's accusers concentrate, above all, on the problem of nature: it is nature, or rather the perversity thereof, its overturning (and hence, surely, the numerous allusions to the devil), which constitute the fundamental problem. For we are dealing with a man who, from the first moments of his birth, was the fruit of nature's overthrow (a bastard: the son of the prince's whore—an historical untruth). From his birth he finds himself in the toils of this irresistible rebellion against nature, something along the lines of Shakespeare's Richard . Everything he does is perverse, inside-out: illegitimate birth, false speech, deceit, acting in the shadows. One might say that, because of his birth, Zbigniew became a pariah, and "perversity of nature and mortal venom so stubbornly took root in this man, that he neither wishes to, nor can he, free himself of them."[43] He is thus in some way condemned to villainy. This pessimistic Christian conception of human nature, based upon a conviction of inherited sinfulness, such that is not even conditioned by one's own sins, but by those committed by one's forefathers, is sweetened only by the perspective of acting on behalf of the common good—loyalty toward one's fellow-citizens advanced to such a degree that negates even one's vital self-interest. Only this (except, surely, life as a pious regular) is able to defend us from the sinfulness of our nature, from the upturning of its sense, and thus, from being swallowed by evil. On the other hand, by concentrating on our own ambitions and needs, by egoism, and thus self-love in place of love of the fatherland, we hasten on the horrid practice of falling into evil. In this way man becomes a beast, a "werewolf," a "horned serpent," a basilisk, an omnivore. According to Zbigniew's accusers, such a tendency is also lined with calculation, which arises from the acceptance of a certain type of outside customs and knowledge. Zbigniew was taken for a person educated abroad, the adherent of "foreign" pragmatism (in opposition to native courage), eloquent, well-read. His contacts with the Germans and Czechs, which today we might call polishing smooth one's rough edges in the West, spoke against him, and were seen as rather grist to the mill of his skewed nature. This sort of equivocal pragmatism, present in the foreign customs acquired by Zbigniew abroad, is, as Master Wincenty presents it, expressed in the form of sophistry, both as far as his carriage and his rhetorical abilities are concerned. It does not elicit much trust; on the contrary—it is a cause for suspicion or scandal ("Be, my son, simultaneously a flatterer and a deceptive man, for there is no easier way to deprive a man of his very soul than under the pretext of healing him of his illness. Pretend to be polite when you really hate; cloak your hatred in politeness").

When he starts to speak to defend himself, Zbigniew attempts to overturn the arguments of his accusers point by point. As we already know from many earlier examples, he is expert in false speech. Above all he poses the question whether in judging people we may refer to categories of nature. For it is circumstances that are decisive, as well as how a person approaches them in a given situation. Not much can be said about the nature of man, the defendant suggests; thus, whether we consider it from the perspective of common sense, or Christian mercy, we oughtn't to take it simply at face value. We ought to reckon that, by his very nature, man is motivated by good intentions. Above all, there is absolutely no way of stating that, by himself, uncoerced, he should of his own free will wish to burn down his own house or set his fatherland in peril. That's only reasonable. "For it is inhuman to suppose even the fiercest man to be so savage; after all, by his very nature man is a gentle creature"[44]—so argues Zbigniew, significantly.

Man as a gentle creature, though intelligent, is confronted by various, sometimes very adverse, situations, such as for example an "unlooked-for accident"[45] to which he must react with cleverness. Yes, he entered the camp of his fellow-citizens at the head of their enemies, but not in order to destroy them, rather to warn and rescue them. Can he be blamed for resorting to deception since his enemies were so numerous, and he had to outwit them? To speak in other words, using a language that will be similar to more than one rationalization in our contemporary quarrels concerning politically and morally doubtful actions, one might imagine Zbigniew saying: "It's true—I pretended to be someone else; I made use of deception, but my intent was never to harm anyone. Just the contrary: I love my fatherland as much as any other man does. I only chose to behave differently when faced with a difficult situation." However, as we know, Zbigniew's falsity of speech was well known already. It is certainly for this reason that his arguments are unconvincing, and he himself must have sensed the weakness of his position, since he brings his defense to a close with a despairing plea for mercy: "It is right, rather, to show mercy, because no other virtue is so proper to the majesty of a ruler as mercy, for in this way we imitate God."[46] But all his efforts are in vain. Zbigniew is condemned to "the punishment of Tiresias,"[47] that is, blinding and exile. In this way the tract on treason is transformed into a political morality play, the motto of which is: whoever comes out against his own Republic will, sooner or later, be justly condemned and punished in an exemplary fashion.

The Problem of Succession, or the Ruler Fulfilled—the Perfect Ruler

The problem of succession is one of the most important matters threading through the entire *Chronicle* of Wincenty Kadłubek, and it is to this that we shall now direct ourselves. One is well within one's rights to assert, I reckon, that this political question is at the center of his attention. Not only in the layer of his description of historical events, but also in his reflections on the nature of politics, especially the nature of government. There is nothing strange in this, since Wincenty himself was a witness to the political situation in the Piast state, which for several decades was defined by quarrels between the sons of Bolesław Krzywousty (the Wry-Mouthed) concerning primacy in the exercise of supreme power. To put it more precisely—he was not merely a witness, but to a significant extent must have been embroiled in the whole matter himself. Kazimierz Sprawiedliwy (the Just), the youngest son of Krzywousty, was, after all, Wincenty's political idol, his superior (if we accept the thesis of his employment in the chancellery), his benefactor and, of course, the one who commissioned the *Chronicle*. How then should Wincenty not concern himself with the succession of rule following Krzywousty? To mention just one small matter: it is Kazimierz, after all, in reaching for the title of *princeps*, who violates the statute enacted by his father concerning the principle of primogeniture. Independent of his own personal engagement as well as the concrete historical events, feudal monarchy is the natural field for Wincenty's political considerations, as is the question of the ideal ruler. The accumulation of Latin, republican ideas, which the author employs, however, gripping and intellectually inspiring as they may be, cannot in this respect draw our attention too far away from the central, real problem of succession.

By taking all this into account, the fact that leaps before one's eyes is: how little space the author reserves in his considerations to the establishment of the new district order imposed by Krzywousty.[48] This can be seen most clearly if we compare the fragment dealing with the so-called Testament of Bolesław with the earlier story, developed into the form of a political tractate, of his conflict with his elder brother Zbigniew. In Wincenty's narrative, we should take Krzywousty as a political and military hero; above all, however, as the restorer of the power of the Piast state, the restorer of its interior might, and its international status. He is, *de facto*, the incarnation of all the characteristics of the ideal ruler, which are evoked in various places throughout the *Chronicle*. If that is so, his political testament ought to be something along the lines of a "constitution," the foundation of a system, stone tablets, the record of the rules of the new political order. One might surmise that it was actually something along the lines of an essential systemic change, which had as its goal the solidification of the interests of his dynasty—above all through the supplementation of the principle of principate with the postulate of seniority, and so, primogeniture. Consequently, what we have here is not only a consideration of a personal lesson deduced by Bolesław from the bloody conflict that came to a head some years before with his own brother in the struggle for the throne, or, more generally, from many other fratricidal conflicts such as took place in the days of the first Piasts. There was something more at stake here: a political intention, a systemic plan, which was to provide an answer to the more complex needs of new political times.

The miscarriage of the political plan of the great prince must have been a severe blow: the eruption of several years of bloody civil war between his eldest son Władysław Wygnaniec (the Exile) and his younger brothers (1142–1146), and then, nearly thirty years of interior squabbling which followed, so suggestively reconstructed by Iwaszkiewicz in his literary work *Czerwone tarcze*, and finally the veritable questioning of the rule of seniority by the youngest Kazimierz, in the Łęczyca Statute (1180)—does this not provide sufficient reasons for us to give deeper thought to the sense of Krzywousty's decisions touching upon the system of government? Meanwhile, Wincenty preserves an exceptional abstemiousness in this matter. That portion of the *Chronicle* devoted to the testament contains some complaints on the unjust treatment of Kazimierz, newly born, on account of his not having received his own district. He also speaks of the division of four distinct and separate districts, as well as the senioral district; about the fact that the senior possesses a supreme power, and the rest of the princes are something along the lines of ancient tetrarchs. On the other hand, the quarrel concerning succession is always to be determined on the basis of seniority and primogeniture. Further, all of this is illustrated by the symbol of four streams: "In the pupil of the eye I behold four streams flowing forth from that tear, the waves of which crash against one another. Some of these [streams] suddenly run dry during their most violent flow. A fragrant spring then spurts out from a golden jar and fills the dry beds of these streams with splendid gems—up to their very banks"[49]—which can probably be understood as an allegory of the unity of the monarchy, or the continuity of the dynasty. And so Wincenty illustrates the principle of the new system in a flowery manner. However, it's hard to find here any political reflection of a profounder sort. Rather, what dominates is general historical reporting and elaborate courtesy. And yet, after all, examples could be found of similar solutions in neighboring states: the rule of a strong seniority introduced in the Czech lands by Břetislav or the model of a weak seniority introduced in Kievan Rus by Jaroslav the Wise. Indeed, there was no lack of material upon which to meditate. But certainly the matter was complicated by the fact that this portion of the *Chronicle* still remained under the watchful eye of Wincenty's benefactor, Prince Kazimierz Sprawiedliwy, who, as we have already said, was first to question the seniority system. And as we will have occasion to mention later, most likely, he infringed against the political plan of his father in more than just this one aspect. So the theme most certainly must have been among the most inconvenient ones, as far as the author is concerned.

And yet, beneath the surface of reportage or courtesy lies, as I see it, intuition, consciousness, and perhaps even a deeper understanding of the real political problem. When, in his narration, Wincenty explains the sense of the governmental plan set forward by Krzywousty with his dying words, something extraordinarily grand, something sublime resounds. To cite in full: "Therefore, let all complaints against a merciless testament cease, for it is a proper thing indeed for the territories of minor children to be entrusted to regents, not to the children themselves. But now I must take myself to that place, where no man hastens without the salvific sacrament of *viaticum*."[50] After this, Wincenty comments upon the last moments of the ruler in the following manner: "Receiving thus the salvific medicine, this most happy of princes, and still happier father, saw the good day of his life come to an end."[51] And so Krzywousty turns out to be the most happy of princes, and a still happier father, whose life ends at the very moment when he establishes a new order of succession. So is Bolesław presented here as a ruler fulfilled? And what does that mean, anyway, to be a fulfilled ruler? Does there exist some form of fulfilled political government? What is this to mean in the concrete case of Krzywousty, who, as Iwaszkiewicz aptly described it, might have secretly shown the crown of his forefathers to the newlyweds Władysław and Agnes, but never succeeded in placing it on his own brow? And one more thing: how are we to understand this evaluation of a ruler fulfilled in the light of the later catastrophe of the seniority system?

The manner of a rational solution to the problem of succession, adopted by Krzywousty toward the end of his life and enshrined in his statute, vividly reminds one of the story of Shakespeare's King Lear, written a few centuries later. Just as in the tragedy of King Lear, so here in the case of Bolesław we have to deal with a ruler who spent his entire life constructing the unity and strength of his kingdom. Both through many military conquests, practically incessant battles, but also thanks to the continual forging of dynastic relationships, an active, often boldly assertive foreign policy in regard to the Empire and Poland's eastern and southern neighbors, and finally through the masterfully woven tapestry of interior connections between his princely throne and various groups of magnates and clergy, step by step, indefatigably, Krzywousty strengthened his rule, elevated his political position, and although, as one might state on the basis of Wincenty's explications alone, during his reign he experienced both great victories as well as crushing defeats, still he never stinted in his labors. Until finally the moment of death arrived, and he was set face to face with the greatest challenge any monarch has to deal with—that of his succession. It was only his addressing of that challenge that allowed Wincenty to declare him, with undisguised admiration, a fully happy, fortunate, fulfilled ruler. And yet that great attempt at crowning his work, that solid construction of power that he was building all his life long, ended in catastrophe. The establishment of a rational mechanism of succession would lead in a very short while to fratricidal war between the sons of the deceased ruler, which Wincenty both witnessed and in which he had his own role to play. The elements of political ambitions are capable of destroying every sort of rational order one might choose to establish.

Someone once said that "most difficult task of statesmanship is that of providing, not for the foundation, but for the perpetuation, of political institutions. If the political institutions are the best, to perpetuate them is not only the most difficult, but also the greatest of all the tasks of the statesman."[52] From this perspective, Krzywousty is shown to be a rather ambiguous figure. Certainly, he does not fall into raving as does Lear banished by his own children, but rather dies, as Wincenty would have it, in an aura of fulfillment and happiness. And yet the order of succession he wished to construct as a foundation for his state and dynasty will not outlast a single decade. As Wincenty tells the story—as we remember at the very least from the history of Zbigniew's treason, which is key to the second book of the *Chronicle*, the figure of Krzywousty swells to the rank of a hero, an ideal ruler. In the face of such a posthumous decline and fall, Kadłubek's prudence in addressing the question of the statute shouldn't surprise us at all.

It is not the success achieved by the ruler in the full wax of his powers, nor his authority in the ambit of the political community, which constitute the measure of his greatness, good fortune, and fulfillment, but rather his ability to transmit said power in a timely fashion, the preservation of unity thanks to succession. Such a capability must be the result of intent, the work of political reason and not blind chance or coincidence. The capability of transmitting the power amassed in a monarchy becomes possible thanks to the creation and cementing of dynastic continuity. It is something of the order of a backbone of the political system, assuring the stable character of the whole. In this sense, care for the endurance of the dynasty is an expression not only of the personal ambitions of the ruler, the realization of his personal prestige, but a rational matter. The institution of the dynasty allows for the translation of the political reality of the community to a higher, general plane subject to the rule of reason. At the same time, it also exposes it to all the dilemmas arising from the insufficiency and weaknesses of rational political models. For the greater the power amassed, the greater the unity built up during a successful rule, the greater the catastrophe, the more serious in outcome is the conflict in the case of its unsuccessful transmission through time.

It would seem that the transfer of amassed power and unity to one's successors, as well as the immortalization of the system, should be the basic measure of political fulfillment and the happiness of the monarch. Considering these things from the perspective of the times in which Wincenty was writing his *Chronicle*, it turns out that in Polish history, only Bolesław Chrobry (the Brave) might be considered a ruler "fulfilled" in this sense, which, to a certain degree, might explain the "nationalization" of his legend in the twelfth century during the times of Krzywousty. The testament of this latter king remains a mystery, as far as its content is concerned. However, there can be no doubting that it was the expression of a clearly-defined, dynastic, systemic concept. It was about the establishment of a rule which was to eliminate internal quarrels and external intervention. Therefore one can assume, I reckon, that its goal was the systemic consolidation of rule, the separation of its continuance from internal and external opportunism and pressure. Practically speaking, rule of seniority created conditions for the realization of the idea of supreme power, and that not only in the ambit of the dynasty. The significant words of Krzywousty found in the fragment above: "for it is a proper thing indeed for the territories of minor children to be entrusted to regents, not to the children themselves,"[53] are not exclusively directed at the rivalry and conflicts among the brother rivals to his throne. The aspect of the pressures such as those that arise in a situation of succession on the part of both interior and exterior powers is also essential. This is a key problem for the continuance and stability of the system of government, and there is no great difference here between a feudal monarchy a few centuries ago and modern democracy. The clear system of the seniorate was to be, according to Krzywousty, the solution to the problem. The influence of the magnates, whose significance was waxing, as well as that of the clergy, upon the intra-dynastic squabbles between the elder and younger brothers were becoming an ever more essential systemic problem. After all, one might see this process of inner differentiation in an evident manner in the very pages of the *Chronicle*. The influence of the magnates received a further sanction from the ancient institution of the *wiec*, or moot, as well as the nobles' right of opposition. Zdzisław S. Pietras sums up the matter suggestively in his book on Bolesław Krzywousty where he writes: "Beginning with Mieszko I, every king of Poland had to receive the acclamation of the *wiec* [moot]. He issued decrees at the *wiec* and there he sat in judgement. And at the *wiec* it was the right of the crowd that ruled; various moods were in play. The gathering might be more or less numerous, the ovations might resound more or less thunderously, and indeed, even hostile cries might erupt, tumults, murmurs of dissatisfaction. The *wiec* was a concrete power, a military one, because it grouped together people who never set aside their weapons, even if for a moment their hands were not on the hilts. The inherited nature of rule in the Piast clan had deep roots in the consciousness of all the tribes of Poland... In the twelfth century, no one would dare choose between a Piast and, for example, an Awdaniec, but everyone was ready to make a choice from among Piasts."[54] One might therefore assume that the systemic conception of Krzywousty was directed at the securing of dynastic interests in the face of ever stronger opposing processes, and in this sense it was an attempt at consolidating power around the principle of continuity and the subjectivity of the throne. It arose from a design essentially different from the one underlying the actual district breakdown that followed.

As Wincenty tells the story, Bolesław Krzywousty might have gone to his rest satisfied with what he'd done, with a sense of fulfillment (with the exception, all the same, of his unfulfilled dream of coronation—of which Wincenty holds his tongue), as he perfectly planned the mechanism for transmission of the power he had accumulated during his lifetime, as well as the unity he'd attained. Of course, this inner sense of the dying ruler, so underscored by his chronicler, or rather the sense that he himself wished to see, stands in stark contrast to the further development of events: civil war, the breakdown of the realm, the constant quarrels concerning succession, and at last, the final negation of the systemic model proposed by Krzywousty. His happiness turned out to be brief. It succumbed, at last—to what? The dark forces of human nature? Too complex and complicated socio-political forces? The general boundaries of politicality? As I see it, the fragment concerning Bolesław's testament, and his death, gives the impression of an argument strongly internally repressed, a sort of gigantic problem, a great historical theme whereby the author lived, of which he was conscious, and of a sort that was jammed into a framework much too small to hold it. It is clear that Wincenty's hands were tied in this respect. All the same, he wants to show that he's tried to grapple with the subject, although he cannot do so using this particular example, which is doubtlessly the most important one—such a paradox for a historian! For this reason he will attempt it later, in the fourth book devoted to the dynastic conflict between Mieszko Stary (the Old) and Kazimierz Sprawiedliwy.

The Eternal Conflict of Youth with Age

As has already been said, for various reasons, Wincenty does not plumb the problem of the destruction of the systemic model established by the prince, whom he describes as "most fortunate." At the same time, the problem of succession returns in his *Chronicle*, and in a manner that fully compensates for the auto-censorship of the author in the question of Krzywousty's (the Wry-Mouthed) testament. In its conceptual breadth it is additionally comparable with his earlier description of the judgement of Zbigniew and the mini-tractate on political treason. I have in mind here that fragment near the end of the nineteenth chapter of Book IV that deals with the time stretching from the death of Kazimierz, through chapter twenty-six, i.e., to the recuperation of Kraków by Mieszko Stary (the Old).

The conflict between Kazimierz and Mieszko is a conflict between politics young and old. It is a generational conflict, which has a direct political and systemic significance, as, quite simply, it touches upon the matter of succession and legitimacy. What is more, the young politics expropriates the rights of the old, carrying out a successful assault on the rule of succession by seniority. At the same time, it also risks falling victim to its own success, as it opens the space for the activity of forces leading to the assumed assassination of Kazimierz Sprawiedliwy (the Just). His tragic death, which occurred during a banquet, following the downing of a poisoned cup of wine, opens anew the problem of governmental succession. However, this occurs in much more difficult circumstances now, as it follows upon a series of interruptions of continuity and the overstepping of established rules of order, which were the work of Kazimierz himself and his elder brothers.

Kazimierz's sudden death in circumstances that are far from clear, as well as its public character (during a banquet, before the eyes of all assembled), was a real shock for Wincenty, who was most probably an eyewitness to the event. For after all, he was present at the sudden death of his ruler, his patron, his benefactor, his political guardian. We are not in possession of too profound a knowledge of the facts, but it can be assumed that the sudden death of Kazimierz, and, in consequence, the return of Mieszko to Kraków, must have meant the end of Wincenty's career at court. And yet for the author of the *Chronicle*, it becomes above all an occasion to pick up the thread of the great theme of the succession of power he had earlier let fall from his hands. Now, the problem seemed incomparably more serious from the point of view of the preservation of the political unity of the kingdom. Bolesław Krzywousty passes away in an aura of fulfillment, as, in his own opinion, he had prepared everything for the successful transfer of power as well as he could. Kazimierz dies suddenly, without any such preparation, and what is more, in the aura of one who earlier questioned the basic principle of continuity, that is, seniority, crucial for the new system. In such circumstances, solutions had to be worked up on the fly, *ad hoc*, in a sense of the highest necessity and the greatest threat. In essence, we have to deal here with the problem of avoiding *stásis*, civil war, through the reconstruction of the principle of succession. Only in such a way can we restore the rules of rationality, which support the political community as a whole. It is significant that, in this dramatic situation, Pełka, the bishop of Kraków, elevated to the rank of a key player (regent, *interrex*), reaches for the traditional, systemically speaking: aboriginal, form of solving a political dilemma, i.e., the *wiec* (moot). Following the sudden death of the ruler, the community must gather to take a decision.

The arguments used by Pełka to rationalize the decision for calling a moot are interesting. The first of these refers to general, commonsensical prudence, which mandates that after the bereavement is over, we should engage with current affairs. "My worthy lords, this pain is a pious thing, but to grow bitter in pain is nothing of the sort. In truth, our suffering is pious, but it would be impious should we lose our reason through our pain. For there is no more ridiculous manner of losing one's reason than to neglect the healing of a fresh wound. It is like not wishing to save oneself from drowning in deep waters, even though one have the power of doing so,"[55] Pełka advises. What is interesting, Wincenty himself expresses a similar thought a little earlier in his elegy on Kazimierz's death. It looks as if, following the sudden, and not fully explained death of the monarch, complete chaos must have reigned amongst his supporters—the sense of a complete fall, of the end of everything. And this feeling must also have impelled many not only to despair, but also to engage in some sudden, rash, extreme evaluations and activities. The sudden blow of fate resulted in a breakdown fueled by a sense of injustice, wrong, and pain. Pełka's call, like that of Wincenty, is to make men conscious of the fact that pain cannot blind us to reality, nor can it free us from our responsibility thereto. We cannot recognize death as the end of everything, as this is a position that is profoundly unchristian. Nor can we recognize the death of a ruler as the end of everything, for this is a position that is profoundly unpolitical. Death, even the most horrid and violent death, remains within the order of faith, and in the order of politics, as the beginning of something new, which constitutes an obligation of sorts for both the Christian and the citizen. Only later, as a subordinate argument, does there appear in Pełka's thought the necessity of choosing a new ruler: "Now I ask you, for what reason is a swarm of bees scattered most often, and completely destroyed, if not because they are unable to choose a new queen to take the place of the former, who passed away, or because they give the matter no heed at all?"[56]

We have already spoken of the political specifics united to the functioning of the moot, and what, practically speaking, the choice of ruler by acclamation of the parties there gathered might mean. It was exactly such consequences that Krzywousty sought to avoid by establishing the rule of seniority; at the very least, he certainly wished in this way to curb their significance. However, the rebellion led by Kazimierz against the legitimate rule of Mieszko Stary in 1177 opened the road to the overthrow of this well-thought-out mechanism, through that very path: the moot in Łęczyca in 1180, which ultimately legitimized the rule of the young Kazimierz. This systemic "counterrevolution" became possible not only because the prince was young, and thus represented the future, not only on account of his readiness to cast aside the excessive fiscalism introduced by Mieszko (of which Wincenty broadly speaks in the fourth book of the chronicle). No, above all, Kazimierz represented an authentic generational change, which in the eight decade of the twelfth century was taking place in many a Polish clan. "We mustn't forget that in the fifties and sixties of the twelfth century, the group of magnates who had already been gathered about Bolesław Krzywousty, and who later realized his political testament at the side of his elder sons, were on their way out. Meanwhile, a generation that learned politics from their example was beginning to come to the fore and was reaching the apogee of its capabilities at the turn of the sixties and seventies."[57] This is what the historian Józef Dobosz writes in his monograph on Kazimierz Sprawiedliwy. Following the death of Kazimierz, the question circled somewhat back to its starting point. For Pełka, it is an obvious fact that the new ruler ought to be chosen at a moot. At the same time, he clearly suggests that this new ruler ought to be Kazimierz's heir.[58] For that king died only in his "own person," whereas he ought to live on in the new, reborn dynasty through his heir. And so dynastic rights are still to be preserved, but in a renewed form. The interests of the magnates also are to receive sanction due to the moot. The only thing that is to be negated is the principle of the seniorate, represented by the hated Mieszko Stary. Such a setting of the matter led, however, to a sharp exchange of views between the participants at the gathering. For Pełka's proposal would lead to the transfer of power to the sons of Kazimierz, still minors, and that would be in disaccord not only with the principle of the violated seniorate or rule of elders, but would also turn out to be irresponsible. "Woe to the land whose king is a child!"[59] cried one of those there gathered. What might happen to such a realm in which authority is placed in the hands of a person who needs to be governed himself? Pełka's response is, in turn, an example of a slyly intricate, although effective, rhetorical deduction.[60] He argues that the moot is not the same thing as the election of a ruler. If that was the case, the choice of the minor Leszek as king would indeed be an expression of the insanity of free, but irrational people. It is, on the other hand, nothing other than the sanctioning of the principle of dynastic continuity in the orbit of the Piast family, established in 1180 and confirmed not only by the presence of the magnates and dignitaries of the Church at the Łęczyca moot, but later too, in individual documents issued by Pope Alexander and Emperor Frederick. In this context, Pełka speaks of the "compulsion of the law,"[61] which constrains the recognition of Leszek as ruler—and here his present age is of no significance.

The bishop's arguments were received with enthusiasm. All doubts were cast aside, and the decision was adopted by acclamation.[62] All very beautiful, except for the fact that Mieszko Stary was already waiting just beyond the city walls, as the lawful senior of the clan, according to the letter of Krzywousty's statute. He is not, of course, a positive character in Wincenty's narrative. Above all, we remember him from the first chapters of Book IV in which he is represented as a tyrant, in essence, exploiting his state unscrupulously, as if it were his private demesne. Without a doubt, Mieszko was attached to the old model of traditional monarchic rule. He felt himself to be the inheritor and the guardian of the dynastic-seniority system of government introduced by his father. His reaction to the election of the minor Leszek by the Kraków moot shows that he perfectly understood the political consequences of supreme power arising in such a way. One sees in his arguments a mature consciousness of the significance that the incarnation of the traditional idea of monarchic power in the feudal world has for the unity of the state and the crown, or—as we would put it today—for sovereignty. "They're choosing children as princes so as in this way to rationalize their own rule over their rulers. In order to totally deracinate the royal clan, so that they might at last be able to rule freely themselves, so that instead of one Head, there should grow among them as many kings as they have heads," states Mieszko, acknowledging at the same time that such a situation threatens the security of the entire country, the entire community, as "the fold thus remains without a shepherd."[63] However, the problem rests in that the monarchic convictions of Mieszko, combined with his earlier banditry of fiscalism as well as his complete refusal to come to terms with the magnate clans then waxing in power, show that, most likely, he was not capable of properly reacting, as a ruler, to the challenges of the new political times. He was incapable of uniting tradition to the exigencies of the future, and understood the power of the monarch in a simple way, as the absolutist rule a prince has over his private domain. But Poland at that time, having become in the twelfth century a much more advanced conglomerate of interests of its constituent districts, magnate clans, men of the Church, and finally all the new social structures that arose as a result of the dynamic, civilizational development—could no longer be ruled in such a way. Remaining, according to the letter of the law, the nation's ruler, Mieszko turned himself into a person incapable of governing, ignoring as he did the exigencies of the new reality. He was also the representative of the old world, which was strongly highlighted by the generational dispute in which he was permanently entangled, be that by his struggle with his much younger brother Kazimierz, the representative of the new generation, or in his conflicts with his own sons. For this reason too, the entire history as told by Wincenty in the fourth book can be understood as a general observation, according to which conditions, relations, circumstances change with the passage of time—the reality that is subject to the power of governance is a living and complex thing, so no political form can abstract from its dynamics. For this reason, no system can abstract itself from its dynamics. Mieszko's return—even if he was well within his legal rights (something that Wincenty clearly relativizes by underscoring the events of the year 1180) and even if the whole matter might play out in accord with objectively correct arguments on behalf of the necessity of a strong, independent monarchical power—in practice would signify the imposition of an old, anachronistic form upon a much changed reality. It is for this reason that Wincenty so clearly stands on the side of youth, and not tradition, which can be exemplified by his eloquent evaluation of Mieszko's motivations: "And yet I cannot comprehend why the vacuity of old men should still so yearn for favor! The older they get, the more they become bent with age, the higher they carry themselves, and the more greedily they curry men's favor. The more they are oppressed by the burden of impotence, the lighter they float about the heavens on the wings of empty giddiness. For although an old man might tame all the monsters of fault he finds within himself, he shall still be subject to two, namely: vanity and greed."[64]

Mieszko is not only old, he is also stubborn. He refuses to submit to the exigencies of the new reality. The struggle for power culminates in the battle of Mozgawa, which as Wincenty describes it, becomes a bloody, senseless, fratricidal shambles, resulting, it is true, in Mieszko's re-occupation of Kraków, but also in the loss of his beloved son Bolesław. What is more, the short time left him renders his rule practically insignificant. For the old world is now definitely fading into the past, while the new has not yet fully been born.

I reckon that this is a proper conclusion for Wincenty's intermittent, unfinished *Chronicle*. Of course, he had no way of foreseeing that eventually history would take the side of his princely protector, Kazimierz Sprawiedliwy. It is true that the dynastic project of the transfer of power invented by Krzywousty turned out to be unreal and ultimately foundered in the blood of fratricidal wars. In undermining the principle of the seniorate, Kazimierz effected a *de facto* coup d'état; something to which Mieszko Stary was never willing to reconcile himself. And yet he established a new Piast dynasty, which, some one hundred years after his death, achieved, at last, the royal crown. For Władysław Łokietek was, in a direct line, the grandson of Konrad Mazowiecki, Leszek's brother, the younger son of Kazimierz Sprawiedliwy.

Dead to the World

Why should we read Wincenty these days? What advantage is to be drawn from it? Why should we bother our heads with an author, whom later, contemporary history has demasked as a mythomaniacal liar? On the other hand, should one undertake a journey to the Cistercian monastery in Jędrzejów in which Wincenty was buried, one might better understand why in their own time those charges might have elicited such a violent negative reaction. The cult that surrounds the holiness of Kadłubek with a nimbus has lasted without interruption for many centuries, leading to his elevation to the altar as one of the blessed by Pope Clement XIII in 1764, just before the first Partition of the Republic. To this day pious Catholics pray before his reliquary, raising their petitions for the intercession of Blessed Wincenty. The walls of the church are covered with the carved initials and names of the pilgrims who travelled there; some even date from the beginning of the nineteenth century. Are they to be understood as praying to a blessed liar?!

Wincenty's flight from the world, after ten years of episcopal service in Kraków, to the Cistercian cloister *Morimondus Minor* in Jędrzejów, has become overgrown with legend. It is rather not true that it was only there, in seclusion, that he brought his *Chronicle* to an end. I shall also risk the thesis that Wincenty never took the

Cistercian habit at all, but only lived there as a resident surrounded by the respect of the brethren who saw in him a great dignitary and learned man, since tradition holds that he was buried in his episcopal pallium. The decision to resign from his bishopric must have been a deeply considered one, and irreversible. The sudden death, in 1194, of Kazimierz Sprawiedliwy (the Just), as the result of an assassination, was a shock for Wincenty. The later meanderings of politics resulting from the battle for Kraków waged between Mieszko Stary (the Old) and the supporters of the sons of Kazimierz made it so that, for his own safety, Wincenty withdrew from direct politics and the interests of the court in Kraków. As the author of a chronicle composed at the request of the deceased prince, he might now feel the pincers of censorship tightening. His investiture in the prebend in Sandomierz looks a little like a desire to withdraw into the shadows. However, it is not the case that Wincenty remained completely without support in the new political situation. He took a stand on the side of Henryk Kietlicz, the archbishop of Gniezno, who had fought against the absolutist tendencies of Mieszko Stary, and later those of his son Władysław Laskonogi (Spindleshanks). Kietlicz won the personal support of the great Pope Innocent III in his attempts at introducing the Gregorian reforms of the Church to the Piast state. In the Polish lands, this reform had been retarded in relation to Western Europe by a full hundred years. However, had he been able at last to introduce them, the position of the Church in relation to the Piast dynasty would have been strengthened to an immeasurable degree. Having so powerful a Roman protector, Kietlicz became a key figure of the reform in Poland, a figure whom the Piasts and the magnates currently had to reckon with. If we take into consideration Wincenty's earlier public engagement, his taking the side of the Gniezno archbishop seems a logical step, independent of his own personal engagement in the matter of the postulates of ecclesiastical reform. In 1208, with the support of Kietlicz and the agreement of Leszek

Biały (the White), son of Kazimierz Sprawiedliwy and now prince of Kraków, Wincenty obtained the bishopric of Kraków. For the next ten years he was to play an active role in the life of the Church and the Piast state, including his participation in the Fourth Lateran Council in Rome. And yet, in 1218, he made the decision, at last, to die to the world. He left Kraków for Jędrzejów on foot, heading to the Cistercian monastery which is set amongst the picturesque meadows of the rolling Małopolska uplands, and there he was to remain in monastic seclusion until his death. His decision to abandon Kraków was certainly linked to the fall of Archbishop Kietlicz, which shook the entire movement of ecclesiastical reform to its foundations. When his Roman protector passed away, and a new Pope, Honorius III, ascended the throne of Peter, the enemies of the archbishop took advantage of the ripe moment to accuse him of the sin of pride. The plot was successful, and Kietlicz's star was extinguished. After his being forced to withdraw from public life, surely Wincenty's situation in Kraków had to change as well. Perhaps he thought that enough was enough; that it was time to concentrate on his own personal salvation and for this reason he chose a contemplative life among the Cistercians. A straight path runs from active to contemplative life.

Wincenty left behind him an extraordinary work. Historians are free to tussle among themselves concerning its historical value. That is beside the point. For the *Chronicle* is, above all, the expression of the authentic political passion of an engaged man, who, in order to understand the sense of human actions centered on government, makes use of all the wisdom made available to him by both classical and Christian thought. For Polish culture, it remains a foundational text for political reflection. In it can be found musings on the wellsprings of political community and the role of evil in politics, on the power of political elements that burst all the reins of law, and on the matter, still important to the Polish tradition, of the tension between the moot-culture (*kultura wiecowa*)—let us say: democratic-anarchic culture—and the institutional order of the state. We find there considerations on treason and civic loyalty, as well as many other fundamental problems of a political nature. Above all, however, Wincenty writes Polish history into the current of the European classical tradition, which remains, perhaps, his greatest and simultaneously most controversial achievement of an intellectual-political character, as he sets the ancestors of the Piasts firmly on an even level with the heroes of antiquity. And one more thing: in the pages of his *Chronicle* we find a key opinion stating that identity is the mother of all societies. This is the most important signpost found in his political reflections. With Kadłubek, identity swells into a paramount political conception, which we cannot do without, and which, in the case of Polish political culture, seems self-evident even today. For to this day our consolidation is above all a matter of our identity, of which we always quarrel in a fundamental manner. By leaving Kraków on foot and heading in the direction of Jędrzejów, Wincenty wished, irreversibly, to die to the world. And yet his *Chronicle* saw to it that his political reflections remain alive for us today. Indeed, they possess an undying significance.

Endnotes

1. T. Wojciechowski, *Szkice historyczne jedynastego wieku,* Kraków 1904, p. 250.
2. See T. Grudziński, "Konflikt króla Bolesława Szczodrego z biskupem Stanisławem w polskiej świadomości zbiorowej [zarys problematyki]" (The Conflict of King Bolesław the Generous with Bishop Stanisław in the Collective Polish Consciousness [a Sketch of the Problematics]), *Acta Universitatis Nicolai Copernici. Historia*, 17 (117), p. 14. *Translator's note*: King Bolesław II (c. 1040–1081/82) enjoyed the honorific *Szczodry* (the Generous) before his part in the murder of St. Stanisław (1079). From that time forward, he was known as the Bolesław Śmiały (the Bold).
3. The accusation of Kazimierz Krotoski. Ibid., p. 10.
4. T. Wojciechowski, "Plemię Kadłubka. Odpowiedź," Lwów 1909.
5. P. Jasienica, *Trzej kronikarze* (Three Chroniclers), Warsaw 2008, p. 390.
6. Ibid., p. 391.
7. Ibid., p. 397.
8. See O. Balzer, *Studyum o Kadłubku* (A Study of Kadłubek), Lwów 1934, Vol. 1, especially p. 210.

9. Ibid., pp. 187–188.

10. W. Kadłubek, *Kronika polska*, trans. B. Kürbis, Wrocław 2008, Book I, 1, p. 3.

11. Ibid., I, 1, p. 2.

12. Ibid., I, 1, p. 8.

13. Herodotus, *The Histories*, trans. T. Holland, London 2015, p. 3.

14. Geoffrey of Monmouth, *History of the Kings of Britain*, trans. L. Thorpe, London 1977.

15. Citation from: J. Le Goff, *Medieval Civilization 400–1500*, trans. J. Barrow, Oxford 1988, pp. 171–172. In French: Jacques Le Goff, *La civilisation de l'Occident médiéval,* Paris 2022).

16. On this topic see the in-depth discussion found in Z. Kałuża, *Lektury filozoficzne Wincentego Kadłubka. Zbiór studiów* (Wincenty Kadłubek's Readings in Philosophy. A Selection of Studies), Warsaw 2014.

17. W. Kadłubek, *Kronika...*, Book I, 5, p. 11.

18. Ibid.

19. Ibid.

20. Ibid.

21. Ibid.

22. Ibid., Book I, 5, p. 12.

23. Ibid., p. 13.

24. Ibid., Book I, 7, p. 15.

25. Ibid., Book I, 5, pp. 14–15.

26. J. Iwaszkiewicz, *Czerwone tarcze,* Warsaw 1988, p. 42.

27. Ibid., p. 38.

28. Ibid., p. 62.

29. Ibid., pp. 64–65.

30. Ibid., p. 70.

31. Ibid., p. 71.

32. Ibid.

33. Ibid., pp. 195–196.

34. Ibid., p. 196.

35. T. Parnicki, *Srebrne orły,* Warsaw 2004, p. 483.

36. Ibid., p. 505.

37. W. Kadłubek, *Kronika...*, op. cit., Book II, 29, p. 112.

38. Ibid., Book II, 24, p. 91.

39. Ibid., Book II, 27, p. 96.

40. Ibid.

41. Ibid., Book II, 22, p. 87.

42. Ibid., Book II, 26, p. 94.

43. Ibid., Book II, 28, p. 102.

44. Ibid., Book II, 28, p. 107.

45. Ibid., Book II, 28, p. 108.

46. Ibid., Book II, 28, p. 110.

47. Ibid., Book II, 30, p. 112.

48. Ibid., Book III, 26, pp. 155–156.

49. Ibid., Book III, 26, p. 157.

50. Ibid.

51. Ibid.

52. H.V. Jaffa, "The Limits of Politics: an Interpretation of King Lear, act I, scene I," *The American Political Science Review*, Vol. 51, No. 2, 1957, p. 405.

53. W. Kadłubek, *Kronika...*, op. cit., Book III, 26, p. 157.

54. Z.S. Pietras, *Bolesław Krzywousty*, Kraków 2000, p. 227.

55. W. Kadłubek, *Kronika...*, op. cit., Book IV, 21, p. 240.

56. Ibid.

57. J. Dobosz, *Kazimierz II Sprawiedliwy*, Poznań 2014, p. 92.

58. W. Kadłubek, *Kronika...*, op. cit., Book IV, 21, p. 240.

59. Ibid., Book IV, 21, p. 241.

60. Ibid., Book IV, 21, pp. 241–242.

61. Ibid., Book IV, 21, p. 242.

62. Ibid., Book IV, 21, pp. 242–243.

63. Ibid., Book IV, 22, p. 244.

64. Ibid., Book IV, 25, p. 256.

ROMAN FORM

My first experience of Rome was quite unique and for that reason I remember it vividly to this day. It was somewhere in the mid-1990s. I had been invited to a conference in Rome, organized by the German Goethe Institute. Their intentions were quite clear. I was to play the role of the poor cousin from the East, according to the well-known script. The star of the debate was a special guest: the German philosopher with Dutch roots, Peter Sloterdijk. I reckon that they were aiming at attracting the blasé Roman public to the event, for whom a German gabbing about Europe must always seem some sort of eccentricity, now as then, since no Italian has any doubt as to the fact that Europe equals Italy. And so the organizers must certainly have had some sort of arch-German pedagogical goal in mind. I travelled to Rome by train—through Vienna, the Alps, Venice and Bologna—a trip that took just about a day and a half. Nor was the trip devoid of sensation. When my night train from Warsaw, delayed for over an hour, finally rolled into the southern station in Vienna at six in the morning, it turned out that my train to Venice had just pulled out. So I had to wait a few hours for the next train, but I didn't miss out; I spent the time on a bench in the Belvedere gardens with a beautiful view of St. Stephen's cathedral, and a panorama of the city. I suppose that someone, especially today, might say that this was a rather peculiar way to travel. It only takes two hours or so to get to Rome from Warsaw by airplane. But the comfort of quick movement from place to place not only tears us away from the earth, it also precludes contact with all the factual differences that make up our unique reality, our world. So let's say that I wanted to experience my first journey to Rome in a fully conscious manner. I wanted to see for myself that oldest route of migration in Europe, which runs from North to South, and believe me—it was worth the trouble. I saw with my own eyes that this path truly leads us to our source, to warmth, to light. The conference itself was a funny sort of show, which gave me a lot to think about. The German organizers went out of their minds with planning, but the Italian public took their sweet time to take their places. We were running about an hour late before the hall was half full. I spoke about the Polish experience of Communism and about Solidarity, in acute consciousness of the fact that my words were falling on deaf ears. For his part, Sloterdijk presented a lecture on Europe that completely surprised me. I had been expecting to hear what one always heard from the side of our western neighbors—unity, reconciliation, Adenauer and Schuman. It turns out that I had underestimated Sloterdijk; as a matter of fact, I didn't know him at all at the time. Peppering his lecture thickly with citations from Vergil, he spoke of how Aeneas created Europe, and finally arrived at Augustus Octavian and Christ. It was a curious thing to witness, for as far as physiognomy goes, Sloterdijk might seem the typical German barbarian from the North: whiskers, big nose, long unkempt locks. All he needed was a metal helmet with horns. He was the complete opposite of the Roman public sitting *en face* to him, who looked at both of us as a couple of wild men. I remember that, because of their bored, glazed eyes I suddenly understood that Sloterdijk and I, that great, self-righteous German and the "poor wretch from the East," constitute a sort of community of barbarian ultramontanists from the Northern regions beyond the Alps. And then the scandal erupted. Now the organizers were very desirous of setting the highest tone possible for the conference; for this reason they also invited a certain important Italian personage, some Italian commissioner from the European Commission in Brussels, I ween, to take part as well. As luck would have it, during Sloterdijk's presentation, the telephone of the important personage began to sound, and he answered it. It must have been some important matter that brooked no delay, some *very* important European issue. Sloterdijk behaved just the way a barbarian from the North ought to behave. He leapt to his feet, threw his papers down on the table in front of him, began fulminating at the important personage, calling him a "Eurocretin," and announcing that such being the case here, he was leaving. Later, he dramatized the situation even more, screaming, or rather bellowing, that it's because of such soulless Eurocrats that Europe is dying today. He left, and then he returned, he threw his papers down on the table again, went out, and so on, for some fifteen minutes. He certainly made an impression. The public was a little frightened and disoriented, but a little fascinated as well. With a tone of disapproval in his voice, the important personage declared his willingness to apologize. As for me, I was delighted, because all this only confirmed my deepest intuitions concerning the fact that the history of Europe might begin with Aeneas, and not with Adenauer or Schuman; that Rome is more important than Brussels, and that Poland's return to Europe after the years of Communism was a return to our source, to warmth and to light, which are to be found here in the South, and that in the face of these sources, all European institutions, that whole legal order of the European Union, that *acquis communautaire,* toward which Poland had been so aspiring at the end of the twentieth century, well, they are important things, and yet very, very secondary ones as well. And there is one other situation linked to my first experience of Rome of which I must speak, as it constitutes an important conclusion. After the conference, I went, *de rigueur*, to St. Peter's Square, which seemed to me truly gigantic in comparison with what I'd heretofore only known from the television screen. Standing in front of the mighty façade of the basilica, I suddenly understood that, for Pete's sake, it's a Polish pope who's residing behind these venerable walls. In other words, this Rome, all of this grand Roman form, can also be filled with Polish content. Now, this would be no discovery to my countrymen in the sixteenth or seventeenth centuries; it was rather an obvious thing. But for my contemporary countrymen, even for those who arrived here in buses in order to see with their own eyes their beloved Polish pope, such a thought was neither obvious, nor even so universal. And at that moment I thought: if we once more acknowledged that we might fill out Roman form with Polish content, and after all, thanks to John Paul II we possessed just such a phenomenal example in our own day and age, not at all some distant, historical image, well, we might, at long last, stop thinking about ourselves as these poor relatives from the East, set into that well-known script that had been cut to our measure, albeit somewhat too tightly.

Teodor Parnicki's Barbarian Europe

Polishness at home in Roman form, our own way of life, our place in Europe, is an idea that allows us to understand the highs and lows of our history. But it's also related to a thought that to a great extent reaches past any particularly Polish experience, and which I'd like to state at the very outset here, with perfect clarity: civilization, as an order, an *ordo*, is not at all in the first place some sphere of comfort, of social, economic, or political conquests, which allow us to organize ourselves on some higher plane of effective rule over nature. We may construct civilization only in conditions of Good, and that means, with a readiness to confront evil, to look at reality just as it is, without fear. In conditions of readiness to such an understanding of valor, which sometimes requires martyrdom—things that, generation by generation, Europe is un-learning.

In order to better understand this, we have to go back a bit in time. For the nonce, just fifty years, but then—get ready for a strong acceleration backward. And so: the start of the 1970s. The first years of the Gierek decade in PRL history. Teodor Parnicki was invited by the Institute of Polish Philology at Warsaw University to deliver a cycle of guest lectures. Throughout the entire academic year, beginning on October 11th, and then in more or less weekly instalments, the sixty-five year old writer developed in one of the lecture halls his narrative of life, and his conception of the historical novel. In his large horn-rimmed glasses, always impeccably dressed in an official suit and tie, elegant in an old-fashioned way, he presented, each time without notes, but always well-planned out, detailed lectures. The auditory was astounded at his perfect memory, lively narrative, and absolutely brilliant eloquence. From the beginning, the lectures were cloaked in an aura of sensation, and the lecture hall was filled to bursting. It's understandable that Parnicki aroused great interest. First of all, there was his biography—far from the standard fare. He had been born in Berlin, the capital of the Prussian Empire, in a Germanized family with Polish roots. Before the First World War he emigrated to Moscow with his father, after which he lived in Omsk and Vladivostok, from which he escaped to Harbin in Manchuria where there was a large Polish colony of some tens of thousands of people. It was only there, in Harbin, a city established near the end of the nineteenth century by the Russians as the central settlement for the great project of the construction of the East-China Railroad, that he became familiar with the Polish language and Polish culture—by reading Sienkiewicz, among others. It was there that he experienced the process of repolonization, as up to this time he'd really only made use of Russian and German. And then, alongside Polish, he began learning Latin as well, discovering in himself an immense interest in the history of ancient Rome. "Interest" is something of an understatement. Actually, it became the passion of his life. In the 1920s, he decided to settle in Poland for good, in Lwów (Lviv). Arrested by the NKVD in September 1939, after his release in 1941 he began working in the Polish embassy in Kuibyshev, after which he travelled through Teheran and Jerusalem with General Anders' army. After the war he lived in Mexico for a long while. But then in the 1960s he decided to return to People's Poland—at that time the Poland of Władysław Gomułka. One can only imagine that, for many of the students listening to him in that lecture hall, whose road through life had, up till now, stretched only as far as, let's say, from Radom, Starachowice or Szczytno to Warsaw, Parnicki's biography must have seemed something absolutely exotic, stupendously so. What a fascinating globetrotter! His books also aroused great interest. Historical novels, beginning with the pre-war *Aecjusz, ostatni Rzymianin* (Aetius, the Last Roman) for which he received a literary prize, or *Srebrne orły* (Silver Eagles), which he wrote in 1944 in Jerusalem—Parnicki's "greatest hit," reprinted again and again thanks to the immense interest of his readers. But even his later novels, which were considered too complicated and unclear, especially on account of their murky character, the ever growing elaboration of style, the sense of some sort of mysteriousness if not to say hidden meanings and messages, all this enflamed interest in Parnicki even more. And now he was sitting in a lecture hall of the Polish Department at Warsaw University, speaking in a tone of complete obviousness of things, which for many of his listeners must have seemed extraordinary. I reckon that they'd never heard anything like it before. Certainly not in the PRL—neither before, during the years of the whiny Gomułka, nor now, during the years of the "worldly" Gierek. From where they were sitting, their window on the wider world might be constituted, at most, by a bottle of Coca-Cola or a packet of Marlboros bought at the PEWEX[1]. And here Parnicki was opening entirely new windows before their eyes.

"My passion was Rome," he said to his auditors, "especially the later Roman Empire, and thus, also, the problem of the triumph of Islam at the cost of the Christian Roman Empire."[2] In another place, in the same lecture, he stated: "For me the idea of catholicity was above all a synonym for the idea of Roman Catholicism; it was linked to the idea of Rome, Latin, culture, the Latin culture of Rome, and so forth."[3] And it is this very catholicity, "some sense of a link to ancient Rome and the universal language of that Rome,"[4] that allows one to always clearly make out our difference in regard to the Orthodox and the Protestants. For Parnicki, Rome was the most important thing; without it nothing could be understood properly. And that was the case during those lectures at the Polish Department in Warsaw. There also occurred something very characteristic there—during one of his lectures, Parnicki listed from memory and in order all of the Roman Emperors. He knew perfectly which of them had died a natural death, and which had been assassinated. Then, after some reflection, he asked—and I imagine that his tone must have been somewhat uncertain—whether he hadn't bored his listeners with that list, whether he hadn't overwhelmed them.[5] Quite early on, for at the age of only twenty-nine, Parnicki poured these Roman passions of his into the form of his first novel, which treated the fall of Rome and Aetius Flavius, the last great leader of the army of the Western Empire, a Roman Patrician, whom perhaps not without reason he named the last defender of Rome. Parnicki composed this debut of his in Lwów, which—also perhaps not without reason—Aleksander Wat considered the most Italian of all the cities of Poland.

That beautiful Lwów was also the setting for a conversation, the eloquence of which is quite essential to us, and which Parnicki recalled during one of his lectures. "I once had a conversation with a professor of History—it was Professor Chyliński, and his assistant. They generally had very pleasant things to say to me, complimenting me on my book, but then Professor Chyliński said: 'Dear Mr. Teodor, are you quite certain, sir, that Aetius might have saved or rescued anything at all, in that situation?'" Of course, he was asking whether Aetius had any chance of rescuing Rome from its fall, or whether his death at the hand of the young Emperor Valentinian, who was quite simply afraid of the power of the great patrician, doomed the Empire, finally. And then his assistant added, pressing the question further: "Was there anything worth saving?"[6] It was a provocation. It opened a whole range of possible, far-reaching consequences. Immediately, Parnicki hastened to explain the matter to his listeners. German historiography of the nineteenth century—and it needs to be stated that at the time the Germans had some significant achievements in this field—had a great influence on university life in Poland. And this assistant found himself absolutely under the strong influence of the fashionable German historical thought, which was of that very opinion—that there was nothing worth saving. According to them, the Roman world was mortally ill. "And so it was a fortunate thing," Parnicki went on, "that new tribes (of course we're speaking of German tribes from the era of the migration of the peoples) entered into the historical arena. For only on the ruins of that rotting organism could new social relations be created, new interpersonal relations, new political relations. And so it is to these fresh people, all these Visigoths, Franks, Burgundians, Saxons, etc.—that Europe chiefly owes a debt of gratitude for its later civilization, for everything that it became."[7] Such theses were more often than not underlined, quite simply, with that new German nationalism, which was preparing the ground for the ideology then on its way, according to which European culture had been created by the Germanic peoples. To put it another way, Arminius, the prince of the German Cherusci tribe, who in the year 9 of our era won a spectacular triumph over the Romans in the Teutoburg Forest, was the harbinger of all future, irreversible dictates of history—the fall of Rome and the victory of the new Germanic peoples on its ruins, which built our Europe. On this same basis,

German historians (Otto Seeck, for example) and theoreticians of culture (such as Gustav Friedrich Klemm) were later to develop their conceptions of the birth and decline of cultures as a natural process of development, which Oswald Spengler was to present in a dramatic form in his famous book *The Decline of the West*, as was Marian Zdziechowski here in Poland. And so the question as to whether it was worth saving wasn't innocent at all. For should one respond in a positive manner, things would look entirely different from the way German historical science wished to see things. Indeed, then it would appear that the one inalienable characteristic of European culture was the effort, constantly repeated, of rescuing the Roman world.

So I will constantly repeat after Parnicki that Europe arose from the clash of North and South. The dramatic process of the destruction of the ancient, Roman world was simultaneously the beginning of a new European form. The barbarian peoples flooding down from the North poured themselves into the old form of *romanitas* as if it were into desiccated vessels, so as, in the end, to become transformed, converted into something good. This was like a collision of atoms which gave rise to the whole chain reaction of European history. We can still catch sight of the faint glow of that explosion in our European culture, even if it is growing ever more weak. Will it, someday, be snuffed entirely? And if so, what will happen to us?

As nuclear physics tells us, a chain reaction might result in something absolutely catastrophic. It was no different in this case. For it was a destructive event that transformed the whole ancient, Roman world. At first glance, the fifth century of our era looked like one great battlefield or a complete, chaotic downfall. It can be accepted that the very process of the decline of the Roman state had been going on, more or less, for a whole century—from the time, let us say, of the disastrous rule of the Arian emperor Valens, which came to an end in 378 with his deserved death in battle against the desperate Visigoths near Adrianople, up to the episodic reign of the final emperor

Romulus Augustulus, which was interrupted in 476. It gives one pause to wonder whether the inhabitants of the empire in decline were at all conscious of the process of decline in which they were participating. Perhaps it was too spread out in time, too complex, for it to be noticed with precision, and this is why the great majority of people lived entirely normal lives, establishing families, building houses, getting educated, climbing the rungs of a profession, engaging in various business, and travelling the world? The great western Empire was dying, but the intensity of social, economic, intellectual, and finally religious life remained for a long while at a high level.

Certainly, it was those living in Britain at the time, in that most northern, distant province of the empire who noticed the fact of old Rome's disappearance most swiftly, before their very own eyes. For they had been cast aside. In the face of the spreading battles with the barbarians in Gaul, in the Balkans, and in Italy herself, no one had either the strength nor the courage to busy himself with such a distant part of the Roman world. What is worse, because of a disastrous strategic error, the island had been left practically helpless, without any defense at all. When, in 396, it was attacked from many sides by Saxons, Angles, Jutes, Picts, and who knows what other barbarian tribes—a real catastrophe was the result! Stilicho, the commander-in-chief of the western armies, the *magister militium*, performed the very last act of rescue in the island's Roman history. While it is true that he beat back the barbarians, he proceeded to withdraw all the more important military forces from Britain, sending them back across to the continent, in order to beat back there the Visigoths attacking Italy. What is interesting here is that Stilicho already belonged to that group of Roman leaders dating from the time of the sunset of the Empire, who most often came of mixed marriages (his father was a Vandal), just like Aetius, Parnicki's hero, or also like Sigiswult, the Roman *comes* in Africa, who was of Gothic blood. Whatever the case may be, Stilicho's decision left the island completely defenseless. As late as 410 the Romano-British were sending letters to Flavius Aetius begging him for help: "The barbarians drive us into the sea, and the sea drives us back into the barbarians."[8] But all for naught, as at the very same time the Visigoths of Alaric were plundering Rome. This must have been a poignant experience, the lot of every distant province, an outthrust portion of the political organism, to learn that nobody's picking up in the home office; nobody's taking any decisions, nobody's in charge. Along with the native Celtic population as well as the remnants of the northern army, the Romano-Britons were all alone on the island. For this reason too they had to create by themselves their own structures for a new government, and to establish their interior political balance on their own. In these events one can discern the wellsprings of today's England and her idea of independent, autonomous rule, the English *self-governance* and *self-confidence.*

However, the unstoppable process of the decimation of the Roman Empire carried out by successive waves of barbarians had been set in motion long before the Romano-British understood that they were all alone on their island. What is more, this process was initiated by happenings so distant from the Mediterranean world, that it must have seemed to the inhabitants of the Empire some completely inexplicable decree of Providence, some horrible punishment falling upon them from Heaven. The verdict that sealed the harsh sentence concerning the fate of the Roman Empire fell in a distant part of Asia, where for long centuries the wild, warrior tribe of Huns had been threatening the existence of another empire, that of the Chinese, located, from the Roman perspective, on some unimaginably distant edge of the Asian continent. As early as the third century BC, in order to defend themselves from the hordes of the savages, the Chinese emperors raised a defensive wall running some two and a half thousand kilometers. Yet ramparts, battlements, and great armies were to no avail. The Huns spread terror and destruction all around them; they were like swarms of locusts that nothing could contain. The most fantastic legends were framed concerning their genesis. For example, it was said that witches, banished from human settlements for their disgusting, murderous practices, had spawned the Hunnish people through sexual relations with the demons of the steppe. Then suddenly, at a certain moment, just as if the wind of history had made a violent reversal to blow in the opposite direction, these frightful descendants of witches and demons chose for themselves a different direction for expansion. Pushed out of the Central Asian steppes by other peoples, the Huns began conquering the Black Sea steppes, driving therefrom the Slavs, Scythians, Alani, Ostrogoths, and Visigoths—all of which peoples, escaping from these new, cruel, and unknown conquerors, were racing in panic to the West. And so with these Huns we have a classic example of the domino reaction. The uprise of these exceptionally cruel barbarians from the East somewhere around 370 AD set in motion the gigantic migration of other peoples into the depths of the western world, which no one was able to halt any more. Further peoples inhabiting the Pontic steppes were conquered by the Huns or forced to escape, which in a violent and completely unexpected manner fundamentally transformed the geopolitical situation of the old Roman Empire and, as it was soon to become apparent, sealed the fate of the Mediterranean world in general. In 377 there occurred some dramatic events of great historical consequence. For some time, for some hundred years, the Germanic people of the Goths had inhabited the territory on the northern bank of the Danube, which had been the old Roman province of Dacia. They were known as "people of the woods." Already in the second half of the third century they had spread terror among the Romans, after first penetrating the borders of the Empire and threatening the security of Italy herself. And yet they had been pushed back beyond the Danube where they were to settle. The situation had changed since those times. Now, especially in comparison with the savage Huns, these barbarians, and above all that portion of them known as Visigoths (or let us say, western Goths settled near the Roman borders), might have seemed quite gentle: they led a sedentary, agricultural life, and the broad bed of the Danube separated them in a natural and safe way from the territories of the Roman Empire proper. They were, you might say, next-door neighbors. There is one other essential condition that should be mentioned in this context: the great majority of the Goths had become fervent Christians. And so, they were an avant-garde in the process of the Christianization of the barbarian peoples. A certain man named Ulfilas played a decisive role in their conversion. Also known as Wulfila, he was the bishop of and apostle to the Goths. Even earlier, when they had settled Dacia, the Goths had met with many Christians among the Roman population, who shared the Good News with the barbarians. But it was only the mission of Ulfilas that turned the tide. This Ulfilas or Wulfila was himself of mixed ancestry; a Greco-German, educated in the monasteries of Moesia, who was later ordained bishop of Tauris, that is, modern day Crimea. From there he set out on his historical mission: the evangelization of the Goths. He won their trust and quite quickly their adherence to the new Faith. In order to make the Word of God fully approachable to the barbarians, Wulfila took up the unusual labor of translating nearly the entire Bible from Greek into Gothic. For this task he had to create a Gothic alphabet, which had not existed before, from a compilation of Latin and Greek symbols. There was, however, one fly in the ointment of this whole exceptional history of the quite smoothly progressing process of the Christianization of the Germanic tribes north of the Danube, and their neophyte piety: Ulfilas was an Arian. And thus, with ardor, he filled the fair heads and raw souls of the barbarians with a heresy incompatible with the Catholic dogma of the Holy Trinity, as it denied the divinity of Christ. At this time in history, the quarrel concerning the consubstantiality of Christ with God the Father constituted the most important matter dividing the Christian community. It is true that, in 325, the Nicaean Council had attempted to solve the problem, accepting the confession of Faith which we still use today, which acknowledges the Son of God as true God, consubstantial with the Father. However, the proponents of Arius' teachings still held to their opinion that there is only One God existing from all time—God the Father of all creation, including Jesus Christ Himself. Wulfila's confession was completely anti-Nicaean, and the Goths converted by him repeated after him that they believed "that there is only one God the Father, alone unbegotten and invisible [...] And I believe the Son to be subject and obedient to the Father in all things."[9] This Arianism of the barbarians, and their heretical nature, quickly became a hot-button political problem. It was not without reason that St. Ambrose, that great figure of the Church of the western empire, a fierce enemy of the Arians, bishop of Milan and teacher of St. Augustine, was said to have stated that the Arian heresy rolled triumphantly into the territory of Rome on Gothic wagons.

But that is a bit of an exaggeration. The entrance of the Goths into the borders of the empire at the time looked completely different from this. In 377, these menacing Goths, although already graced by civilization and religiously converted, and above all, well known to the Romans, firmly settled down on the other side of the neighborly fence, realized that there was no way of saving themselves from the savage Huns pressing down on them from the north. And so it came to a Gothic exodus, with hundreds of thousands of them crowding the northern bank of the Danube, desiring at all costs to cross over to the other side. To speak in today's language, we might say that in a completely unforeseen manner a regional conflict had arisen on the north-eastern border of the Empire, which resulted in a humanitarian catastrophe. The leaders of the Goths appealed to Valens, the emperor of the East, begging him to open the borders of the Empire to them and permit them to settle in Thrace, within the Empire, thanks to which they might find safety from the Huns beyond the broad bed of the Danube. Bishop Ulfilas himself interceded on their behalf. And it could not have been an insignificant fact in this regard that Emperor Valens was himself an Arian. Ulfilas might then appeal to him, an Arian Emperor, to rescue his Arian, barbarian brothers from the waves of truly vicious, unfaithful savages, the descendants of witches and demons. But Valens was probably of a more practical bent of mind than the bishop. He imagined that the assimilation of the warlike Goths on the lands granted for their settlement would help him to exploit them for the strengthening of the Roman army. Still, he didn't trust them completely, and for this reason, in giving his permission for them to immigrate into the bounds of the Empire, he set as a condition their complete disarmament, and dictated that the sons of the more important Gothic warlords were to be transported into the depths of the Empire as hostages. The whole action of transferring the desperate Goths from Dacia over the Danube most clearly exceeded the imagination of the Romans, as well as their technical capabilities. The undertaking was completely without precedent. As Gibbon was later to write: "[...T]he most experienced statesman of Europe has never been summoned to consider the propriety, or the danger, of admitting, or rejecting, an innumerable multitude of Barbarians, who are driven by despair and hunger to solicit a settlement on the territories of a civilized nation."[10] Many families were drowned in the attempted crossing, while the weak, the ill, and the aged were left to the mercies of the Huns on the farther bank of the river. In the face of the ubiquitous chaos, the attempts made by the Roman officials to count and register the refugees was a complete fiasco. The entire process of disarming the Goths, and separating children from their parents, immediately fomented a rebellious atmosphere. At any rate, the Goths were often successful in bribing the officials, in this way to retain their weapons and children. The Roman politics of settling and integrating the new arrivals also ended in complete failure.

It soon turned out that there wasn't enough land for them to settle, that in the face of the coming winter the Goths were threatened with famine, and that the imperial authorities were not all that concerned about their fate in the first place. The Goths, driven to desperation and self-reliance did indeed revolt in the end, and set to pillaging the nearby cities. When Valens decided on the pacification of the barbarians, the latter routed the imperial forces in the battle of Adrianople, slaying the emperor himself. As a result of this catastrophe, for the next thirty years or so the hostile Visigothic people took up residence in the very heart of the empire, and the Romans were simply unable to come to terms with them. Finally, in 410, under the leadership of Alaric, the Visigoths turned their attention to Italy where, after two failed attempts, they forced the walls of Rome and plundered the old imperial capital. Then they occupied Gaul, settling at last in Aquitaine and on the Iberian peninsula, where they established their own kingdom.

It was probably the inhabitants of the seven African provinces who were the last to learn that Rome no longer existed—the populations of such great cities as Carthage and Hippo Regius. Their fate was sealed by a coincidence, or, rather, a certain unexpected natural anomaly. The winter of 406 was extraordinarily severe, which led to the freezing-over of the Rhine. That natural barrier, which had up until now protected the Empire from the north, suddenly ceased to exist as such, and became rather a bridge for the tribes of the Vandals to cross. They headed south, wreaking destruction. It was they who finally separated Britannia from Rome, and less than three years later they became lords of the entirety of Hispania. This time, along with the Sarmatian Alani, those same tribes who, a few dozen years earlier, had been escaping the Black Sea steppes with the Huns on their heels, they founded a new kingdom, the state of the Vandals and Alani, a strange alliance of two barbarian peoples who had invaded the old world from opposite directions. The key figure in the conquests of the Vandals was Genseric, an uncommonly cruel man and ambitious leader, the son of Godigisel, who in 406 had led the Vandals across the frozen Rhine, and one of his slave concubines. Genseric, who had abandoned the orthodox Christian faith for Arianism, united under his scepter the Vandals and the Alani and in 429, crossed over into Africa from Gibraltar, initiating his African campaign. Here, the cause of catastrophe was no longer any natural anomaly, but unforgivable human error. The seven African provinces of the West embraced the narrow and long coastal belt, which, on account of its fertile land, constituted one of the most valuable territorial possessions of the Roman Empire. It was essentially the granary of Rome, which nourished the city. It was from here that hundreds of ships delivered grain to the millions of inhabitants of the metropolis, as well as to the ports of the northern coast of the Mediterranean Sea. Three great cities: Carthage, Sirte, and Hippo Regius constituted the administrative, economic, and intellectual centers of the area. They were also centers of intense Christian religious life, sometimes decidedly too intense. For beginning with the fourth century, the African provinces of Rome were shaken by the great religious quarrel between orthodox Christians and the so-called Donatists. The latter considered themselves to be the true Church of the martyrs, insisting that clergymen who had renounced their faith during the great persecution of Diocletian had lost, once and for all, the sacrament of their baptism as well as Holy Orders. For such men, there was no way of regaining the favor of the Church. However, the opposite opinion, which allowed apostates to return to the bosom of the orthodox Church, won out. Still the Donatists remained stubborn in their beliefs—we may take them for radicals, and as such they were understood at the time. The quarrel lasted until the days of Genseric's invasion. Neither the severe penalties meted out by the emperor, which included capital punishment, nor the admonitions of the Church, including the bishop of Hippo, St. Augustine, were to any avail. As early as a few years before the expedition of the Vandals from Gibraltar to Carthage, a stormy episcopal synod, at which some few hundred hierarchs were gathered, led to the condemnation of the Donatists and forced them to abandon their churches and other properties. However, this only sharpened the conflict. Organized into partisan units, the deracinated Donatists prowled throughout northern Africa, stirring conflict and attacking Christian churches. Doubtlessly, for Genseric, such religious chaos constituted a prime opportunity, especially as, being an Arian, he might set himself in the role of a protector of the minority persecuted by the Catholics. And indeed, at the beginning, the Donatists saw the Vandals as their allies. However, the most fatal mistakes occurred at the very summits of Roman power. At the time, Africa was ruled in the Emperor's name by the *comes* Bonifatius, who was just as unlucky a leader as he was an ambitious one, locked in a rivalry with an even more ambitious Roman leader, the afore-mentioned Aetius, the hero of Parnicki's novel. Gibbon states the matter straightforwardly: "Amidst the decay of military spirit, her armies were commanded by two generals, Ætius and Boniface, who may be deservedly named as the last of the Romans. Their union might have supported a sinking empire; their discord was the fatal and immediate cause of the loss of Africa."[11] Aetius, who had fought with the Huns and Visigoths in the north, cleverly exploiting them, after all, one against the other, was supposed to have intrigued the ouster of Bonifatius. But the latter not only did not submit to the orders he received, he decided to threaten Rome by entering into an alliance with Genseric. It was these personal settlings of accounts that permitted Genseric his entry into Africa and swift occupation of the province. Bonifatius tried to control the situation but, following an unsuccessful battle against the Vandals, he could do nothing more than ensconce himself behind the walls of Hippo and beat back the furiously besieging barbarians for a few dozen months. During the siege of Hippo in which the inhabitants of the surrounding areas also sought refuge, St. Augustine's life came to an end. Then, in 431, taking advantage of Genseric's withdrawal from the city walls, the inhabitants of Hippo were evacuated by ship to Sicily and Italy. When the Vandals at last entered Hippo, it was an abandoned city. Carthage would defend itself for a few more years before also foundering in 439. The ambitious Genseric was to transform that entire area of Africa into a new bandit state, which would support itself by conquest, piracy, looting, and the exploitation of others. Roman law was liquidated. Genseric would requisition all Roman wealth by decree. The Roman population would either be murdered, or sold into slavery to merchants from the East, like cattle. Those who could, would escape over the sea-lanes north. Genseric would also introduce a new religious order into his bandit state. Not only the remnants of the Donatists would fall victim to him, but all orthodox Christians as well. And this piratical, Arian state of the Vandals, founded by Genseric, would last for a whole hundred years, until the thirties of the next century.

The Hunter and his Prey

And this, in broad strokes, was how the great drama of the fall of the western Roman Empire played out over the space of decades. Many variables had a role to play in this gigantic catastrophe: natural anomalies, ethnic reshuffling in faraway Asian lands, hasty, rash decisions taken by the political élite, and the usual incompetence or corruption of officials. However, above all, it was that epochal event that we call the Great Migration of the Peoples, which once more moves the imagination of contemporary Europeans with epic images of columns of Islamic nations flooding into Europe from the Near East and Africa. The Roman Empire couldn't handle the sudden flood of the barbarian peoples. But there was something else that Parnicki noted in his lectures given at Warsaw University, and it was this very problem that played a key role in his literary interests.

Especially there, where the writer refers to his first novel of Aetius, the last Roman, where he suggests that the Empire was done to death by a much more serious mortal illness—the interior barbarization of the Romans themselves. Parnicki arrived at that conclusion through his detailed research for his historical novel. The fall of the Empire was not only a systemic catastrophe, as if, quite simply, the structure couldn't bear the blows raining down upon it from without. No, the matter was a much more serious one, because on account of their ever stronger associations with the barbarians, the Romans became ever less Roman in form and in spirit. And this is the topic of Parnicki's first novel, published during the interwar period: its theme is the barbarization of the Romans, which finally determined the annihilation of their world. It is necessary to remember that this interior decay of the ethical principles of the Roman world, resulting from their growing spiritual barbarization, saw to it that the greatest civilizational achievement of the Romans, their idea of order, of *ordo*, practically expressed in laws and general rules as the *Pax Romana*, that order of peace, was squandered and negated by the Romans themselves. The world of the ancients was, in comparison with ours, much more cruel and ruthless. And yet, all the more, that *Pax Romana* transferred its cruel character into something better, more civilized. Under the rule of Roman law, on the vast areas encircling the *Mare Nostrum*, incomparably fewer sudden, violent deaths of innocent victims occurred. Even in comparison to the Greek world, the culture of which we have become so used to praise to the skies—but where, as Parnicki reminds us, in the name of freedom and autonomy, through ages entire the Greeks committed the most horrid slaughters amongst themselves—that Roman peace and Roman order of law constituted a completely other, incomparably better world.[12] And that world was the complete opposite of the barbarian world, head and shoulders above it, by its very essence something better. Being ordered toward the Good and a universal goal, it allowed in practice the realization of Stoic, and later Christian ethics, and man became something more than just a wretch or a predatory beast. That world expressed—as Paweł Hertz, Polish poet and, like Parnicki, a great lover of Rome, put it—the Roman legal canon that regulated the principles of the coexistence of different human communities as well as the individuals in their orbit. The result was the creation of a visible form of public institutions and laws, which were at the same time set in general values: a social order, an economic order, a local order, and finally an aesthetic order. This form molded the most varied manners of existence into the shape of *romanitas*, providing them, above all, with the figure of a comprehensible, enduring, peaceful whole. In her *Distant Mirror*,[13] Barbara Tuchman explains how, thanks to so formalized an order, based on the power of the legions, the Romans could live a happy life, free of fear in their unfortified villas surrounded by open gardens. For in essence, within the borders of the Roman Empire, man was no longer a wolf to his fellow man. But during the last, let us say, one hundred years of the decline of the Roman Empire, that wolven nature crept back into Roman souls. This was also the moment when very many innocents met with violent deaths within the Roman Empire, and faith in the efficacy of the *Pax Romana*, the order of law and the order of peace, was irretrievably undermined. Parnicki suggests that this was not primarily caused by the hordes of savage barbarians, but rather by the very élite of the Roman powerful themselves; more precisely, as a result of the decline of their souls.

Aetius, as described by Parnicki, a Roman patrician, leader of her armies, often referred to as the "buckler of Rome," was himself a Roman with a barbarian soul. Following the death of Emperor Honorius in 423, a war broke out among the pretenders to the throne and Aetius took his stand on the side of the usurper John, on whose command he introduced the Huns to Italy. He lived among them for a certain time—at the court of King Rugila, where, in Parnicki's powerful description, he underwent the peculiar transformation in which his barbarian soul was reborn in the body of a Roman. Along with the king of the Huns he took part in invasions, participated in looting, murder, rape, and torture. The more there is of that, the more this last Roman discovers in himself emotions he had not known up until now, the more he "loves himself and his gigantic vital power"[14]—which is a blind, barbarian power. Aetius calls these emotions a new truth of life, the truth of the Huns, and in these words he is to engraft that truth into his own son: "Life is nothing but a hunt, an endless, pitiless hunt. If you won't be hunter, you must be prey, hounded, killed—but no, always alert, always predatory, pitiless... always conquer!"[15] This image of the world as hunter and hunted, of a world of constant predation, is the complete opposite of the Roman *ordo*, the *Pax Romana*, where citizens can live securely in their unfortified homes, tending their gardens in peace, and travelling the straight, Roman roads without fear of a violent death. But the truth of the Huns conquered the truth of the Romans, as it penetrated their souls and awoke therein cruel human nature, stifling righteousness. The *Imperium Universalis Romanum* more and more became the *Imperium Universalis Barbaricum*. The other main protagonist of Parnicki's novel, the famous, beautiful Empress Elia Galla Placidia, undergoes a similar interior transformation. The fierce rival of Aetius in the struggle for power, she was the daughter of the last Emperor of West and East, Theodosius I. However, she was brought up in the home circle of that Stilicho who, as we recall, was a Vandal—a barbarian with a Roman soul. Following the plunder of Rome in 410 by the Visigoths, she was betrothed to their king Ataulf, Alaric's heir. As Parnicki sees it, it was her contact with the barbarians as well as the real love she had for her Gothic husband—who was actually shortly to perish in Barcelona, murdered by his rival Sigeric—that turned Placidia into a horrifyingly cruel person. He describes the death of John, who wished to deprive her of her inherited rule over Rome. It was a Goth who executed him publicly, on the command of the Empress, but his death was preceded by a public shaming and the torture of the condemned man before the eyes of a jubilant crowd. Only a small number whispered that such things are improper; that Roman law does not allow for the cruel treatment of persons condemned to death, and that what the Empress was doing was an imitation of the barbarian customs she'd adopted. And so those who were standing on the very summits of power in the western Roman world were the ones who were undermining the foundations of its values. Ambitious but weak Emperors, and equally ambitious military leaders like Stilicho, Bonifatius, Aetius, Litorius, and many others besides them, faced off against one another, making use of barbarians as instruments of destruction. Of course, the Huns were the worst, being impossible to tame, but as a blind, destructive force, they were perfectly suited to the realization of the plans of the ambitious Roman generals when they wished to abase the Emperor or the senate in Rome. They served the Romans, defeating other barbarians like the Goths or Vandals. On the other hand, when arguments of blunt force were lacking, treaties were made with the Goths, Vandals, and other tribes, the so-called *foedus*, which granted them land and allowed them to found their own states in Gaul, Hispania, or Africa. In practice, this amounted not only to the loss of political control by Rome, but also to an abdication of legal jurisdiction over these territories, with the exception of the retention of the rights of Roman landowners, the so-called possessors. The barbarians introduced their laws and customs to the territories they'd acquired, and if the Roman population rebelled against them, their answer was extermination—a policy often carried out with the help or acquiescence of the Roman government, who were above all interested in the preservation of the *foedus* so that they might wage war with other barbarians on other fronts. The *Pax Romana* retreated ever more in the face of the completely new reality in which people arranged their predatory expeditions; where human life, law, and property no longer had any significance; where once more there was so much violent undeserved death and where captive people were treated like booty, and where if such people should rebel they were sent to the gallows in such incredible numbers that lumber began to be lacking with which to build the necessary scaffolds. Along with the fall of the *Pax Romana* people perished, as did their culture. In the final scene of Parnicki's novel, Carisius, a fictional figure, poet and friend of Aetius, describes his historical role in such words: "And so, the barbarians are pressing in on the Empire from all sides, looting, destroying, conquering. [...] You stand in defense of everything that the ages, dozens of centuries, have created... you are defending not only Roman peace and power, and the glory of the Roman name, but also Homer, whom you do not know, the Etruscan sculptures on which your eye never rests, and for which the rich Lausus, that eunuch of Constantinople, has paid hundreds of pounds of gold [...]. And so as long as you live, rule, and fight, here on the frontiers of the Roman world, on the land of my fathers, I may finish my translation of the *Iliad* in peace, certain that neither I nor my work will meet with any evil, as long as you are defending us... And when you shall be no more, Aetius, then all will crumble into ruin... the Empire and the might of Rome, the *Pax Romana* and, along with them, I and my Homer, and everything beautiful, wise, and good that time ever created under the aegis of Roma."[16] Now, murdered by the jealous, youthful Emperor Valentinian, Aetius would not defend Rome. However, all those beautiful, wise, and good things, including Homer, did not perish. On the other, African edge of the Roman world, not that many years beforehand, another representative of Roman thought in the ages of decline, the historian Orosius—this time a figure completely authentic, a disciple of St. Augustine of Hippo—was to write, under the impression of the great events: "And yet, if the barbarians had been admitted into the territory of the Romans for this reason alone, because, in general, throughout the East and the West the churches of Christ were replete with Huns, Suebi, Vandals, and Burgundians, and with innumerable and different peoples of believers, the mercy of God would seem to be worthy of praise and to be extolled, since, even if with our own weakening, so many peoples would be receiving a knowledge of the truth which, surely, they could never have discovered except with this opportunity."[17]

The Earth Void and Empty

The problem of Roman form returns again and again in these meditations. But in order to understand why the problem of form is the fundamental question of our European culture, we need to consult once more the writings of St. Augustine of Hippo, who was also an eyewitness to the events of the fall of Rome described above. Augustine is the author of one of the most interesting texts on the matter of form ever written in Christian literature; what is more, it was written exactly at the time when *romanitas* was being devastated by the barbarians. I have in mind here the twelfth book of his *Confessions.* It is a fragment that is frequently overshadowed by the preceding chapter, because of the famous analysis of time it contains, so often commented upon by later philosophers ("So what is time? If no one asks me, I know; if I want to explain it to someone who asks me, I do not know").[18] Ruminating on the sense of Moses' description of the act of creation in the book of Genesis, in chapter twelve Augustine strives to unravel the problem of the relation between the Creator God and the material reality formed by Him into the shape of our world. In a natural way, this leads to the question: where in all this is there a place for man as a creator? Augustine understands the act of creation as an act of shaping. In what manner and why something comes about, and further, why things must perish—this, in the context, is the basic question for which he seeks an answer. From a theological perspective, in the case of God, creation has, naturally, its own unrepeatable specifics. It is something exceptional and irrefutable.

From the perspective of man, it is also an archetype, a pattern of sorts, which allows one to understand the Christian view of the situation of man confronted by the world as creation. At a certain point in his meditations on this subject, Augustine states that "every formed nature, and all formable matter, has its being from the One who is supremely good because He supremely is."[19] This of course refers to God. But what does it mean for us people? How are we to understand this desideratum of being good to the ultimate degree, and existing to the ultimate degree? Is he trying to say that we are to strive for the maximum good and to exist as truly as we can, because otherwise one cannot create anything? To be good means to take a decision, on which all else depends. But how are we to understand existence to the ultimate degree? What does that mean?

Struggling with form, shaping, endowing something with a character, is a basic trait of the human condition—the historical destiny of man. In each individual case it signifies an attempt at orienting oneself to the practical, daily dimension of reality, through its shaping. And this, certainly, is related to a striving to be maximally good and to exist to the greatest degree. In the case of man, however, it is something that is burdened with constant uncertainty and a tragic quality. For to whatever degree shaping is, by itself, a source of man's sense of his own executive might, power, glory, or quite simply satisfaction or even happiness, to the same degree reality constitutes a cause for constant concern, fright, or even doubt and dread. For at the foundations of reality shaped by man, lurks the constant dread of the vacuum.

Augustine was perfectly familiar with these dreads and fears. After all, he himself had earlier succumbed to the fatalistic charm contained in the Manichaean understanding of material reality, opposed to the spiritual forces of life: at the foundations of everything lay aboriginal, unformed matter of a force so great, that it is thought to possess its own, autonomous status. According to the Manichaean conception, matter swells into an ur-deity, in rivalry with God, becoming *eo ipso* a stubborn, self-extant force in opposition to all human efforts to shape reality—a malignant opposition to pure or artificial acts of creation. Following his metaphysical shock and conversion, the circumstances of which he describes in the eighth book of his *Confessions*,[20] Augustine devoted the larger part of his intellectual, Christian life to battling against this harmful Manichaean viewpoint. The result of this argument is the aforementioned twelfth chapter in which Augustine concentrates on an explanation of what matter actually is, and on overthrowing the mistaken ideas on this subject that characterize Manichaeism. Only a proper understanding of what matter is allows us to comprehend the significance of form, and what sense there is to the human bestowal of varied traits upon reality.

Before the divine act of creation "this earth was invisible and unorganized," Augustine writes, referring to Genesis, and adding from himself that it was "an unfathomably deep abyss."[21] Before the shapes imposed by God elicited our world from non-being, some sort of matter existed—shapeless and deprived of all characteristics. As Augustine freely admits, this is a state that is difficult to imagine, but one that also fills us with horror. In the old, classic, Polish translation of the Bible by Jakub Wujek, this fragment sounds even more stirring and is probably even a more adequate rendition of the original: *A ziemia była pusta i próżna* (and the earth was empty and void). Before the creation of our world, and thus before its shaping, before it had been endowed with forms, the world was completely empty and void, and darkness and silence reigned therein. All that existed was shapeless matter having no characteristics at all—a shapeless abyss, a desert self-enclosed, incapable of creating or transforming anything: perfectly sterile, fruitless, a waste. This is something we need to understand: we are not speaking here of nothingness, but rather the wasteland of existence. Nothingness is nothing: there is nothing terrifying about nothing, but as for a wasteland... nothing is so terrifying for man than a wasteland, as it is the most incomprehensible of experiences. So we might say the following: God, in His boundless goodness, through the act of creation, chased away that terror, that barren, fruitless, empty continuum. He filled existence with shapes and initiated all subsequent human transformation and activity in the world. From this Christian perspective given us by Augustine, shaping is an act of creation capable of liberating all the richness of existence, all the possible forms of life, from the waste. Shapes elicit the world from non-entity, endowing it with concrete traits, a whole diapason of characteristics, colors, aromas, and meanings. Extracted from the darkness and the abyss, they change barren into fertile. Shaping—as Augustine suggests several times—sets existence in a full light, thanks to which its richness, that powerful range of capabilities found therein are discovered. This is equivalent to making being not only visible, but also recognizable, comprehensible, and therefore it constitutes the very basis of its cognition. Only when shaped does reality become recognizable, and thanks to this, a possible point of reference for man. What is more, only at this moment does history begin. Before its formation, matter endures unchanged in its silence and darkness. On the other hand, when shaped, the world changes, transforms itself or is transformed. The act of creation signifies not only the act of formation, but is also the commencement of the whole history of the transformation of reality. "[...] For after all," Augustine notes, "changeability itself is visible in this world [...] For where there is no form, there is no order; nothing comes to be, and nothing passes away. And where nothing comes to be or passes away, there are no days; there is no change over any spans of time."[22] By its formation, matter is set in motion.

It is easy to train our attention on the exterior manifestations of the forms of life, discovering the multiplicity of traits which uprise suddenly from the empty darkness. This must, understandably, give rise to delight. It is beautiful, it attracts us dynamically, it becomes a source of fascination such as can even make one giddy. But that's not what Augustine is after, nor is it this immensity or beauty of the exterior results of the act of creation that holds his interest. The capability of a positive orientation to reality thanks to form carries within itself many of these above-described results. However, all of them have a deeper and more important significance for Augustine—above all as the result of the ethical choice of the good, which makes them possible. This is a decision taken by each of us, inwardly. This capability of positive orientation to reality thanks to form is only made possible by conversion, which signifies a readiness to turn away from the vacuum.

That unformed world at the beginning of things is so terrifying not only on account of its barrenness, that yawning chasm, its horrid silence and its paralyzing cold. For Augustine, it is incomprehensible and horrible, above all because it offers no place for good and love, and no transformation can possibly occur within it. This lack is what makes it so entirely fruitless. Only through the act of creation does God change this state of things, indicating to us at the same time our own proper road. Capability to form is the result of an ethical turning toward goodness and love, and this must occur in each of us. Without it, we do not exist, really, and we see nothing at all. Without it, we remain barren ourselves and our efforts in the face of reality are nothing more than a wretched struggle against hostile resistance, which can bring us no more than temporary victories won through the bitterness of much loss. The forms of life arise only then, when we accept reality as ours, rather than fighting against it or seeking to pervert it. It is this, certainly, that differentiates the forms of life from the "formatting" which universally pertains in this contemporary world of ours. Metanoia is possible—as Augustine notes—as is hope, but only as the result of a profound, spiritual recognition of ourselves, which constitutes true liberation: "Certainly, Lord, this is a struggle for me, a struggle within myself. I have become for myself a stretch of ground to be worked with difficulty and much sweat. We are not now exploring the expanses of the sky or measuring the distances of stars or inquiring after the weight of the earth. I am the one whom I remember: I, the mind."[23] The entire effort put forth by Augustine in his *Confessions* is, therefore, directed at an understanding of who he has been, so that he might be capable of becoming who he ought to be. The indicator contained in this Christian thought turns out to be the road which led the barbarians from the North. Through their collision with the form of *romanitas*, which they overcame in a military sense, they could, thanks to Christianity, recognize their emptiness, chaos, and barrenness. And this recognition provided them with the chance of conversion, of choosing the good, thanks to which, instead of fruitlessly struggling with a hated reality, they might transform its forms and participate in the work of creation. And the fruit of that transformation became our Europe.

The Calvary of Aleksander Wat

The question of the fall of European civilization, that Western, Latin civilization, resulting from a barbarian flood, will return again and again in our reflections upon past ages. Catastrophism has never been foreign to European culture, among other reasons, due to Christian apocalyptic thought. However, the view has prevailed that destructive events such as those which passed through the Roman world at the turn of the fourth and fifth centuries were something absolutely exceptional. Gibbon brings his great work on the decline and fall of Rome to an end with this conclusion: "The savage nations of the globe are the common enemies of civilised society; and we may inquire, with anxious curiosity, whether Europe is still threatened with a repetition of those calamities, which formerly oppressed the arms and institutions of Rome." Still, as he sees it, "today we are secure." Today "the great republic of Europe" is impressive in its civilizational potential thanks to the progress of trade, craft, and social organization. Oh well. Gibbon is perhaps the most representative voice of the enlightened, optimistic eighteenth century, and it is for this reason that he fostered such a profound conviction that civilized Europe is no longer threatened by any barbarian flood from North or East. "Europe is secure from any future irruptions of Barbarians; since, before they can conquer, they must cease to be barbarous." Interestingly enough, in formulating this very opinion, Gibbon turned the reader's attention to the Russians as an example of his thesis. Jacob Burckhardt, another historian, but a less optimistic one representing in turn the nineteenth century, also stated that the migration of the peoples in the fourth and fifth centuries, as well as the fall of the Roman Empire, were gigantic crises, but, historically speaking, completely unique, unrepeatable, and thus with all certainty events of a non-cyclic character. And yet that history *does* return to us again and again in different guises.

Conversations dealing with the Huns, those descendants of witches and demons, with the fall of Latin Roman civilization, and also with... the Russians, have also returned in certain circumstances, crucial for us, to which I would like to devote a little more attention. For some of these circumstances connect the fate of Parnicki and his intellectual fascination with Rome with another character, whose path to Rome and Latin civilization led through a search for faith, beginning with the thoughtless deconstruction of the 1920s (Dadaism, Nihilism), through a fascination with Communism, Stalinist prisons and labor camps, and a desperate struggle with his own human condition, with the burden of historical experience and the search for the absolute. Here I would like to introduce to our considerations the figure of Aleksander Wat. The conversation I'd like to evoke took place in Lwów, that most beautiful and most Italian of all Polish cities, in 1940, in the prison in Zamarstynów.

As described by Aleksander Wat, Lwów was an exceptionally colorful city, a carefree place, where the charm of Polish life took on its fullest character. But at the beginning of 1940, it was a little different. Just a few months of Soviet occupation had changed the city unrecognizably: it got uglier, greyer, becoming also the scene of some terrifying events—a hunting down of human beings. The first wave of arrests took place in October 1939, the second in November, and the third in January. It was representatives of the administration who were being arrested, as well as lawyers, teachers, policemen, military men, journalists, high schoolers... The third wave of mass arrests swept up Aleksander Wat and Teodor Parnicki into the prison located in the borough of Zamarstynów. They probably were unaware of one another, placed as they were in separate cells. I don't even know if they even knew one another at the time. Parnicki was never an activist. If at all, he was rather attracted toward *endecja*—the National Democracy party. At the time Wat was a fervent Communist, whose name was often to be found in the records of the police and security services of the II Polish Republic. He lived in Warsaw, whereas Parnicki, right after his return from the Far East, had settled in Lwów. And yet both of them, at the same time, along with a whole host of other Poles, Jews, and Ukrainians arrested in that third mass wave—and, it seems, even on the very same day—landed in the Soviet prison in Zamarstynów. The conditions there were horrible. I reckon that none of us today are even capable of imagining them. Wat's description of the existence in Zamarstynów is piercing, and yet at the same time completely incomprehensible in its totality for anyone who has never experienced such things—and our generations have been spared the like. Twenty-eight prisoners were crammed into one cell measuring eleven and a half meters square. Perhaps it's worth giving two, maybe three short descriptive passages. The first experience: "The winter of 1939-1940 was terribly severe as you know. The nights were hell in winter, and especially when the weather turned suddenly hot in the spring of 1940. As a matter of fact, the most abominable physical memories that Soviet prisons left me with are those nights in Zamarstynów. Sweat streamed down both sides of you, your own mixed with other people's. That's terrible. You have to experience it to know what misery that is—somebody else's sweat mingling with your own. We really were packed in like sardines."[24] The second experience: "The worst thing about the bathhouse wasn't those jets of dirty water or those wet, smelly clothes thrown on the floor but that the process infuriated the lice, a rage that would last at least two days. They never bit you as they did for those couple of days after the baths and the delousing."[25] The third experience: "The prisoners slept on their own things, piles of dirty rags. I was afraid. My eyes were gaping and my instinctive reflex fear in those first few moments was very bad. I was frightened by the prisoners' faces, by the way they looked."[26] To this let us add that monstrous, unimaginable hunger, and the twenty-some ways of chewing one scrap of bread for several hours on end.

Yet, perhaps the most striking experience of that horrible prison described by Wat, was to see with one's own eyes how in such inhuman conditions the very thing that is most human crystallizes. The more that human physicality was humiliated there, torn, tortured and the more meaningless it was seen to be, all the way to complete annihilation, the more close-knit the social character of human life became, and the more its spiritual and religious dimensions came to the fore. Each cell organized itself into a complete social world as well as a spiritual, religious community. Reciprocal relations were knit amongst the prisoners, a structure uniting their loyalties, obligations, self-help, joint responsibility, honor, prestige, and common religious and metaphysical experiences. The exchange of trifles carefully squirrelled away, the bandaging of wounds, the recollection of whole fragments of books once read, common prayer. It was just as if everything that constitutes our understanding of civilized human life was suddenly concentrated in the microcosm of the cell, under the pressure of mortal danger, in order to assert itself in self-defense and endure. Our entire Latin civilization was locked up in the walls of a Soviet prison cell measuring eleven and a half meters square. For Wat, who up till then in his normal, pre-war life had rejected all the "bourgeois" forms of Catholic, Polish life, with some imagined "better" Communist paradise constantly in his mind, the crystallization of such a penal microcosm was a true revelation. During the course of discussions in the cell, which Wat terms philosophical or historical consolations, much was also spoken of what had just occurred, the war—and above all, Communism and the Soviets, because in Lwów at that time, except for the German bombardments of September 1939, the war with the Germans and the German occupation were something abstract. There, the war and the occupation were Soviet. During one such consolations, Wat recalls, a lawyer gave a lecture on the basis of Communism in Russia. He believed that Communism, in its bases or in its essence—however you wish to put it—is nothing but a barbarian invasion. The barbarians from the East, like those from Tartary or Tartarus, like those of Genghis-Khan, have their own order, their own "civilization," but their fundamental aim is the destruction of the civilization of the West: Latin, Christian civilization. Of course, depending on circumstances, in its superstructure, Communism might appear a more finessed and attractive conception. And that's how it always is, because whether we're talking about nineteenth-century England, or Latin America toward the end of the twentieth, or even today, in Europe, due to the loss of faith in liberal capitalism, there will always be found people ready to defend various principles of Communism, making use of sophisticated arguments. But the foundation always remains the same: whether in Europe, or Latin America, or Asia—a barbarian invasion. And in the conclusion of this particular historiosophical consolation in Zamarstynów dealing with Communism, Wat states: "Communism's anti-Christian aspect was fundamental, and that was brought home to all of us, from the most overly intellectual to the simplest."[27]

Gibbon, that English progressive of the Enlightenment, that civilized gentleman living nearly two hundred years prior to the events in the Zamarstynów section of Lwów, was convinced of the fact that the great republic of Europe was secure because thanks to progress, it had become a rationally ordered potency, looming over the entire world that surrounded it. The essence of that gentlemanly perspective on order, *ordo*, on European civilization, is, however, a reduction of her essence to usefulness, need, comfort, and therefore everything that allows us to be "civilized." Meanwhile, both in the case of the religious and philosophical assurances and comfort provided to the terrified inhabitants of Hippo under Vandal siege by St. Augustine, as well as in that of the comfort found in discussions and prayer by those Polish, Ukrainian, and Jewish sardines packed into the eleven and a half square metres of the Soviet cell, it turned out to be, in my opinion, something completely different. For the Latin, European order is based above all upon a choosing of the good, on a love of the good—upon *agape*, and that choice is at times a heroic choice, especially when confronted with absolute evil. I myself remember, in quite pleasant circumstances—in a time of peace and relative security—during a conversation at the University of Warsaw, in a city that had once been flattened to the earth—during a faculty meeting, a Marxist-leaning professor colleague of mine set out to prove that the most important post-war success of European culture was its realization of the necessity to abandon the theological language of good and evil. My hair stood on end, as I realized that each week he was cramming such contemporary "wisdom" into the heads of his students, and that this was the nightmare that, in the end, might completely destroy Europe. Wat's book is perhaps the best antidote to such a contemporary Europe beyond good and evil. His shocking description of life in the Zamarstynów cell of the Soviet prison allows us to see, despite the assurances of different gentlemen, that "The filthy square of our cell floor became the battlefield for the enormous thousand-year war between the barbarians and civilization, between nomads and settlers."[28]

Both Wat and Parnicki had a fair bit of good luck because after some months of that horrid prison in Zamarstynów they were transported East—Wat to a prison in Kyiv, and later to the Lubyanka in Moscow, Parnicki to Gorodnia, Chernihiv, Novgorod. Those who remained behind most likely thought that it was they who were fortunate—and yet all of them perished. Before the entry of the Germans into Lwów, the Soviets decided to liquidate the prison. They lured all the prisoners out of their cells into the corridors, where machine guns were waiting for them. They were shot to pieces en masse. In those cases where the prisoners succeeded in withdrawing into their cells and closing the cell doors, grenades were heaved inside. Practically no one survived. Such a great number of violent, horrid deaths in a world in which people once more became hunters and hunted. At any rate, that part of beautiful, Italian Lwów called Zamarstynów became a sort of place marked by evil, cursed. It was where the Germans built their ghetto and where, after the war, the Soviets levelled the cemetery where their victims were buried and built a school, a playground, a recreational park and a housing development over the bones. According to Wat—and it seems to me that this was one of his most important perceptions concerning Communism—the entire scientific, materialistic character of Marxism is nothing but a smokescreen for a truth concealed in Communism: that, in contrast to Western materialism, Communism never negated the existence of the soul. Bolshevism, says Wat, is a reengineering of the soul. "I want to stress this point: the essence of Stalinism is the reforging of souls, the Stalinist *paideia*."[29] The soul exists and it is the true battlefield in the war waged by Communism. Here we must add that the same thing is true in the case of Nazism. It is no meaningless fact that Wat arrived at his fundamental discovery while imprisoned in Lubyanka, in Moscow, which in so many ways was the opposite of Zamarstynów.

For however much Zamarstynów might be seen as a place in which human chaff was separated from the more promising cases, Lubyanka constituted a level absolutely higher. One might even say that this prison was a pattern for the new Stalinist *ordo*. As the central NKVD prison, the lion's den, Lubyanka surprised Wat with the high level of perfection of its organization, the ubiquitous cleanliness and silence that reigned there—the intentness, the focus, as in a laboratory. Cells with beds for four, eight people, the availability of books—at the time, Wat was devouring, among others, Machiavelli, Boetius, and... St. Augustine. Truly, as Wat describes it, Lubyanka does not resemble a place of torture at all. Rather, it seems a perfectly organized department for the working-over of the human soul, a great factory of projects for the new Stalinist *ordo*. "Perhaps," Wat muses, "in Stalin's ark, which contained the prototypes for everything—wealthy collective farms, model cattle feeders, the most modern factories—there was also a place for a model prison."[30] In Żamarstynów and the other Soviet prisons through which he passed, Wat met, above all, brutal and primitive executors of the Soviet apparatus of repression and extermination—devils of a baser sort, one might say. In Lubyanka, on the other hand, he had to deal with a true diabolical aristocracy, the cream of the crop of the engineers of human souls. Following his experiences in Lubyanka, frequently, even obsessively, Wat began to associate Communism with the devil. The historical vision of the ultimate battle waged between the remnants of Latin civilization and the Turan civilization of barbarians overflowing its borders, of which he and his cell mates in Zamarstynów were so convinced, began to be transformed into a theological vision of the battle of good and evil. This he developed under the influence of conversations held in Lubyanka and through a reconsideration of Krasiński's *Nie-Boska komedia* (Undivine Comedy). Wat admits that Communism is the work of Satan, the incarnation of evil in history: "I knew that evil takes one incarnation or another in every epoch. And I thought that in the twentieth century evil had incarnated itself in history and that Bolshevism was the devil in history. [...] I didn't know about Nazism, what it was. I tended to minimalize Nazism all the time I was in Russia. [...] But, you see, I considered Nazism a provincial phenomenon. I hadn't imagined its dimensions." For this reason, he saw Bolshevism as "a phenomenon that had come out of history, that it was a disease that was surfacing—but a disease of European, Christian, Western civilization."[31] If that be the case, mythologically speaking, an accession to Communism signifies a betrayal of the principles of the good. It is for this reason that Wat constantly returns to his prewar entanglement in Communism, not as any settling of accounts with the shameful mistakes of his youth, or a decision, taken in the thirties, to make a stand *de facto* on the side of the mortal enemies of his own country, his fatherland, but perhaps above all as a struggle with the sense of his own horrid fall, his abandonment of the good, which only became obvious and clear to him in Soviet prisons.

The outer barbarian became an inner barbarian—and so the barbarian is reborn in the soul of the European. Wat's way of the Cross that led through Soviet prisons was for him not a path of suffering, but a path of conversion—of jettisoning Communism and discovering Christianity. What is important is that this process of conversion, which played out in several stages, was concomitant to Wat's re-acquisition of clear sight, of a synthetic vision of reality and man, of the truth about both, which is found exactly there and nowhere else. The first station of Wat's Via Dolorosa was his imprisonment in Zamarstynów. There he saw how the prisoners, squeezed into a cell measuring eleven and a half meters square, children of God in the power of executioners, stripped of their humanity, defended themselves from evil thanks to the communal function of their Christian faith. This experience helped him to understand that "it was in this very cell in Zamarstynów [...] that religion preserved its deepest social sense. Just as the piety of the Counter-Reformation was born in an era of national catastrophes and wretchedness, so here, in the wretchedness of the Bolshevik invasion, the piety of my fellow prisoners, the Marian hymns they quietly sang, their common prayers, discovered to me their unsuspected depths and their rock-like strength."[32] These Zamarstynów experiences led Wat further to the question: "If Catholicism were a Pascalian affair in Poland, the Catholicism of Maritain: philosophical, constantly questioned and found anew, and not something ritual, customary, could it be for these millions of people such a firm rock in the struggle against the police oppression directed at the spirit, the diabolical deception?"[33] Still, this experience of a religious community as a firm rock was an experience of something outside of Wat himself. It was a discovery, a wonder united to a desire to become part of that community—a flock huddling together around their Shepherd while the storm rages around them. For the time being, it was the desire of a person who once abandoned the religion of his Jewish family, and accepted Marxism in order to fill up that unbearable hole, and who now was not only experiencing the horror of the practical dimension of Communism but who also saw in his fellow prisoners the Christian *agape*, which up until now had been a world unknown to him. As he was to write later of his Zamarstynów experience: "It's not that I refuse to pray; I just don't know how."[34] And even more literally: "After all, I wasn't converted here. I didn't believe that I believed. I knew that a strong impulse of desire to believe was at work in me, which I took with me upon leaving the cell in Zamarstynów; of believing in a community with my brothers, who had been thrown into those dungeons like the first Christians chosen to be tossed *ad leones*."[35]

Wat was to write that just as his Via Dolorosa was to lead further East, this social aspect of Christianity would progressively disappear. Already in the prison in Kyiv it was missing—there were only individuals there, scattered, who fought for their survival alone, like animals. In that way, they became an easier target for the absolute control of the new, Stalinist *ordo.* The next station on his path to conversion was the Lubyanka prison in Moscow. It was indeed there, in that central, Stalinist department for the *pieriekovka* of the soul, in that diabolical laboratory where the new man was in production, that Wat took his first decisive step. In the very center of absolute evil, where the strength of social ties is no longer valid, there is nothing left but man, isolated, set in front of the questions concerning the absolute God and his own salvation. One early spring night in Moscow, on the roof of the Lubyanka during an exercise walk with the other prisoners, Wat heard a radio broadcast of Bach's *St. Matthew Passion* resound from a loudspeaker. This was a few days before Easter. As he was to admit years later, that very night on the roof of the Satanic, central department for the destruction of human souls, the music of Bach, as well as the sap of life set in motion again by the coming spring appeared as a grand epiphany of the Absolute, the ultimate victory of God over evil. "If the human voice, manmade instruments, and the human soul can create, even once in all of history, such harmony, beauty, truth, and power in such unity of inspiration—if this exists, then how ephemeral, what a nonentity, all the might of the empire must be, that might that a beautiful Polish carol says "quakes in fear."[36] Bach's music, his *St. Matthew Passion*, or maybe it was some other cantata by Bach, for after the passage of so many years Wat was no longer certain what exactly it was that he heard on the roof of the Lubyanka, in the very depths of the third, Stalinist Rome, worked it so that with all clarity and now no longer separate, from without or from the side, but with all of his being he experienced the divine Absolute, the resurrected God. Resurrection exists, and therefore life will conquer death, even violent death on a mass scale; good will overcome evil, the truth will triumph. Significantly, Wat was also to write later: "In Lubyanka, to my joy, I rediscovered the sense of integrity—the whole that "precedes" the parts and is their soul. I had fully recovered my ability to see things synthetically."[37]

Yet faith in the Resurrected God is worth nothing without preparation for a confrontation with true evil. Only in this confrontation does the Good become a real choice. And for this reason, the last station on Wat's path to conversion took place in the prison in Saratov on the Volga—there, where the actual, historical border between Europe and Asia is said to run. It is the place where Wat caught sight of the devil—a real Mephistopheles. What is interesting here is that while he relates his experience of the Christian *agape* in Zamarstynów with seriousness and engagement—with precision, he speaks of his experience of the Resurrected God in Lubyanka in an elevated manner, yet strives to blur its sharp contours, excusing himself with a faulty memory of details. Instead, he fits his vision of the devil in Saratov into the convention of *buffo* and reduces it to the *delirium* of a man worn out by bloody dysentery and starvation in prison. This he does consciously, although the Saratov station of his way of the Cross is its culminating point. Can it be that he felt awkward speaking of his vision of the devil, face to face with his interlocutor Czesław Miłosz—can this be the reason for his seemingly indispensable caution? It is hard to say. "It was then that I had a vision of the devil. I won't even try to reconstruct that night because I wouldn't succeed. But it was then that the breakthrough occurred. Evidently, there had been something missing. There had been some obstacle, some last partition, and then it broke with that laughter of the vulgar, the most vulgar devil of all, flourishes of vulgar laughter that kept approaching, then receding far away for a long time, a very long time. I saw the devil. Well, I saw a devil with hooves, the devil from the opera. I really did see him—it must have been a hallucination from hunger, but not only did I see him, but I could almost smell the brimstone. My mind was working at terribly high revolutions. It was the devil in history. And I felt something else, that the majesty of God was spread over history, over all this, a God distant but real. I can't decipher it fully, I can't remember it all, but it was so actual, so sensual, as if the devil was in my cell, the ceiling of the cell was lifted away, and God was above it all."[38] The experience in the prison in Saratov changed Wat and let him find faith in the end. He became a Christian, although later he would be troubled with the thought that there was something wrong in this conversion of his—that it didn't come about through love, though.

It's terribly difficult to write about Wat's conversion. His story is full of contradictions, as is that of every person who sets off in search of God. At any rate, it seems that by passing through Soviet prisons he did indeed experience an authentic conversion, although after the war he was not sure whether he converted toward goodness and love, or was to die as a person longing for God, who once more had lost his faith. In later years he would speak of his conversion with doubt, distance, uncertainty, wondering if it were a full conversion, or merely a temporary and conditional affair. But for all that his transformation was authentic and profound, not merely based upon a final condemnation of Communism and of his own communist-influenced convictions. For Wat's conversion was linked to a reacquisition of the ability to clearly see the world and people as they really are, something he was also to mention frequently in his memoirs. *Etre! Et ne pas paraître!*[39] To be! And not merely to seem! To arrive at living, bloody reality, as he was to put it. To struggle with it and to bear that struggle to the end. To not avert the eyes, as most people do, locking themselves up inside themselves or escaping to illusion for in such cases conversion is not possible. The experience of that *Etre*, which Wat underwent during his way of the Cross through the Soviet prison system, is, of course, something completely unique, incomparable to anything, individual—it is quite difficult to take its measure, but still it has a universal, general significance as well. Modern man has made Europe a place of comfort and security. For exactly that reason, he no longer knows who he really is. The ability to see reality has been entirely lost in favor of illusion. I wonder if, in our culture, we'll ever be able to return to *Etre*, to existence in its fullness and concreteness, to the truth that lies where it lies. For otherwise we won't be able to rescue our Latin civilization. But must we too experience all those monstrous things that Wat underwent in his path toward God in order to rise to the challenge and catch sight of real reality? In order to free ourselves of illusion, must man once more become hunted and hunter, and the world fill up, *en masse*, with violent, horrifying death? Wat was a man who suffered horribly—not only on account of his passage through the Stalinist *ordo*. He was plagued by a horrible illness—Wallenberg syndrome (Bulbar palsy), which led to long-lasting, unbearable headaches. I also believe that, for someone who had experienced conversion and a vision of *Etre*, a return to the Polish People's Republic, which was an absolute illusion, must have been a source of diabolical suffering. When in the end he liberated himself from it, remaining in the West, in France, he attempted to soothe his soul and nerves by travelling south, to Italy or to Mallorca. This resulted in some absolutely beautiful Mediterranean poems, some of which have a biblical content. And yet, in 1967, Wat did something that no Christian ought to do—so perhaps his doubts concerning the endurance of his faith weren't baseless. He took his own life, ingesting a fatal dose of pain-killers. This suicide of his is terrifyingly understandable. I would like to believe, and I deeply do believe so, that later, in Heaven, the Good Lord received Wat into his mansions with arms wide-open.

The Forms of Life

Europe today and its imposing potential are now fully secure—so various gentlemen still would convince us, despite the news items to the contrary with which we are constantly being bombarded, each and every day. Why do we not believe them? As we look upon the present state of Europe, upon its ever deepening devastation, it is indeed difficult not to return with anxiety to the question that

Professor Chyliński posed to the young Parnicki in beautiful Lwów, that most Italian of Polish cities, in reference to the fall of Rome. For, taking into consideration the present circumstances in which Europeans are living today, can we really hope that our contemporary Europe may still be saved, rescued? And is it worth the effort? For after all, the temptation will always return to cast it aside like some old husk, leaving it to its own, fatal destiny, and to set off in search of something completely new.

On the other hand, we are also aware—after all—that we won't have any other culture; that the only new thing that we were capable of creating in Europe was merely the old barbarity of our nature in a new guise, and that the essence of European culture, that culture which allowed the taming of the barbarian within its borders, is a constant, unending re-assumption of efforts to save and rescue Roman form. Without that, there will be no European culture, and along with it, Polishness will also completely disappear. If not in this way, how can we understand the work of people like Parnicki, or the Calvary and conversion of Wat? They also constitute for us some essential signposts, and here I especially have in mind Wat's re-acquisition of a capability to see past illusion to the real world. The point is to stop averting our eyes. To re-acquire synthetic vision, which is a radical act of an ethical nature, and which can lead us to where we see that the West, that West as understood in a certain postmodern meaning, no longer exists or is vanishing ever more, being as it is a blind alley. And this would be a transformation of epochal significance, of fundamental consequences for all of us, at which more than one of us would feel terrified. I myself won't hide the fact that I was born, and grew up, in a concrete time and a concrete place in Poland, in the Polish People's Republic during a time of transformation, and the possibility that the West no longer exists, that we must seriously consider such a possibility, fills me with fear. But if the West does no longer exist in this one sense, in the sense of fully concrete ideas and imaginations: faith in the power of markets and finance, in the Faustian supremacy of man over nature, in the emancipatory power of modernization, and the conviction that today's European Union is the fulfillment of human history in Europe, then there is also no sense to the division of East and West, which would be a liberation. Even should fear conquer us, the dread of abandoning this status quo that defines today's Europe, then our further, knee-jerk holding onto a faith in the existence of just such a postmodern West will have no real significance, and no one will any longer be able to blackmail us into thinking that some alternative road must, necessarily, lead us only to the East. After all, if we allow for the possibility that the West, in its specific, postwar form no longer exists, we are not at all breaking away from European culture, executing some revolutionary leap into a historical unknown, even though the necessity of a definitive abandonment of this zone of comfort with which it has provided us over the last three decades will fill us with dread. For—where should we go now? What would take the place of that sort of West?

North and South, about which I have been writing, indicate a certain possible direction. But this would mean a return to an earlier understanding of form, and casting aside postmodernity that will lead us to no new salvation whatsoever. For what indeed has the postmodern West to offer us? A bureaucratic tyranny executed universally in the name of a state respecting the rule of law, the ubiquity of supranational corporations perfecting the irrationality of markets, or perhaps autonomous artificial intelligence that will determine the end of human existence? This is an erroneous path, which must be abandoned as quickly as possible in favor of a renewed creation of our own forms of life, from which we would draw our advantages on the basis of the most important principle of European culture—the transformation of Roman form. On such a basis, we will never have complete agreement between us in Europe as individual European nations have related differently to that Roman form during the course of their history, the French, the Italians in a different way, differently the Germans or the Poles. But the goal is not the creation of some new illusion of unity or a synthesis—after all, European culture isn't any sort of accomplishment, any highest stage of development. There is not the slightest reason to bend ourselves to something which we ourselves would acknowledge as unnatural. The point is—and it's an important one—to turn our eyes in the proper direction and to once more take advantage of the varied forms of life, from the perspective of our own form of life; thus, so that European culture might regain its vitality and survive. Actually, I should speak of this in more precise terms. For when I talk of the probable necessity of casting postmodernity aside, I don't have in mind any rebellion against the West—although I might be misunderstood in this very way. I see around a lot of people eager for such a silly crusade. Now, such a rebellion is senseless. It's always reactionary and doomed to failure. Beyond that, in our particular, Polish, case it is always lined with a horrid sense of guilt on account of the last two hundred years, which induces us to reach for the most idiotic rationalizations—that Poland is this great, worthy nation deserving respect, etc. It is enough if we cease turning our eyes away and turn our backs on that Western postmodernity, which can no longer be saved and which does not want to be saved at all. Rather, taking advantage of our own form of life, we should strive to save Europe, save it by ourselves—at least a portion thereof. Let us always remember that Europe is no relay-race of achievements, as our Western neighbors believe, and there is no reason why anyone should bend to what they consider to be unnatural.

Endnotes

1. *Translator's note*: Pewex was a chain of shops founded during the Communist era in Poland that accepted payment only in US dollars and other hard currencies or special bank cheques, instead of the złoty. Pewex offered a large number of imported Western items not available for purchase on the normal market, offered outside of the rationing system then in place, and customers did not have to queue up for items. Due to that and the high cost of the

items it offered when compared to the average salary at the time, Pewex was seen a symbol of luxury and privilege.

2. T. Parnicki, *Historia w literaturę przekuwana* (History Re-Forged as Literature), Warsaw 1980, p. 69.

3. Ibid., p. 67.

4. Ibid.

5. Ibid., pp. 146–153.

6. Ibid., p. 110.

7. Ibid., p. 111.

8. Cited by N. Davies, *The Isles*, Oxford 2000, p. 173.

9. Cited by S.J. Vicchio, *Jefferson's Religion*, Eugene, OR 2007, p. 32.

10. E. Gibbon, *History of the Decline and Fall of the Roman Empire,* Basil 1789, vol. IV, Chapter XXVI: "Progress of The Huns, Part III," p. 308.

11. Ibid., Volume VI, Chapter XXXIII: "Conquest Of Africa By The Vandals," p. 7.

12. T. Parnicki, *Historia...*, op. cit., p. 114.

13. See B. Tuchman, *A Distant Mirror: the Calamitous 14th Century,* New York 2011.

14. T. Parnicki, *Aecjusz—ostatni Rzymianin* (Aetius—the Last Roman), Warsaw 1957, p. 41 (German translation: *Aetius, der letzte Römer,* trans. F. Griese, Frankfurt am Main 1989).

15. Ibid., p. 45.

16. Ibid., pp. 360–361.

17. Paulus Orosius, *Historiae adversus paganos,* Book VII, 41. English translation by R.J. Deferrari, *The Seven Books of History Against the Pagans,* Washington 1981, p. 358. For a fuller discussion of the providential concepts of Orosius, see K. Ilski, *Idea jedności politycznej, społecznej i religijnej w świetle pism Ambrożego z Mediolanu* (The Idea of Political, Social, and Religious Unity in the Light of the Writings of Ambrose of Milan), Poznań 2001.

18. St. Augustine, op. cit., Book XI, 14, p. 210.

19. Ibid., Book XII, 15, p. 232.

20. Ibid., Book VIII, 12, pp. 136–138.

21. Ibid., Book XII, 3, p. 225.

22. Ibid., Book XII, 8–9, p. 228.

23. Ibid., Book X, 16, p. 176.

24. A. Wat, *My Century* (Mój wiek), trans. R. Lourie, p. 133.

25. Ibid., p. 132.

26. Ibid., p. 127.

27. Ibid., p. 141.

28. Ibid., p. 184.

29. Ibid., p. 232. The quote is supplemented with Wat's words: "The Stalinist *paideia,*" which appear in the Polish original of *My Century,* but are missing from the English translation.

30. Ibid., p. 207.

31. Ibid., pp. 225–226.

32. A. Wat, *Mój wiek*, Vol. 1, Kraków 2011, p. 360. This fragment and the three following ones are not contained in the English translation of Wat's book.

33. Ibid., p. 359.

34. Ibid., p. 362.

35. Ibid., p. 134.

36. A. Wat, *My Century* (Mój wiek), trans. R. Lourie, p. 241. *Translator's note:* The carol in question is "Bóg się rodzi" (God is born), with words by Franciszek Karpiński (1741–1825). The first two lines read: "Bóg się rodzi, moc truchleje / Pan niebiosów, obnażony" (God is born, power quakes in fear / The Lord of heaven, denuded).

37. Ibid., p. 210.

38. Ibid., p. 291.

39. Ibid., p. 151.

CONCERNING THE BLACK CHANCELLOR

To this day we live in the shadow of the Polish-Lithuanian Commonwealth, the legacy of its great power and its horrid fall. Some five centuries ago, our Polish ancestors took a decision which left us an inheritance of a political culture, but simultaneously took from us the chance to build a state. One can evaluate their choice variously, but one cannot deny its greatness. At the same time, more or less, when a certain Orthodox monk, Philoteus of Pskov, was writing letters to convince Tsar Vasili III that Moscow was the third Rome,[1] and Emperor Maximilian I had decided that the Holy Roman Empire belonged exclusively to the German nation,[2] our forefathers began their revolution, which led to the establishment of a noble, democratic Republic. In doing so, they decided to set off on an entirely different path than that of the Muscovites or the Habsburgs. While those were dreaming fondly of the *translatio imperii*, of establishing once more a single rule over the entire world, one powerful empire, some sort of supreme government of a universal empire on the pattern of the ancient Augusti, Constantines and Justinians, here in our country obedience to such a one supreme government was rejected in the name of life in liberty. *Vivere libere, civitas libera* became the longed-for goal of our splendid, Polish revolution of the sixteenth century, when it was believed that the destiny of Poland wasn't the construction of any third or fourth Rome at all—that is to say, some new empire ruling the world—but rather a state in the line of the ancient Roman Republic. In other words, a state of Catos, Brutuses and Cincinnati, a life in common to the advantage of all and under our own laws—and all this so as to take the fullest advantage of our liberty. And so, they chose their own liberty over the liberty of the ruler, or the liberty of the state. As we have said, this decision can be evaluated variously. For sure, they were not the only ones who chose to set out on this very road. The Venetians tried it, the Florentines, the inhabitants of other Italian republics, the Swiss, the Dutch, and even the English—with mixed results, eventually. But what our forefathers believed in, that one might live just like those Romans, without the oversight of state or monarch, or any other sort of authority above one, this was a path from which, in our history, there was to be no return. It was to define us for good and bad, forever more. What happened with us in the sixteenth century was, therefore, the great victory of an idea over necessity.

I'm not entirely sure if we have ever fully taken the measure of this exceptional experience of the Republic. Our approach to this matter has always been lined with fear. Are we afraid of it, because we're afraid of seeing what we are, or what we might be? In 1979, that memorable year of the first pilgrimage of John Paul II to his fatherland, when the Poles "evened the score," when the Poles saw what they were like and how many of them there were, the now-legendary exhibit authored by Marek Rostworowski and titled *Polaków portret własny* (The Poles: a Self-Portrait) opened at the National Museum in Kraków. In his own idiosyncratic way, Kazimierz Kutz would later express his impressions of the exhibit: "Sarmatians! Those foul, monstrous mugs! 'Run wild, my soul, there is no Hell,' but… All that was to be seen in those mugs: limitless drunkenness, arrogance, idiocy. We went to have a look at the *Self-Portrait* out of zoological curiosity, to have a gander at what that real Polish monster looked like, what its contours were, how it dressed, and whether it was anything like the contemporary monster. This was a marvelous, marvelous Polish fabric, an element, nothing but meat. Nothing pretended, nothing colorised."[3]

Polish monster? That very significant opinion of ourselves expressed by Kutz toward the end of the 1970s, at the beginning of the decline of the PRL, a view at any rate quite out of step, as I see it, with Rostworowski's intention and the exhibition itself, sums up for me our whole problem with our inheritance from the Republic. It is almost as if he were to say that the Poles could only be "normal" in the tight frames cut for them by Stalin and Roosevelt; as if they could only survive in Europe today in hiding, camouflaged. But should they wish to be otherwise, well, from the get-go they're monstrous and horrid. Indeed, in our approach to the Republic there are contradictory feelings of delight and disgust. How many times have we seen in the faces of our interlocutors that glow of bliss, of dreaminess, self-adoration, and relaxation at the thought of that Republic, a republic of many nations, tolerant and without stakes, reaching from sea to sea, so powerful, so great, so awesome. And how many times do we see something totally different: the arched brows, the grimacing lips, the belittling shrug of the shoulders, or the smile of mockery? What is it that we don't want to see? What is it we don't wish to catch sight of?

I think that the decision taken by our ancestors to live, in defiance of all, that unwavering, Roman, republican liberty, to have here on the banks of the Wisła our own Roman republic; this truly revolutionary step taken by them, which was brought into life over the space of a mere two generations, however mad it was, however full of many evil consequences, practically speaking, overtops us completely and in every respect. Never again were we capable of attaining their greatness or courage. It is for this reason that we later looked, and still do look, upon what they accomplished in our country in the sixteenth century from a crooked perspective of latter-day malcontents, failures, hard-luck types, or dreamers. Torn between a dream of power and a terror of the next catastrophe. Hounded by history; skittish dreamers. I sometimes wonder—dear God, if only after 1989 we had just a bit of the courage and sense of liberty of those forefathers of ours, everything today might be different. That is not to say that it would be better, but it would certainly have been something done "our way."

It's true, and it must be admitted, that these forefathers of ours, besides exceptional courage and a thirst for freedom, and also not a little bit of peculiar fantasy, additionally enjoyed some uncommonly advantageous circumstances in which to effect their revolution. The Jagiellons, due to some specific sweetness rooted in their nature, turned out to be a surprisingly weak dynasty. And so, that specific type of political organization characterizing the Republic could be quite freely constructed in our country in the sixteenth century, on the rubble of monarchical ideas which had never been fully realized. The Republic brought about the triumph of the democratic political community over the state and the crown. As I see it, it is impossible to fully understand this phenomenon of victory without a consideration of the fruits of that great noble revolution, which was above all assimilated with complete sincerity and devotion to the idea of a democratic identity. It found its full expression in the principle of a free, universal, elective monarchy. In this revolution, the democratic identity is above all the political image of people who are free and equal, who by stages augment their independence from the king's rule, as well as in the face of the interests of the remaining social strata amongst which they live and over which, as a final result, they would win a complete primacy—and that one subject to no appeal. It is in this that the entire radicalism of the democratic revolution in Poland consists, thanks to which a political caste took in hand the exclusive responsibility for the fate of the common weal and interpreted it according to its own lights. The consequences of this are immense, since in such circumstances the objectivization of the state as a supreme political category cannot come about, nor can any separate principle of state interest make its appearance. And thus, the Republic became not only the source of many values and attitudes familiar in our political culture, such as liberty, equality, deliberation, and participation, but it also inaugurated our entire toilsome history of yearning for a real presence of the reality of a strong state, such as would lift the yoke from our shoulders—in other words, it initiated the whole nature of our political culture, in all its ambiguity, such as exists down to our very own day.

However, the picture remains incomplete without two other important elements. The idea of a republican community, united in equality and liberty, would not be possible in Poland without Cicero and, along with him, the other great minds of the Mediterranean, classical world. The Roman Republic was the pattern for our idea of a Republic, or, rather, this pattern was constituted by all that our forefathers had read in the books of Cicero, Livy, Sallust, and Tacitus. In this is to be found an awe-inspiring executive power of the imagination as well as the fascinating geographical-spiritual phenomenon of the noble Republic. After all, it had its concrete, specific geographical location, and developing as it did from the territory of the Polish Piasts, it experienced a giant swelling eastward, but during the Jagiellonian period it was also present in the kingdoms of Central Europe. Throughout the sixteenth century it was to be constantly hesitating as to the direction in which it was to focus its potential: toward the East, or toward Central Europe. Whatever the case might be, mentally and culturally speaking, that great potential had always been inseparably united to the Mediterranean South, which to a great degree was solidified by Italian humanism. We're not only speaking here of the political ideas derived from the pages of Cicero or other authors read anew during the political Renaissance. Something greater was at play, since along with the uprise of the Republic, the Poles accomplished an imposing and enthusiastic entry into Mediterranean culture, the culture of the South. The transplantation of the idea of the Roman Republic onto the soil of their own political imaginings would not have had such profound consequences, had it not been accompanied by the acceptance of southern culture, as a direct, main point of reference. For this reason the introduction of Cicero's ideas was accompanied in Poland by the development of a universal, but sublimated as well, rural culture of life of a Mediterranean character—a southern way of life in the Polish style, the material expression of which was the noble manor, a way of life expressed most beautifully and unsurpassably in our language by Jan Kochanowski.

There is also one final element about which I'm very concerned, because for me it is indirectly linked to the state of our contemporary Polish condition. For I understand the foundation of the Polish Republic also to have been an effect of a great shift, a great revolution of the old order in Europe, which was accompanied not only by new currents of thought (Humanism) or religion (the Reformation) but also significant technological developments (moveable type). The Republic remained in a positive relation to all these, becoming here our own, Polish response, impressive in its results, both to the liberation impulse flowing out of Renaissance Humanism and the radical individualism of the Reformation, as well as the shattering of the traditional hierarchy of government and communication by the discovery of moveable type. There is something absolutely fascinating and grand in the manner in which our forefathers grasped and embraced all these transformations, how they entered the new world laid open by humanism, the Reformation, and print unapologetically and with aplomb. It was as if they wanted to take advantage of the force of the growing wave of transformations, mount it and ride it as far as it would take them. I reckon that never again have the Poles risen so high in their spiritual courage; never again have they ever been so free; never again have they been so much themselves.

All these powers, interior and exterior, urged our forefathers in the direction of that great, courageous step, toward that noble revolution establishing the political community of the nation high above ruler and state. It seems to me sometimes—and I will not dissemble here—that there was too much optimism and imprudence to be found in this; that perhaps on these our distant sands and mire of the North a solid structure of stone and iron would have been more suitable than the idea of a republic of free people taken from the pages of Cicero. The only thing is, my opinion in the matter is meaningless. They took their decision, the greatest in all our history, and we have been living with the results to this very day. However, there is a certain curious story related to it, to which I find myself constantly returning in thought, as it gives me no peace—and now has led me to write this essay. That great revolution and decision of our forefathers to build their republic on these sands lifted one extraordinary man to the heights: Jan Zamoyski, a man of the new type, who as both chancellor and hetman had gathered immense power over the Republic into his two hands. And this is why I am constantly nagged by the question: why, having all that, did he not decide, in the end, to seal his power with a crown, to establish a new dynasty of Polish rulers and transform the republican community into the structure of a modern state of stone and iron? In order to find an answer to this question, we must gaze into the very heart of that Republic.

Armed Election

The free election was the pearl in the crown of the Republican system; the political culmination of civic liberty: the possibility of choosing one's king. Can anything make us freer than that? But the third free election, the one that took place in 1587, was exceptional for many reasons, and that in an ominous, evil way. For it was taking place while an open civil war was raging. It was an armed election, a wartime election, and its conclusion played out in the midst of fratricidal military operations. However much the first election—that unfortunate choice of Henri Valois in 1573—was something of a spontaneous, civic improvisation in the face of the loss of dynastic continuity, and the second, that of Stefan Batory, an attempt at solving the matter of the basic political issues of the structure of the new Republic or, at least, naming them, this third, following Batory's sudden death, meant open war between two hostile parties—the Zborowskis and Zamoyski—who were mutually determined upon the destruction of their rival. This fully militarized election of 1587 became, thus, a culminating point of the interior conflict—a struggle for life and death. But did it solve the matter? Who won? The Zborowskis or Zamoyski? And what was the conflict all about? The crown for Zamoyski?

For the people of the time, a growing sense of looming civil war must have been a very gripping matter, arousing general anxiety following the death of Batory, since so many voices give so many testimonies to the fact that on the field in Wola where the election took place, the nobles gathered armed to the teeth—heavy artillery in tow, as if they were approaching a battlefield for the final, bloody act of a conflict rather than a meadow where they would gather to choose a new king together. The escalation of tension was gigantic and violent. As early as at the Diet of Convocation, in February 1587, and thus hardly six weeks after the death of the king, Zamoyski was charged with the heaviest of crimes, including treason, while simultaneously the Zborowskis were lifted beyond suspicion. In Warsaw, this led to some serious rioting since, if certain sources are to be believed, during the sitting of the convocation, between 2 and 26 February, as many as one hundred eighty seven persons were totted up as having been killed. This is why, when the Diet of Election was inaugurated in June of that year, people observed the militarized entrance of the nobility into Warsaw with fear and uncertainty. The Zborowskis were supported by Stanisław Górka, the voivode of Poznań, a Lutheran and former rector of Wittenberg University, as well as many other magnates inimical to Zamoyski. But the real ideologue of the party in these last reckonings with the chancellor was Stanisław Sędziwój Czarnkowski, a man possessed by a real, personal hatred of Zamoyski. He arrived at the field of election in Wola towing up to twelve heavy cannon in his train as well as many pieces of lighter artillery besides. Zamoyski arrived in Warsaw with his own numerous army: one thousand infantry, three thousand cavalry, and eight heavy cannon. His entrance into Warsaw made a huge impression on the people. It wasn't a triumphal entry at all, but rather seemed a well planned out military operation of lightning-like aggression. It must have been a terrifying sight, certainly aimed at striking fear into the hearts of all the Chancellor's opponents, the Zborowskis and Górka above all. At the head of several thousands of troops dressed in black, himself dressed in a black armor of mourning, he led his troops over the wooden bridge across the Wisła with such clatter that, most likely because of the excessive weight of men and military equipment, it suffered serious damage. He then set up a commanding position on the meadows at Wola, right near the Powązki woods. It was there that he had his camp pitched with expedition—or, rather, his field fortress, encircled as it was by a secure defensive rampart and a moat intended to secure him from a surprise attack by his enemies. He himself went off immediately to present himself at the palace to the queen, and after this, to the papal nuncio. It all must have been very theatrical and premeditated: to dress up several thousand men in black uniforms as a sign of mourning for the king, and to enter Warsaw at their head in black armor; a masterful public relations coup. The days of July slipped by in ever greater tension. The senators of the Republic debated nearly every day in the temporary Senate building set up on the field of election. Despite the fact that during the High Mass in the Cathedral of St. John at the beginning of the election assembly, Archbishop Karnkowski lifted ardent prayers to the Holy

Ghost for swiftness and concord in the election of the new king, no one proved brave enough to take the first step in the direction of making a choice. The building stood in the middle of the field of election, surrounded by a rampart, around which the equestrian cadres (*koło rycerskie*), in other words, the noblemen, gathered. The atmosphere thickened with the conflict of two hostile camps dug in: that of the Zborowskis with Górka at their head, and the black camp of the Chancellor. Both sides brought their accusations before the Senate. The Zborowskis wished to "set the insults suffered by their house before the judgment of the Republic"[4]—above all, they were after the condemnation and punishment of Zamoyski for the shameful death of Samuel Zborowski, condemned to beheading by the deceased King Stefan Batory, in whose judgement the Chancellor was understood as having been complicit. They also demanded the lifting of the sentence of banishment laid upon the second of the Zborowski brothers, Krzysztof. But fundamentally and above all they were after the punishment of the mighty, abhorred Zamoyski, at whom they hurled every imaginable charge, calling him tyrant, murderer, and "venomous dragon."[5] The Chancellor placed his own matter before the Senate, demanding to be cleansed of the charges and insults. In his speech, he stated that he arrived in Warsaw at the head of such a large armed escort not in order to stir up trouble, but rather to assure the safety of his supporters. As hetman, he was also responsible for the security of the entire Republic. He noted that the same could not be said of his opponents, for, unlike them, in his camp there were no foreign mercenaries, but only noble citizens, which itself should testify to the purity of his intentions. However, the problem was that each of the Chancellor's explanations merely evoked still more rabid attacks from the side of his opponents, who did not restrict themselves to mere threats and verbal insults, for they had also been known from time to time to shoot into the ranks of Zamoyski's supporters with firearms. Once more, just as in February during the convocation, some incidents of manslaughter occurred. The chaos in the Senate was augmented still more by the Lithuanians, who from the very start of the election did not hide their great dissatisfaction, desiring above all to have their own matters taken care of. They made their camp, ostentatiously, on the eastern bank of the Wisła, far from Wola. Stubborn as only Lithuanians can be, they stated that they would not take part in the election until the militant moods had ebbed, and unless the quarrels between Lithuania and the Polish Crown lands be resolved to their satisfaction. And as far as the system is concerned, that quarrel was of an explosive caliber. For ever since the foundation of the Republic of Both Nations and the Union of Lublin in 1569, the common election of the monarch by Lithuania and the Crown constituted the most sublime confirmation of the endurance of political unity. For this reason then, the open declaration of the distancing of the Lithuanians and their separation from the Crown and the field of election by the Wisła must have made those assembled there painfully aware of the real threat of the dissolution of the community, which at the time was less than twenty years old. And as if that were not enough, the extraordinarily raucous Mazovian nobility, also the numerically largest group, began to stridently demand that all quarrels cease so that the election might begin, and call to the throne... Fyodor, the Tsar of Moscow, son of Ivan the Terrible. Only one spark was needed here for the powder keg to explode. And so, when the nobles of the Crown gathered in the elective entrenchment in order to debate what ought to be done in this situation, close nearby, in an open, brash provocation, the armed contingent of Górka and the Zborowskis—more or less five hundred infantry and just as many hussars, reiters, and Tatars began to march by, loudly dragging with them about ten cannon and sixty harquebuses. Such a demonstration of might aroused strong emotions in the circle of those debating, until it was decided that from henceforth the supporters of the Zborowskis and those of Zamoyski would gather in two separate groups, far from one another, so that they wouldn't be at each other's throats. All of these extraordinary and upsetting events only displayed all the more clearly that free elections, that pearl in the crown of noble freedom, was ceasing to be—if it ever really was—a great holiday of the community of the Republic, where each free citizen, armed with his vote and supported by the Holy Ghost, participated in the choice of the future ruler. Instead, it was becoming a battlefield on which the victors would be those who were most capable of organizing themselves into a strong, disciplined, and well-armed party.

Miechowita's Mushrooms, or What's Amiss with Polish Politics

Well, there you have it. But what was the whole conflict about? The "venomous dragon," the *oppressor libertatis nostrae*, the tyrant, the hangman, the usurper, the new Palatine Sieciech, elevating himself above all others—it would take a long while to list the whole catalogue of insults so eagerly tossed at Zamoyski. There was a whole slew of venomous verses agitating against Zamoyski circulating about the country at the time, like, for example, this delightful little couplet: *Najadszy się ta gnida, jak wszystkim dogryza, / A powstawszy z niczego, sprośnie je poniża* (Having sucked his full, that louse, after he's bitten everyone, / Having arisen from nothing, he foully tramples others down).[6] So the Chancellor was, doubtlessly, a figure who aroused hatred as well as awe. After all, following the death of Batory, Horatio Spanocchi, the secretary to the papal legate Cardinal Bolognetto, had written—and not by chance—of Zamoyski, that "no one else, certainly, might be found in the entire Republic more worthy of the crown than he."[7] Such opinions helped on the growth of the Zamoyski myth, which he himself eagerly fostered. However, at the same time, they also increased the hosts of his bitter enemies.

Even if, formally speaking, Zamoyski was not the king, in question of fact he possessed an authority equal thereto, and perhaps even greater. Matejko perfectly represented this paradox in his canvas *The Sermon of Piotr Skarga*. All attention seems to be focused here on the expressive figure of the preacher. Skarga is in the middle of one of his famous tirades prophesying the inevitable downfall of the Republic. But the real political drama is being played out in a completely different area of the painting. To the side, on a chair, sits King Zygmunt III Waza (Vasa), surrounded by his courtiers, in black Spanish-style clothing with a snow-white lace collar. He is pale, absent, with drooping eyelids—he's nearly asleep. Meanwhile, high above him, in halflight, towers the great figure of Zamoyski, sitting on some sort of monumental throne. In gazing at this painting, I wonder whether, had Zamoyski actually stretched out his hand for the royal crown, would all of the charges against him and slanders have grown quiet with the current of history, and the black legend of the great Chancellor been forgotten? The essential thing is that Zamoyski never decided upon this ultimate last step. Neither in 1587, during the third armed election, nor several years later, when the attempted flight of young Zygmunt III Waza to Sweden, in league with the Habsburgs, was discovered, and it would have been an easy matter to knock him from the throne. Perhaps he could not do this, although that is a problematical hypothesis, considering the fact that he was the most powerful man in the Republic. So, of course he might have done it, but he decided not to do so, and this becomes more understandable if we take into consideration the nature of the Republic—which he himself had so much helped to establish. It is common to acknowledge that following the death of Batory, Zamoyski quite simply became the hostage of earlier political events and decisions, which in consequence blocked his route to the crown—the most fatal of which events being the execution of Samuel Zborowski.

Jarosław Marek Rymkiewicz has described in beautiful and suggestive colors the history of this execution in his book on Samuel, but what is more significant is the way in which he opened the floodgates of his own extraordinary dislike of Zamoyski—writing himself into that black legend. Rymkiewicz, quite simply, does not like Zamoyski at all, exactly for being that monstrous "oppressor of our freedoms." He hasn't a single kind word for him in all his story, and thus the Black Chancellor becomes for Rymkiewicz a black character. With obvious ostentation Rymkiewicz much prefers Samuel Zborowski and his brothers, namely, Krzysztof—the royal cupbearer, universally known as the "villainous rabble-rouser" (*krzyknik niecnota*), who, following the election of Waza, will lay siege to Kraków along with the armies of Archduke Maximilian, as well as Andrzej, the court crown marshal, a person, we might assume, less violent and more eloquent than Krzysztof, although himself prompt to dangerous intrigues and not at all adverse to violence—to Zamoyski. At this time, the Zborowski clan—six daughters and seven brothers—was numerous and influential.[8] The most noble of this numerous gaggle was probably Piotr, voivode of Sandomierz and later Kraków, the initiator of election *viritim*, but he died in 1580. Jan was also well known: as Court Hetman, he vanquished the rebellious burghers of Gdańsk in 1577, and earlier still, after the first election, travelled along with Zamoyski as a member of the Polish embassy sent to Paris to bend the knee in Notre Dame before Henri Valois after settling the terms of his reign in Poland. It was Jan who faced down Valois, when the latter didn't wish to agree to all of the conditions, with the famous riposte: *Si non iurabis, non regnabis.*[9] Above all, though, Rymkiewicz prefers Samuel, known also as a "retarded bully," whose head was separated from his body in 1584 at the advice of the Chancellor. The king was supposed to have stated the famous, ominous phrase that says a lot about Samuel's reputation (and about at least some of his brothers): "a dead dog doesn't bite."[10] There are good reasons to suppose that as much as Andrzej was indeed a very clever schemer, a skillful opponent of Zamoyski's, and Krzysztof a common thug capable of doing anything on behalf of the Habsburgs if the price was right, so much did Samuel not belong amongst the sharpest knives in the drawer, and one can assume with a good bit of probability that, independent of his swashbuckling, he became a sort of unwilling victim of his brothers' intrigues against the king—an easy patsy. For all that, his severed head became a sort of peculiar symbol of an attack on Polish freedoms. In Słowacki's drama, that head of Samuel's becomes a sort of lantern, from the interior of which comes an uncanny glow of the inner freedom of the Poles.[11] And that glow becomes a major accusation laid at the Chancellor's feet under the pen of our bard, something that Rymkiewicz picks up with alacrity. It is a charge formulated against the man who committed such great violence against the golden freedom of the nobility. Setting off, then, in the footsteps of Słowacki, Rymkiewicz sees in Zamoyski not only a tyrant, but, for the author from Milanówek, he becomes the prefiguration of all those élites in Poland who throughout the history of the nation were to raise themselves above all the rest of the Poles, the nobility included. He even discovered a concrete statement uttered by the Chancellor, with which, he reckons, "there commences the long (now four-centuries old) history of Polish contempt held by those who govern for those who are governed. And there begins the history of the contempt on the part of those Poles who feel themselves to be better than the Poles whom they take to be worse."[12]

That Zamoyski would exalt himself above others—as he does on that canvas of Matejko's? Of course he does, naturally, he sees himself as a *primus inter pares*. Zamoyski's history is one of staggering success. In 1571, some twenty years old, he was the owner of three and a half villages given him by his father. At his death in 1605, he left to his heirs one of the largest estates in the Republic, his own freehold property consisted of eleven cities and two hundred villages. On top of that, he gathered in his hands the royal holdings (królewszczyzny) comprising twelve cities and six hundred twelve villages. His possessions embraced an area of seventeen and a half thousand square kilometers. Toward the end of his life, Stanisław, the father of Jan, was awarded a seat in the senate by the king: number eighty-six in a camera of one hundred. In less than fifteen years he became the mightiest man in the state—Chancellor and Great Crown Hetman. And he was not to raise himself above the rest! However, the problem lay in that he himself had created such a system for the Republic in which every power was a scandal, every might something horrible, to say nothing of a situation in which the government, for its own reasons, some reasons of state, could effectively chop off a citizen's head—even if it was the head of an open roisterer.

That frightful statement, which so moved Rymkiewicz and which he flourishes in his book as a grand accusation against Zamoyski, crowning evidence to confirm his decided thesis concerning the beginnings of the history of our homegrown, Polish contempt of our own selves, is something that the Chancellor was to have said following Samuel's imprisonment. Actually it is unknown whether he indeed said it or not, as the whole matter is related to us by the declared opponents of Zamoyski, and the history of the execution of Samuel Zborowski became in its own time, as we would say these days, highly politicized. In other words, it is unknown whether he said it or not, but it sounds good and fits the theory well. Upon mention of the general unrest amongst the nobility at the news of Samuel's imprisonment, the Chancellor is supposed to have said that *Polacy są piwo, które kisa z przodku, a potem za wodę stoi* (Poles are like beer. Strong at first, but then they piss out like water).[13] Rymkiewicz, ever the professor of Polish literature, submits this sentence to close analysis, as it sounds to our modern Polish ear quite incomprehensible. He arrives at the convincing explication that sees Zamoyski as meaning more or less that "Poles ferment at the start, bubbling and frothing, or at least are sour or bitter (as if they were displeased at something), but later they become like water, growing apathetic, and are worth no more than water."[14] The Chancellor truly must have been pleased with that bon mot concerning his fellow countrymen since I have been able to find it elsewhere too, spoken by him in other circumstances, and in my opinion, in a form much more interesting. For when, following the unexpected death of Batory, the Diet of Convocation called in Warsaw in 1587 devolved into a bar fight between hostile factions of the nobility (let us recall that one hundred eighty-seven persons were killed in the conflict), and Zamoyski was warned not to travel there for his own safety, he is reported to have said that this fracas was nothing more than *piwo z sieczki uwarzone, prędko będzie tam, gdzie Miechowicine grzyby*" (beer brewed of chaff, which soon enough will find itself among Miechowita's mushrooms).[15] But so saying, he still did not go to Warsaw himself, sending rather his in-law Stanisław Żółkiewski. I was fascinated by this line when I came across it, because it strongly recalls the former expression to which Rymkiewicz refers as the beginning of four hundred years of Polish reciprocal hatred. But here the statement sounds different; there is a slightly different intent behind it, and, above all, what are Miechowita's mushrooms? Miechów, the Miechowice or Miechowskie woods, must be loaded with mushrooms. It took me a while to track it down, but at last I was led onto the most obvious path, leading to Maciej Miechowita, one of our most splendid humanists, a renowned Polish geographer and author of the *Kronika Polaków* (Chronicle of the Poles), professor of the Kraków Academy. Above all, however, Miechowita was by education a doctor *in medicina et philosophia*, our own Polish Hippocrates. He treated kings: Władysław Jagiellończyk, Jan Olbracht, Aleksander Jagiellończyk, and was the personal physician to King Zygmunt Stary (the Old). Amongst the many questions that piqued his curiosity was the problem of a healthy lifestyle—a topic to which he dedicated an entire work entitled *Conservatio sanitatis*.

I reckon that, had he lived in our day and age, with this passion of his for healthy eating habits, which had him concoct various recipes for dishes and preserves, Miechowita might easily have become the celebrity star of some popular culinary program. And here we finally arrive at those mushrooms of his. Miechowita was a great advocate of beer drinking. He was of the opinion that if beer were to be brewed from barley and wheat, it would be good for one's health—and thus, no chaff can be used. On the other hand, he was decidedly not fond of mushrooms. One of his recipes for their preparation has survived: Mushrooms should be stewed a long while, seasoned with various roots, fried with butter, after which they should be tossed out the window so that they do no harm to anyone. It's hard for me to judge whether in this case Zamoyski, making reference to Miechowita's joke, were opening a new chapter in the contempt of one group of Poles for another. Perhaps he just wanted in this way to express his opinion on the nature of Polish politics, which since the times of those free elections in the Polish-Lithuanian Commonwealth developed in rhythms similar to the life of a capricious river. In exceptional moments it swells suddenly, violently overspilling its banks, only to return to its old channels just as suddenly, as if nothing at all had occurred. Was he so very mistaken in this? How many splendid plans, announced with fanfare, bold visions drawn with panache, firm declarations or iron-clad, steadfast decisions taken in our Polish politics have come to their end—right there, among Miechowita's mushrooms?

Rector of the University

In the year of our Lord 1560, the young Jan Sariusz Zamoyski, son of Stanisław, the starost of Bełz, set off for Padua—at the time the most renowned and indeed best university in all of Europe, generously supported by the mighty Republic of Venice. He was eighteen at the time, and had already studied in Paris and Strasbourg as well—in the famed gymnasium of Johannes Sturm, whose aim was to make its charges over into people like the ancient Romans: bold politicians and citizens. But absolutely no seat of learning at the time equaled Padua, a true center of the academic life of Renaissance Italy and Europe as a whole. It was there that the real intellectual adventure of the future Chancellor got underway—an experience that was to have a gigantic significance for his later career. We know that in June 1561, Zamoyski, a diligent and ambitious student, purchased books proper to the study of Roman law; his enrolment records are written in his own hand. Here it is important to note that there were two universities in Padua. Today we'd call them two separate campuses, independent of each other. The *Universitas iuristarum* provided instruction in civil and canon law as well as theology. Lectures there were attended by men set on making a stellar career, whether in Church or state. The second campus, the *Universitas artistarum*, gathered to its halls more restless spirits, those in search of new ideas, and artistic types. There were taught: the liberal arts, astronomy, dialectics, philosophy, language studies, medicine, and rhetoric. Medicine especially enjoyed great interest; at times an even unhealthy excitement was aroused there by autopsies conducted in its especially designed anatomical theatre, which were open to all students. The university itself already had a solid three centuries of tradition behind it. It had been founded in 1222 with the permission of the eccentric Emperor Frederick II. As rumor had it, this foundation was the work of a group of students and their Bolognese professors who were dissatisfied with the relations then prevailing in that oldest university of Europe. In search of greater personal and intellectual freedom, they found a new place for themselves in the ancient city of Padua. It was therefore no coincidence that the motto of the new university claimed that "the freedom of Padua is absolute for all men,"[16] which beautifully dovetailed with the republican spirit that reigned in nearby Venice, and which certainly was very pleasing to the young Polish nobility, who from the start of the sixteenth century began travelling there in droves for wisdom and adventure.

When Zamoyski arrived in Padua, Venice was already past the prime of its political and military might. The republic was in a slow decline. All the same, for many in Europe it remained *the* most splendid republic, a pattern for all—both in regard to the respect paid to its ancient traditions and the awe in which its systemic solutions and civic freedoms were held. Thanks to the popular texts of Donato Giannotti and Gasparo Contarini, Venice was acknowledged as being possessed of the most perfect republican system. It was an oasis of freedom and peace, in glory surpassing Florence, which was constantly shaken by coups and gnawed at by revolutionary fever. For those in Jagiellonian Poland or Elizabethan England searching for new political inspirations, Venice was continually referred to as an unsurpassable pattern of good republican order. In essence, however, in the middle of the sixteenth century, this glory was something more of the effect of good Venetian PR than any factual political excellence. During the course of the so-called Italian Wars, it was becoming ever more difficult for the Venetians to defend themselves against the aggressive expansionism of Habsburg and Valois absolutism. And so their main concern became a clever balancing act between the Empire and the French. As late as 1509 they succeeded in driving Emperor Maximilian away from the walls of Padua, but ever more frequently they had to enter into pacts with their more powerful opponents, securing their independence not by strength of arms, but rather deft diplomacy. Still and all, thanks to this Venice was to avoid the tragic fate of Papal Rome, humbled in 1527 by the Protestant landsknechts of the Emperor, who plundered the Eternal City for a full eight days, committing slaughter and rape, and disgracing the graves of the Popes in St. Peter's Basilica. To the east, on the other hand, Venice began ever more to be subject to the expansion of Suleiman the Magnificent, losing one after another key maritime possession to the Ottoman

Empire. And so here too the Venetians were forced to negotiate, to make concessions, and to accept disadvantageous peace treaties. And yet, paradoxically, the republic's ever more unpropitious geopolitical situation had no malign influence whatsoever on its potential for development and further advancement. The luxury and wealth of the city, the elegant lifestyle there, the costly celebrations and entertainments, the generous patronage of the arts, the palaces constructed with élan, which aroused universal awe—on account of all these Venice remained an imposing, cosmopolitan melting pot in which all the different races, cultures, and religions described by Shakespeare in his Venetian dramas combined. Here, the most important European trade routes as well as those of diplomacy, finance, and international politics, still crossed. Despite its ever more defensive political posture, the star of the Republic of Venice shone continually on the firmament of Europe, and that shimmer of liberty still attracted to her people from all over the continent. Stanisław Reszka, one of the excited throng who visited it in the sixteenth century, was to write these beautiful words: "You behold Venice with awe, as sprinkled about her waters, like magic, are palaces, churches and squares, where the streets are blue and wooden horses serve as transport, where the population is divided amongst people and fish."[17]

As has already been mentioned, by the time that Zamoyski directed his steps toward Padua, the city had been the goal of Polish educational pilgrimages for several dozens of years. The myth of nearby Venice and its liberty certainly played a significant role in this. But nor was Padua lacking in its own charm and beauty. When speaking of the cities of Europe at the time, it is always worth reaching for the unsurpassed *Civitates Orbis Terrarum* of Georg Braun and Franz Hogenberg. They describe contemporary Padua as a city within a city, all on account of its truly marvelous military engineering, the pride of the most modern Italian art of fortification: the *mura veneziane.* Encircling the old, crowded structures of the center city themselves surrounded by mediaeval walls, widespread areas of new city quarters, gardens, and fields were protected by mighty, contemporary fortifications—a clear mirror-image pattern of how Zamość was to be built later on. Guarded by six defensive gates and a deep, natural fosse, these constituted an unsurpassable obstacle even to an enemy outfitted with the most modern artillery. More than one such learned this the hard way—the Habsburg Emperor no less. In the city itself was erected the grand Basilica of St. Anthony, where the tomb of its patron was situated (the goal of many a pilgrim), striking the beholder with awe. The fantastic Palazzo della Regione, with its gigantic main hall, its gorgeous loggia, and Europe's largest roof unsupported by columns—the great pride of Padovians—was another source of wonder, as was, of course, the Scrovegni Chapel: small, with only one nave, but all the same graced with the breathtaking frescos of Giotto. However, the true center of the city, its heart, remained the university located in the Palazzo del Bo—formerly the Tavern at the Sign of the Ox—renovated into a beautiful Renaissance structure with a wide-spreading courtyard. Without exaggeration, one might state that in the course of the sixteenth century that university educated an outstanding majority of the governmental élite of the Polish Republic. The list of influential and famous Polish alumni of Padua is long and impressive. According to the careful calculations of the historian Stanisław Windakiewicz, some one thousand Poles graduated from Padua at the time, in which number he finds thirty seven bishops, twenty abbots, fourteen voivodes, twenty-four chancellors and royal secretaries, along with three vice-chancellors.[18] It is no strange thing then that, especially beginning with the second half of the sixteenth century, it seemed as if the political destiny of Poland was directed by the influential group of the so-called Padovans—at a certain moment, including King Stefan Batory. In short—a Padua education opened wide the doors to a grand career in Poland, permitting one to find oneself in an influential circle, something that for the young, ambitious Zamoyski must certainly have been of first-rate importance, decisive in his choice of alma mater.

The popularity of Padua amongst the young Poles of the time must truly be acknowledged as a real phenomenon, something extraordinary. Naturally, there were also Paris, Bologna, Prague, and good schools in Germany. But the decided majority chose Padua, creating there a large and vocal Polish community. Padua was full of them—predominantly students, but also such youths as treated their stay there less practically, as an adventure rather than an important stage in their educational career. Most of them were the sons of more or less wealthy aristocratic families (Zamoyski would be counted among their ranks); there were representatives of the great magnate clans, but there were also commoners as well, who because of their exceptional talents enjoyed the support of a mighty Maecenas. For one example of these, we might point to Klemens Janicki, who not only achieved the degree of doctor of philosophy at Padua, but was also awarded the laurels—*poeta laureatus*—from the hands of Pope Paul III himself. The Poles at the University of Padua were grouped into their own "nation," the interests of which were represented by a *consiliarius* chosen from among their number. "Nations," as the chief bodies of student autonomy at the university, were generally constituted along geographic lines, according to the regions from which the students came. The two largest nations, of course, were the German and the Italian. They were divided, generally speaking, in two categories according to the line of the Alps: the Cismontane nations, those to the south of the mountain range, and the Ultramontane, those to the north. And so, in a literal sense, the University of Padua was a place where people from the North met those from the South. In practice, the nations busied themselves with the organization of their members' lives at the university, resolving their quarrels, conducting their own documentation, and organizing financial aid necessary to their members. They were mini-nations, communities within the framework of the great, common organism of the university. An important role was also the preservation of relations between the nations themselves, which had a special significance, for example, in the election of the university government, above all, in choosing of the rector. Frequently, misunderstandings, rivalries, conflicts, and even open brawling occurred in the reciprocal relations of the nations, which the university governors had to pacify with the use of force. It was these very relations between the nations that constituted the first school of diplomacy and foreign relations for these young people. The Polish nation was at the apogee of its growth and strength, perhaps, toward the middle of the sixteenth century, since at that time it enjoyed its own tavern in the city and something of the sort of its own club—the academy, of which Łukasz Górnicki writes as being initiated by Wojciech Kryski, later secretary to Zygmunt August. The Polish nation also possessed its own chapel of St. Stanisław, established in the Basilica of St. Anthony.

Why Padua? The first and simplest answer to that question has already been given: the university there had become the gateway to a career back home. Yet the extraordinary interest of Poles in Padua and its university had its cause also with the general transformations that had already arrived at northernly-situated Poland. Along with the appearance of the new currents of humanism in our land, the innovative ideas of the Renaissance—here Callimachus is perhaps the clearest, and most controversial, example of the transformations in the Jagiellonian monarchy at the end of the fifteenth century—the Poles of the time were gripped with an extraordinary mobility, arising most likely from great intellectual and spiritual anxiety and curiosity. Of course, Poles had travelled about the world earlier than this, studying at foreign universities, but those were individual cases, at any rate, no mass phenomenon, such as began to take shape at the turn of the sixteenth century. Józef Szujski was to call this a true travel mania,[19] a mass migration of Poles into foreign lands, to the South, in search of what was new; an intellectual migration of the peoples. At the University of Kraków, which at the time was internationalizing itself only with difficulty, and which fundamentally remained conservative toward the new currents flowing in from foreign parts, this trend was not warmly welcomed. A lot of blustering against it took place; some efforts were even made to put a stop to it, legally. Of course, all in vain. And this mobility and curiosity of the Poles were directed above all toward Padua, which was certainly their preferred destination. Naturally, they also travelled to Bologna, but less willingly now to Rome, to say nothing of Naples.

Padua reigned supreme. More precisely, Venice and Padua reigned indivisibly in the minds of many Poles open to the world. This had something to do with their own ideas concerning the roots of their ancestors, buried deep in the mists of ancient Slavic history predating the Polish nation. At least since the time of Virgil, a conviction had solidified that ancient Padua had been founded by the Trojan prince Antenor,[20] one of the heroes of the *Dismissal of the Grecian Envoys* (Odprawa posłów greckich) of the Padovan Jan Kochanowski.[21] Antenor was that unsuccessful advisor to Priam who had urged the king to return Helen to the Greeks and in this way to avoid war with the Achaeans. As we know, the king did not heed his advice, which led to tragedy for the city of Troy. But the destruction of that city was to result in the birth of Padua. Antenor, and other Trojans, leading the Veneti people, defeated the Euganeans inhabiting the area of today's Verona, and founded their own city called Patavium. At least this is what Livy teaches us in his description of those events long-ago.[22] The ruins of the ancient Patavium might still be seen in Padua. The history of the Veneti, who were supposed to have arrived with Antenor, is an interesting question not without its significance for us; not only because—obviously—they gave their name to mighty Venice. It is a fact that when Patavium was threatened by Attila's Huns during the period of the migration of the peoples and the fall of the Roman Empire, those descendants of the Veneti, that is, the Romans seeking to escape extermination, found security on the little islands of the lagoon, and this is considered the legendary beginning of the new city and Republic of Venice. But there is one more mysterious circumstance associated with the Veneti—namely, where they first came from. It is reckoned that some 950 years before Christ, this particular group of Indo-Europeans had inhabited Central Europe before making their appearance on the southern side of the Alps, where in the third century BC they became fully Romanized. This, of course, doesn't fit well with Livy's theory of the bonds shared between the Veneti, Antenor, and the Trojans. Nonetheless, the background of those forefathers who were to become Venetians is very intriguing. For they were associated in the minds of many with the Venedi, a people who in the Roman era, between the first and fourth century of our millennium inhabited the Baltic territories. These in turn were associated with the Vandals, although for a long period the Germans referred to the Slavs quite simply as Venedi. Now, did those ancient Veneti, who had inhabited the northern territories of Europe, have anything in common with the later Slavic Venedi? Clever Callimachus, for reasons perhaps none too clear for his contemporary Polish auditors, did not hesitate to take advantage of this obvious association. He sets the thesis of the generation of the Poles from the Veneti into the mouth of Grzegorz of Sanok,[23] and this also in the course of a radical historical revisionism that bats aside all the theses on the origin of the Poles found in the first book of Kadłubek's *Chronicle.*

The idea of the ancient, indeed mythic ties that bind us with the founders of the great maritime republic, inculcated by Callimachus—a Venetian himself by family—took deep root in the minds of the Poles of the sixteenth century, all the more so as many questions of a practical and current nature seemed to their eyes to be obvious confirmation of the peculiar relations that united the Republic of Venice and the First Polish Republic. Both Glorious Republics of Europe set the idea of civic freedom as a central value upon which the order of their governmental systems were based, along with the traditions of classical Roman republicanism from which both deeply drew. Both saw the greatest danger to their ideas of liberty in the growing ideologies of absolutism and imperialism, especially as represented by the Habsburgs. Both of them approached the political ambitions of Papal Rome with reserve. And finally, the common struggle in which they were engaged was not only for their own security, but was also conducted on behalf of the peace of all Christian Europe, the greatest threat to which was presented by the Turkish empire. Both republics often felt that in these struggles, they had been left by the other Christian states and rulers to fight alone—whether through calculation or cowardice. The memory of the gloomy tragedy that once took place near Varna was ever vivid, and closely interwove the fates of the both, the Republic and Venice, in the universal thinking of the Poles, bearing eloquent witness to the existence of a peculiar type of bond between the republics. And so, these bonds were deeply historical, but also current, intensely felt on account of both states' geographical location on the map of Europe as well as their common interest. In sixteenth-century Poland, where the concept of a mixed system ever more began to acquire the status of an ideal, on account of the widespread lecture of the ancient authors as well as the growing conflict in the Republic concerning systemic reforms, Venice was often referred to as the most effective pattern of government—indeed, the realization of such an ideal. In discussions, the balance that was developing in Poland between King, Senate, and Chamber of Envoys was compared to the systemic triad of the Venetian Republic: Doge, Senate, and Grand Council. Stanisław Orzechowski, himself a Padovan, was to write (certainly patterning himself on the well-known opinion of Machiavelli from his *Discorsi*) that Venice was a city praiseworthy on account of its organization in all things,[24] and therefore a *città ideale*. The esteem in which Poles held the Venetian system was, however, greatly exaggerated. For at any rate, in practice, Venice itself was systemically more of an aristocratic republic than a republican democracy of the nobility, with which system at the time the fevered political minds in Poland were obsessed. There were other differences too, after all. On the one hand, a republic of equestrians and landowners stretched out over measureless spaces, on the other, a republic of unarmed merchants concentrated in one city, who paid foreign mercenaries to defend them. For this reason, the menacing and severe Skarga was to try to call the Poles to their senses: "There's no need to look towards Venice!"[25] because they are two completely different states, nations, and systems. However, the sense of common interests as well as reciprocal curiosity remained strong between both republics. In 1592, the Venetian envoy Pietro Duodo was to weave before the Venetian Senate a plan for a peculiar union between Venice and the Polish Republic out of regard for the geopolitical situation in Europe: today we would say that he was suggesting a "strategic partnership". It is true, he notes, that it was a strange thing for a great and powerful country like the Republic, which had so many ports and access to the sea, not to possess its own fleet. It was here that he saw a gigantic potential for relations in the transport of wine, proposing the creation of a north-south trade route through Bolzano, Innsbruck, and Vienna to Kraków. For, as he notes: "The Polish Kingdom is rich to excess in all things necessary to life. The only thing in which it is lacking is wine, which only the rich can afford to drink."[26] On the other hand, the myth of Venice injected into Polish thought by Callimachus made it so that young Poles in search of wisdom, attractions, and adventure were constantly making their way to nearby Padua. Toward the end of the 1570s, the Papal Nuncio Caligari was to bemoan the fact that so many Poles were travelling to Italy, that he was no longer able to keep up with providing letters of recommendation for them.[27]

Zamoyski went to Padua to study law. There was a certain regularity to this. Many Poles in Padua chose the liberal arts as a second area of study as well—Jan Kochanowski, for one example. But those who planned a political career, or one in the state apparatus, were drawn to Padua because, above all, it offered very high quality lectures on Roman Law. For the formation of the new type of modern politics and the modern state, the spread of learning and knowledge concerning Roman law had a colossal significance. Toward the end of the fifteenth century, Emperor Maximilian made a breakthrough by establishing Roman law as the universally obligatory, streamlined legal system on the territory of the Empire, with the Imperial Chamber Court (*Reichskammergericht*) as the supreme instance for the settling of legal disputes. This romanization and streamlining of the legal system of Germany, especially in connection with the simultaneous wave of Reformation, determined the further direction of legal and political development and its practice among the German peoples. In Poland, things looked completely different, as Roman law had not yet won such great support here, and now, especially following the decision of Maximilian, was treated as "Cesarian" law, Imperial law, law usurping to itself an unconditional superiority and demanding obedience at the cost of republican freedoms. It is also worth remembering that neither in the fifteenth nor in the sixteenth century was the teaching of Roman Law to find an enduring place for itself at the Kraków Academy, where Canon Law was queen. If, therefore, someone was interested in the functioning of the state as well as contemporary politics, Padua offered all the best. Above all, excellent lecturers taught there, like the renowned experts in classical Roman Law and Criminal Law Guido Panciroli and Tiberio Deciani. It was at their feet that Zamoyski commenced his legal studies. However, another great intellectual power of the university, Carolus Sigonius, began to exert a decided influence on Zamoyski. The interesting thing is that Sigonius, or Sigonio, was not a legalist at all, and did not teach law, which after all gave his colleagues a reason to attack and criticize him, as they were legal romanists and certainly jealous of the great popularity he enjoyed amongst the students who crowded his lecture halls. He was interested in ancient literature, ancient history, the theory of politics and rhetoric. Above all, however, he gave himself passionately to the study of Livy and Cicero, those two pillars of classical Roman republicanism. His publishing in 1555 of the texts of Livy, with commentaries, cemented his fame as a renowned academic, and his lectures on the speeches of Cicero, on the basis of which he reconstructed the republican system, were of sincere interest to the students. And so Zamoyski was to write his diploma thesis under the direction of Sigonius, which on the one side is an expression of his intellectual interests, but also mirrors his own current political preferences. For Sigonius found himself involved in a violent quarrel with another renowned scholar of Padua, the conservative Aristotelian Francesco Robortelli (who taught Kochanowski, by the way). The conflict between these two figures enflamed the political and intellectual passions of the students, who were divided into the supporters of Sigonius, understood also to be sympathetic to France, and the pro-Habsburg supporters of Robortelli. While it is true that Zamoyski supposedly studied Imperial law carefully, as well as the statutes of the Italian cities as practical examples of the spreading influence of Roman law on European legislation, at the same time he maintained a strong antipathy to the Habsburgs and the Empire. But he was more interested in the systemic questions of the ancient Roman Republic, its legislation, as well as the entire historical and philosophical context of ancient republicanism. Sigonius, who didn't directly busy himself with Roman law *per se*, and was more of a historian and philosopher, concentrated his attention above all on the Roman system, on the theory of Roman politics, basing himself upon the texts of Cicero. This certainly was welcome to Zamoyski, who was only to a lesser extent interested in the theoretical side of

Roman law, and much more in the institutional and political practice of Roman republicanism. For it was the latter that also allowed him to consider the current processes taking place in his own country. For this reason the subject of Zamoyski's thesis—the Roman Senate—was certainly no haphazard choice.[28] It must be taken into consideration that, beginning at least near the end of the fifteenth century, a great discussion concerning the systemic shape of the country was underway—for just one example, the "Kokosza" ("Chicken") War, and one of the key questions in this quarrel was the place and role of the Senate. It is obvious that references to the traditions of the Roman Republic played an important part in this debate, with such references often settling argumentative points. And so the thesis was a scholarly attempt at analyzing the functioning of the Roman Senate with the intention of exploiting the wisdom so formulated for the constitutional discussion at home. The fact that at first the Roman Senate had merely a consultative role must have been for Zamoyski an inspiring issue—after all, he mentions this in his work—for its decisions had no power of coercive law whatsoever. The real legislators of the Republic were the people gathered together in consultation. The resolutions of the Senate only took on the might of obligatory law in the times of Augustus—and so this was an important element in the process of the evolution from Republic toward a more centralized government of the aristocracy, and thence in the direction of the imperial government of the Caesars, the Roman Emperors. Therefore, in composing his work on the Senate, Zamoyski sketched his own attitude toward the systemic quarrels currently taking place in his contemporary Poland as well. When his thesis was taking shape under the direction of Sigonius in far-away Padua, in Poland the great "executionist" movement among the nobility was reaching its apogee. Generally speaking, this movement, which had been increasing since the start of the sixteenth century, was aimed at fundamental reforms of the state that in effect would lead to the domination of the democratic nobility in Poland. And yet the Senate was standing in the way of these reforms; the senate understood as an institution representing the aristocratic privileges of the few, who wished to amass power and influence over the king in their own hands. And so we have to deal here with the classic conflict between democracy and oligarchy as if lifted straight from the theories of Aristotle and Polibius. In this quarrel, the successive Jagiellonians stood now on the side of the great mass of the nobility, seeing in them an ally in the great work of the reform of the state, and now on the side of the Senate, understanding that in this way they might all the more easily preserve their control over the political process. In other words, their attitude was somewhat like that of old Augustus Octavianus, who took legislative power away from the popular gatherings on behalf of the Senate, which he himself stuffed with members. In 1562, at the time during which Zamoyski, perhaps, was collecting the materials for his work, a sort of symbolic breakthrough in this quarrel occurred. For King Zygmunt August arrived at the Diet dressed not as usual in the Italian style, but in the dress typical of the nobility—signaling his agreement, in the main, to the postulates of the executionist movement. On which side of the barricade did the young author of the work on the Roman Senate, and rector of Padua University, stand at this time?

In 1563, Zamoyski crowned his career at the University of Padua with his election to the post of rector of the *Universitas iuristarum*. He is not the first Pole to be so honored. The choice made by the *consiliarii* of the nations was preceded by a stormy campaign not devoid of masterful intrigue, thanks to which it proved possible to break the opposition of the German nation and that of a portion of the Italians. These had argued that in questions of Roman Law, Poles are not the most competent, and such competencies are absolutely necessary for a rector. Yet it seems that Zamoyski enjoyed great respect at the university, and his competency and knowledge—in the fields of Imperial, Roman Law as well—were not to be cast into doubt. In the final voting, the Pole received as many as seventeen votes out of a total of twenty-five. In winning the position of rector, Zamoyski was to obtain a great influence over the life of the school, including the seating of professors called to their post by the Venetian Senate, as well as the reformation of the university statutes. With so many administrative matters to be settled, he often had to take himself to nearby Venice where, now not only in theory but also in practice, he was able to examine the functioning of the Republic and its institutions. This again allowed him to develop some widespread contacts among the Venetian governing élite, which he would later maintain and have advantage of throughout his life. He returned to his country in 1564 as a man formed: a doctor of both laws, an experienced administrator and a talented politician with a bright future, a diplomat, an orator, and a negotiator. He brought back with him not only a copy of his thesis on the Roman Senate, but also a letter from the Senate of the Most Serene Republic of Venice addressed to King Zygmunt August, recommending to him his talented subject, who has won the respect of many students and countless officials of said republic. The script of the Senate begins with the significant words: "Having as we do a special affection for the Polish nation..."[29] In later years, reminiscing of his stay in the Republic of Venice, the grand chancellor and hetman would repeat with pride: "It was Padua that made a man of me."[30]

A Digression on State Interest

It was indeed in the sixteenth century that Italy became the setting for a stormy and fascinating debate on the topic of politics and the modern system of statehood. Among others, this discussion touched upon the Republic of Venice as an example of a mixed system that had functioned perfectly for centuries; a mainstay of civic liberties, which especially stood out not only against the background of the absolutist powers of Spain and France, but also the despotism of the neighboring Medicis and Sforzas and the popes. The views of the Florentine Niccolò Machiavelli had an immense significance for this systemic debate, as they provided a strong impulse toward completely new considerations of the nature of politics, free from moral and religious constraints. The majority of the Italian states, the variety of their systems, and certainly the temperaments of the inhabitants of the sunny lands gave rise to an unusually fruitful bumper crop of ideas. The ferocity of the conflicts at the time, the unhealthy ambitions of politically wanton individuals, which quite often approached the level of complete degeneracy, but also the elaborate forms of bureaucracy, administration, finances, diplomacy, and law, so similar to those of our own day and age, in a natural way directed men's interest toward questions related to the very techniques and arcana by which authority is obtained and maintained. At the same time, these Renaissance, sixteenth-century, Italian reflections on politics swung decidedly toward the formation of an innovative concept of the state, which was later to provide the foundation for the absolutist monarchies of Enlightenment Europe. The new idea of politics and the state arose in an atmosphere of great upheavals, uncertainties, the decline of earlier hopes, and things that had been taken for granted to become—as is usually the case with new solutions—the fruit of the crisis as one era comes to an end, and a new begins. Above all, however, it was born in obvious tension with the republican idea of *vivere libere*, life in freedom.

Stanisław Grzybowski, who authored a book on Zamoyski, formulated such inspiring thoughts concerning the inter-epochal intellectual and political atmosphere current in Padua in particular, and Italy in general, at the time in which our hero was studying there: "In the mediaeval system of values, basically accepted by the Renaissance, a hierarchy of non-antagonistic values making up the ideal order and arrangement of the universe was of immense significance.

Renaissance thought wished to combine into one consecutive and harmonious whole the crowd of new facts and new ideas, or ideas renewed after the passage of centuries. This tendency to order and harmony, to unity and consequence, percolated through all areas of life, from scholarship and art through economics and politics. [...] At the same time, into this paradoxical, ever fecund attempt at reconciling the Renaissance revolt, the Renaissance desire of liberty and fullness of humanity with the non-antagonistic mediaeval harmony of values, there penetrated a doctrine teaching that man is by nature evil; that human interests are by nature antagonistic, and that for the preservation of order and harmony it is absolutely necessary to acknowledge one basic value, the highest interest of all—in this case, the interest of the state. This doctrine is in the nature of things just as paradoxical, as it attempts to rescue mediaeval universalism through the attribution of the highest value to that which is the very denial of universalism—the modern state."[31] This interesting philosophical-political insight of the Polish historian throws a strong light upon the essence of the breakthrough taking place in the West during the sixteenth century, which was to lead to the primacy of the freedom of the state in the realization of its own interests, above and beyond the liberty of its citizens.

State interest, *raison d'état, della ragion di stato* or *ragione di stato, Staatråson*—only the poor British, significantly, did not come up with their own exact version of the idea, translating it into the crippled term *national interest.* The concept of state interest would certainly have emerged without Machiavelli, as an expression of indispensable changes, but he, of course, was the first to give a decided pretext for the acceptance of a new manner of thinking about politics and the state. This impulse primarily consisted in his conception of political necessity and in the way he saw the meaning of a political decision as an independent act of power by a political agent. This provided a basis for the modern conception of the state, which was to develop later.

The Republic of Venice to which Machiavelli looked as an example of a perfect republic, a pattern to be followed, but also, naturally, the nearby University of Padua, became that place in Italy where the new conception of state interest found an exceptionally broad resonance as well as many advocates. Meinecke, who devoted an entire, detailed analysis to the idea of state interest,[32] went so far as to claim that at the time spoken of, the very conception gave rise to such great interest that it constituted a topic of general conversation among peddlers at the market and craftsmen in their workshops. There is certainly more than a little exaggeration in such a statement. However, the sowing of new ideas, which Machiavelli initiated at the start of the sixteenth century, was to bear impressive fruit at the turn of the seventeenth in the guise of a large corpus of texts touching upon the question of *ragione di stato.* Many of the thinkers, historians, and politicians referring to this idea were either directly linked to the Republic of Venice, or alluded to it as an important example. For instance, the Padovan Paolo Paruta, author of the *Discorsi politici* from 1599, was a great advocate of the balanced, Venetian system of state. In all probability, Zamoyski had become personally acquainted with him during one of the many public functions Paruta attended in the Republic in the 1560s. Another was Paolo Sarpi, historian, lawyer, the chief theologian of Venice in its quarrels with Rome, a declared defender of the freedoms of the republic in its struggle with the Papacy, as was Trajano Boccalini, Sarpi's friend, who fiercely crossed swords with Spanish absolutism in his writings, only to be murdered in Venice by an assassin sent there for the purpose by the Habsburgs. Finally, there was Giovanni Botero, who was in complete opposition to the political amorality of Machiavelli and held that politicians should be guided by the moral dictates of Christianity, although admitting, in his famous tract published in Venice in 1589, *Della ragion di Stato,* that the state is directed by its own interests, the attainment of which it has the right to approach along various paths.

All of these authors, as well as many not mentioned here, found themselves faced with the problem that ever more strongly described the setting of Europe as a whole in the sixteenth century, namely: how political life might reconcile the irreconcilable—the need of unity, hierarchy, and order with the desire for freedom, as well as the conflicting interests and needs of ambitious individuals, who through humanism are to attain their full, human subjectivity and autonomy in decision-making. How can this human element be restrained? Once loosed of its mediaeval forms, will it subject itself to some new principles, and if so, of what sort? Can it be the principle of state interest, which is, after all, based upon the acknowledgement of the primacy of government over all men? And who is to describe the principles of government, if we are to acknowledge that it is completely independent of the dictates of religion and the Christian morality arising therefrom? Can the simple conviction of how human elements may be the source of evil, and the state the only real universal good, suffice for the recognition of government always being in the right? Does not such a doctrine itself lead to evil, to the abuse of force and the destruction of all freedom? The new, cardinal situation, created by the Renaissance and humanism, posed many such anxious questions. And many authors writing of the doctrine of state rights had to tread carefully through a minefield in order to find the answers to these questions—how to reconcile the interests of the generality, the state, with the personal interest of the ruler and the religious principles dictated by the Law of God.

However, it was only to be in the next century that the politics of state interest would be fully developed in practice, at the hands of a true master. If we are to believe the words of Henry Kissinger culled from his renowned work *Diplomacy*, the great virtuoso of the politics of state interest was Cardinal Richelieu. "Under his auspices, *raison d'état* replaced the mediaeval concept of universal moral values as the operating principle of French policy."[33] According to the principles of such politics, the good of the state and its interests are the only moral rationale for its actions. And so, there are no restraints in politics such as would force a state agent to act against that overriding goal. And it is to just such a principle that the Cardinal was to hold fast during his epic struggles with the Empire and the Habsburgs during the Thirty Years' War when, in support of the Protestant princes of the Reich, he was to foil the rebirth of the Catholic Empire. And all this only to ensure the power of France over its mortal enemies, the House of Habsburg. Zamoyski did not live to see this, but he sensed the coming spirit perfectly.

The conception of *raison d'état* led inexorably to the recognition of the primacy of state interest. In his activities the politician is to be directed by this imperative alone: he is to do everything necessary in order to ensure the state's power and advantage over its neighbors. Ethical principles, religious norms and morality, the personal interests of particular groups acknowledging these, or any particular groups of persons must be unconditionally subjected to said state interest. In consequence, such an understanding of politics also had to lead to the negation of the primacy of universally valid legal or ethical principles in favor of strength and force: the primacy of governmental power. The only thing that counted was necessity, *neccesitas regni*, as Pope Innocent III, the chief jurist of the still mediaeval Church, once stated. For this reason, the advocates of state interest, and in fact all those who confessed to political realism, were to repeat with glee the famous phrase that "necessity knows no law"—it knows only strength. In essence, then, the conception of *raison d'état* made reference to politics as activity undertaken in a state of higher necessity, which, for the politician, is perhaps the only convenable state. It is not at all strange, then, that monarchs interested in the centralization of governmental power exclusively in their own hands, so as to usurp to themselves the right to final decisions, appealed to this idea with relish. However, independent of the motives of kings' personal ambitions as well as their struggles with all sorts of interior rivals, the conception of state interest also still had its own autonomous, historical significance, at least in reference to two aspects. First of all, it objectified the state as a self-sufficient creature, as a political body living a real life, the *stato*, which all its inhabitants are to serve and to which they are to be obedient, each within the framework of his own particular functions and duties. This includes the absolutist monarch, who, appealing to state necessity, may even infringe upon the most universally acknowledged laws, but only—after all—in the service of the highest interest, that of the state. Second, the apparatus of power subjected itself in full to the dispassionate reason, which, paying no heed to any other human considerations, set its inerrant goals. As has been said, or rather, as Kissinger said, all this was brought to perfection by Cardinal Richelieu in his politics. Doubtlessly, it was his mastery of the art of *raison d'état* that saw to it that his beloved monarch Louis XIII, despite hating him personally, was able to achieve so great a position in France and in Europe as a whole. There yet remains the open question: was all this the great achievement of modern politics, or the beginning of its horrid degeneracy?

A Temptation Hard to Resist

It's hard to believe that after his years in Padua and Venice, Zamoyski would not pose to himself questions touching upon the idea of *raison d'état* as a conception capable of overmastering the contemporary political elements unleashed from the ancient framework of the mediaeval order. And yet in the case of the Republic, because of the executionist movement of the first half of the sixteenth century, these were mass elements, of massive might, having the potential of practically unrestrainable transformations. How might this wave be directed? Does the state, as well as its reasons and interests, provide any indispensable indicators for such effective restraints on Polish ground?

As a realist, Zamoyski was certainly aware of the fact that, once the avalanche of the democratization of the nobility should be unleashed in Poland, there would be no way of restraining it in the least; one could only try and ride it. He himself, after all, came of the masses of the nobility aspiring to a chief role in the political might of the state. He also knew perfectly—and certainly had brought this awareness with him from Padua—that the basis of success in politics unhinged from its framework of tradition is might, the concentrated will of power, capable of breaking through the opposition and resistance of the ruler. Such a show of strength was, without a doubt, the execution of the warlord Samuel Zborowski, orchestrated by the Chancellor. All the same, aware as he was of the significance of a demonstration of might in politics (in this Zamoyski was a real master of staging), he was never to decide to stretch out his hands for the fullness of power in such a way that would set him on the other side of the barricades in face of the democratic, noble masses of the Republic.

Zamoyski is often spoken of as the man most responsible for the establishment of elections *viritim* in the Republic, and thus for the universal, personal election of the king by the entire massed nobility. This is not completely true, since the principle of an elective monarchy had made its appearance in the minds of various leaders of the nobility earlier—as early as the times of the last two Jagiellonian monarchs. With all certainty, Piotr Zborowski, Samuel's oldest brother, was an ardent advocate of the introduction of the universal election of the king, as were Jan Firlej, the voivode of Kraków, and Mikołaj Sienicki, Zamoyski's close friend, although significantly his elder, many times marshal of the Diet. All of these, it should be pointed out, were Calvinists. The introduction of the free election was the crowning of the whole process of the noble revolution, and had a simply epochal significance for both the Polish system and our entire political culture. For one might state that, with the principle of free election, the history of Poland as a *regnum*, a kingdom, comes to an end, and that of

Poland as a Republic, the common weal of all its citizens, begins. The attribution of a key role in this transformation to Zamoyski arises, of course, from his engagement in the first election in 1573 following the death of Zygmunt August and later, that immediately following the flight of Henri Valois back to France in the next year of 1574. However, at once we are faced with a clear inconsistency in his attitude toward free election. It is as if the ideas of a strong government, the state and the *raison d'état*, brought back home with him from his studies in Padua, collided in his head with the practical recognition of the absolute supremacy of the democratic sovereignty of the noble caste. For from the start, Zamoyski did not at all take the side of the adherents of free, universal election, but was to advocate for the election of the monarch via a system of representation, the key role therein belonging to the Senate—or, in other words, the principle of an aristocratic republic (as in Venice)—not the people. Here we arrive at a fairly important question, namely: what were the political views that Zamoyski brought with him to Poland from Padua? Is he a democrat, or rather a partisan of the aristocratic republic? Is he an elitist or a populist? One thing is beyond doubt: he was opposed to the *absolutum dominium*, the centering of all authority in the hands of the monarch, believing that absolutism cannot be reconciled with the idea of republican freedoms. He probably sincerely believed in the principle of a mixed system, the stability and balance of which he had been able to observe in the Republic of Venice. But were the ideas just being born in Italy concerning the reasons of state, and a powerful state at that, completely foreign to him? Well, considering the evolution of Zamoyski's attitude toward the universal election of the ruler in 1573, in 1574, and then considering his behavior in 1587, during the third, this time armed, warlike election, I reckon we may assume that he was guided by a certain idea that had been slowly maturing and taking on more and more the clean lines of a determination, to know: that it was he indeed, Jan Sariusz Zamoyski, and only him, who was the man best prepared for such a task. It was him who with time had accumulated the most real power in the Republic, as Chancellor and hetman, to bring about the establishment of a strong state, founding it thanks to the universal election of himself to the Polish throne. From this new position, with a strong arm, he would be able to direct the elements of the nobility in a concrete, perfectly thought out and precisely managed direction—the direction of an undefeated power. In such a case, of course, the abandonment of the aristocratic republic on behalf of the universal, democratic election of the king by the nobility would seem quite comprehensible, and cease to be the mere expression of some interior dithering or conflict. As the son of a low-level senator, who started out as the client to the grand magnate clans, Zamoyski would never have had the slightest chance of being elected king by a narrow coterie of aristocratic electors. Should the election be universal, however, by laboriously building up his position as the tribune of the noble masses, and on account of his ever more powerful personal position, those chances of his would look completely different.

Zamoyski was no political idealist. He was a born politician. Concrete ideas served to attain concrete goals, which he himself set, directed by his political instincts. Even if he did return to the country with his doctoral dissertation on the theme of the Roman Senate under his arm, even if as a *homo novus* he aspired to win the recognition of mighty senators, acting in accord with the interests of his powerful protectors like Mikołaj Krzysztof Radziwiłł Sierotka, he was a realist and saw that in Poland there was only one supreme political force capable of bearing the matters of state, and his own matters—the movement of the mass nobility. It is for this reason that he cast his lot not with the Senate, not with the political élite, not with *lo stato*, but with that democratic, and in the end unpredictable, noble *identitas*—that newly-arisen political identity—for which reason in today's world he would be included amongst populist politicians. So, even if in July 1573 he was still proposing the Senate as the electors of the king, already in September he proclaimed himself in favor of election *viritim*. This turn in his views was therefore a quick one—and one that was exceptionally effective. Zamoyski was not only openly declaring his support for new democratic systemic solutions, he was not only finding legal rationales for the same by making reference to the old act of confederation of the nobility of Rus' from 1436, sniffed out from its pigeonhole somewhere in the yawning royal archives[34] (and we know, after all, that the nobility adored such arguments referencing the ancient rights of their antecedents), he quite simply and consecutively hammered into the heads of the nobles the idea of the universal election of kings as the most important symbol of political freedom. Thanks to this, he became the unquestioned leader of the noble brotherhood, pushing old Sienicki out of that role. He was also a clever salesman of this idea, as he crafted in the minds of the aristocracy a consciousness of himself as an irreplaceable man, who alone is able to control the elemental force of the nobility. On this, indeed, he built his impressive influence during the reign of Batory. He amassed in his hands the great power of the most supreme offices, becoming the Great Crown Chancellor, and therefore, the supreme official of the realm, let us say: something along the order of a prime minister today, and Grand Hetman—this latter title granted for life, which gave him immense authority in the state, while in times of interregnum, a power well-nigh dictatorial. Zamoyski energetically made use of the possibilities granted him by the power he possessed, forming, kneading, shaping the systemic character of the Republic like some kind of Pygmalion, stamping it with his own trademark. And so I think that, psychologically, Zamoyski must have been something of a "self-made man," someone conscious of the fact that he'd scrambled doggedly to the summit under his own power. Perhaps even more than that: he clambered to heights where previously no foot had ever trod, borne upward by the broad, rushing current of noble democratization. He was the true father of the noble nation and the creator of a new, democratic system. But of the state? It seemed that there were no limits before him, that he might, by strength of will and his own power, shape the Republic in every situation, overcoming every opponent—that the only thing lacking for the fullness of his glory was one small step, one small motion, but one that would decide everything—stretching forth his hand for the crown. But it was in 1587 indeed that, perhaps for the first time in his life, he saw before him an impenetrable wall which constituted the limits of his power. The plastic material of the new Republic, malleable up until now, so subject to his will, began to crumble in his hands.

The Senatorial Shack Aflame

In considering the events surrounding the 1587 election, it is impossible not to notice that something in the great Chancellor cracked, something within him began to falter. That great power of his, which for several dozen years so ably shaped the form of the Republic, got bogged down somewhere in the ruts of fate. This gives rise to the disturbing question whether it might not be that the disadvantageous current of events during the third election drove the great Jan Zamoyski to a nervous breakdown? I know that this question might seem inappropriate. In his book on Samuel Zborowski, Rymkiewicz insists, and perhaps not without justice, that the Poles at the time of the First Republic were completely different from us today—that there can be no comparison between us. Back then, in the sixteenth century, they were real knights, people of great courage, of simply extraordinary stamina, manliness, as strong as bulls. And so the question as to whether Zamoyski, the man who was doubtlessly the most powerful person in the entire Republic, might have had a nervous breakdown seems entirely out of place. It fits our condition better, the nerve-wracked, aspirational Poles of today, so full of complexes, but not those giants, those super-humans who created our old-Polish power. It simply cannot be. And yet… Different evidence suggests that something along the lines of what we call today a nervous breakdown, hysteria, or even frenzy, took hold of the most powerful man of the Republic, the Grand Hetman, Chancellor Jan Zamoyski. And it happened in that crucial year of 1587, the year of the extraordinarily stormy election that brought Zygmunt Waza (Vasa) to the Polish throne. It was a bloody election; the first truly militarized one that gave rise to the outbreak of a fratricidal civil war. It was exactly then that the mightiest man in Poland realized that there are some situations which even he was incapable of surmounting. Elemental forces aren't always that easily directed.

In order to understand this better, let us go back to the field of election at Wola at the time of those key events of the third free election. For after Górka and Zborowski had arranged their bold, unaccustomed provocation, marching at the head of armed units in the very presence of the equestrians governing the election from their entrenchment, nothing could be done to restrain the fatal current of events. The emotions had reached their zenith. Primate Karnkowski's separation of the two hostile camps as well as his attempts at mediation were fruitless. They merely provided Stanisław Sędziwój Czarnkowski, blind with personal hatred to the Chancellor, an excuse to pound his staff into the ground and, plucking at his long, grey beard, summon the supporters of the Zborowskis and Górka to an act of sedition: the establishment of a grand, revolutionary tribunal of all the nobles which, before the election should commence, would sit in judgement over all the crimes and treasons of that venomous, horrid dragon—the Black Chancellor. With this call to rebellion he aroused a great furore amongst the nobility. He lifted his crooked hands to the sky and, his entire frame trembling with emotion, moaned dramatically: "Is there no one to respect now, no king? Then there is no Lord above us. Who then must be feared? Only one person. I, though old and blind, shall take to horse myself, staff in hand. And happily I'll bring to order whomever I come across in the name of freedom, and I trust that God will aid me. Let us then organize a *Rokosz* (armed rising of the nobility), and let's see who is on our side, who wants to serve the good." These words had the effect of a clarion call. Someone else in the crowd of the nobles strove to make himself heard, but shots were fired, blood spilt. Someone fell to the ground, dead. Now there was nothing to restrain the horrid catastrophe on the field of election, since "there is no king," since there was no lord over any of them there.

It was clear that a real clash of might was now inevitable. This conflict could only be broken by force. The political community, lacking a king, was divided into camps at each other's throat. Furthermore, in defending himself, the Chancellor had to commit a sort of self-destruction as far as his royal plans were concerned. For should he reach out his hand for the crown of the Republic following a successful, fratricidal battle in Warsaw, there wouldn't be the shadow of a doubt in anyone's mind that he had become exactly what his fiercest enemies said that he was—a bloody tyrant. The case would have been different had the crown fallen into his hands as the result of even the stormiest of elections. It was a sweltering day in July. The Chancellor positioned his units in battle-order, on the eastern edge of the field of election. From the western walls of the city, Górka and the Zborowskis arranged four thousand of their armed men. The field of elections was to become a battlefield. A portion of the senators, terrified, along with the widowed queen and the envoys of foreign monarchs, retreated behind the walls of the city of Warsaw. The church bells were ringing a loud alarm. The artillery was primed and waiting tensely. And thus, in battle order, the two hostile camps faced one another all throughout the day. It was a battle of nerves. Between the two armies a handful of negotiators sped back and forth. The very last hope consisted of Wawrzyniec Goślicki, the Bishop of Kamieniec, and Stanisław Szafraniec, the Arian voivode of

Sandomierz—so-called "neutrals." This dangerous *danse macabre* on the cliff-edge of a great national tragedy went on until dusk, when, clearly, emotions began to abate, giving way to exhaustion. Things did not arrive at a grand settling of accounts by military means—which was in a certain sense a political victory for Zamoyski, who proved himself a moderate against the background of enemies thirsting for blood. This was much to the taste of the conservative nobility, jittery at the development of events. But given all these circumstances, could Zamoyski still advance his candidacy to the throne when the election commenced? It's highly doubtful—things had gone too far. In all the confusion which must have been roiling just beneath the walls of Warsaw all that hot July day until dusk, I note especially two things, on account of their symbolic content. The first is those "neutrals," men of good will, concerned with the good of all, above all. I see Szafraniec and Goślicki, the Arian voivode and the Catholic bishop, tirelessly traipsing beneath their white flag all day long between the two hostile forces, patiently giving ear to pathetic declarations and fierce threats from both Górka and Zamoyski; how they strive to convince all that bloodshed is senseless, that in the end, the good of the Republic is the main thing, and that this needs to be elevated above all partisanship. Supposedly, Szafraniec even had a huge banner with the legend *bonum publicum* planted on the field of elections[35] dreaming of the creation of a great political party comprised of neutrals prepared to bury the hatchet of the divided nobility. There's something very moving in this quixotic pair; their faith in common sense and the possibility of accord in the very midst of a military fracas—and so there, where neutrality has no right to be, where one can only choose between two opposing sides—it can dissolve one to tears. It turns out that the chronic incapability of the Republic to tear itself away from the noble, democratic community, from an elemental political identity and a transformation of the same into a more abstract form of the objectified state, did not only disallow any chance for the establishment in Poland of some practice of state interest, but nor did it allow for the intervention of appeals to the common good in situations of profound crisis. Szafraniec's political program was shrugged off by the fevered nobles. It flowed away like water off a duck's back, never to be realized. However, we must deal justly with these idealists of ours. For then, on the fields of Wola, beneath the walls of Warsaw, it was them, most likely, who saved the Poles from cutting each other's throats.

There's another thing too that cannot be forgotten—the temporary pavilion raised to be used by the Senate members—the senatorial shack, which had stood at the central point of the fields of election, and which at the start of the process the primate always blessed as a place where men were to gather under the special care of the Holy Ghost. Shaken by the events of that July day, Karnkowski, the Archbishop of Gniezno, the *interrex*, ordered that the shack standing on the emptied field of election be burnt to the ground that evening.[36] There was to be no election of any Polish king in this place disgraced by the shedding of fraternal blood. The earthen battlement was evened with the ground and soon the great wooden shack roofed with deal was aflame, great sheets of fire shooting into the dark night sky. This great bonfire must have been a stirring sight, a symbol of something truly evil having occurred. The forty-five year old Chancellor had seen many things in his life, but I reckon that when from his camp he gazed upon the tongues of fire reducing the senatorial shack to ashes, one horrid thought might have crept into his mind, gripping him with terror: truly, matters had got too far out of hand; the crown, which seemed to be within his reach, was now lost to him forever.

The Only Truly Great Revolution

The king never dies—and yet. Ernst Kantorowicz's famous book of the king's two bodies—the human, mortal frame, which dies and decomposes, and the sacred, divine, imperishable body of the kingdom—published in 1957[37]—explains the manner in which the idea of the immortal, eternal crown was shaped in the European kingdoms. And so, when, on the day of the death of the great King of France, Henry IV, in 1610, Queen Marie Medici was to cry out to the chancellor Nicholas de Sillery: "Alas! The king is dead!", the latter replied without skipping a beat and calmly: "Your majesty will forgive me, but in France kings never die."[38] And not only in France, for that matter. To this day, in Westminster Abbey we can inspect a whole collection of so-called funeral effigies, life-size figures of deceased monarchs, usually carved from wood, the more realistic of them from wax. During the funeral ceremonies of the ruler they were set upon the bier, and following the ceremonies—placed above the tomb. They were to symbolize the enduring, intransient, real presence of the dead monarch, God's anointed—for the king never dies. In Jagiellonian Poland, which constantly stressed the unity of the body of the kingdom, the *corpus regni*, in symbols, as well as the unity of the crown, *corona regni*, this particular position of the monarch, the anointed of God, the inherent lord, endured up until the time of the noble revolution, which introduced free elections. In the Republic, the king, of course the most beloved, anointed by the primate with holy oils in the Cathedral, surrounded by respect and obedience, was all the same just the outward face of the kingdom; he had become a participant in the Republic along with the senators and the nobles. As the journal of the Diet from 1592 stresses: "Each of us is heir to this kingdom, the king of which we elect, so that he might command us in accordance with the law."[39]

The sacred continuity of the royal power can be best exemplified by the rituals of funeral and coronation, which also endured throughout the entire history of the reign of the Polish monarchs, beginning with the unification of the Piast districts by Łokietek. Here a peculiar principle was obligatory, that is, that even after his physical death the king still ruled, in accordance with the legal maxim of the Italian jurist Baldus de Ubaldis, stating that the *regia maiestas* never dies.[40] Such being the case, the physical, earthly, human death of the ruler was decisive of nothing. For this reason, the date of the king's funeral was recognized as the ending date of his reign, which burial ought to take place in the presence of his successor, who would be crowned the new king without delay. For such a sequence of events guaranteed the continuity of succession: death—funeral—coronation. The king is dead, long live the king! And so, in practice, this signified that during the entire period between the death of the king and the funeral ceremony, the still unburied monarch exercised unquestioned and undivided authority. Through his majesty he was constantly present, and his subjects still owed him obedience. Such a situation might last quite a long time if, for example, the election of the new king were to drag on significantly. Till then, the already mute, but unburied king continued to exercise his power from the heights of his imperishable, timeless majesty, guaranteeing the factual immortality of his *regnum*.

In reality, however, it was not always possible to hold to these conditions, which led to various complications, some with serious consequences. We know, for example, that Jan Olbracht, the son of Kazimierz Jagiellończyk, was buried toward the end of July 1501, whereas the coronation of his brother Aleksander took place in mid-December of the same year. This means, neither more nor less, that the Polish kingdom was deprived of symbolic continuity for over four months. And this was no coincidence because at the time, during that hiatus of several months when it was unknown whether the king dies, or never dies, one of the most basic steps was taken on the road to that great systemic revolution that led to the establishment of the democratic, noble Republic: the price of Aleksander's crown was the Privilege of Mielnik, which introduced a *de facto* oligarchic-aristocratic republic in Poland, subjecting the new king to the senate. Certain complications with an all-too-hurriedly arranged funeral of the dead ruler had already taken place in our history. For example, the famous case of the funeral of Kazimierz Wielki (the Great), which happened twice. The first funeral took place two days after the king's death, on 7 November 1370. It turned out that it had been performed a bit too hastily, for the man named by Kazimierz to succeed him, Ludwik Węgierski (Louis the Hungarian, of the House of Anjou), wasn't able to arrive in time. It seems that he was only half a day late, so his tardiness cannot really be compared to the disruption of several months that occurred between Olbracht and Aleksander. Still, it was fully sufficient to give rise to speculation that the haste and tardiness might not have been entirely coincidental. Kazimierz's decision to pass the Polish crown to the house of Anjou, while still there existed some collateral lines of the Piast dynasty, inevitably gave rise to great controversy in the country. Certainly for this reason Ludwik Węgierski, an energetic and decisive ruler, determined that all doubt must be unequivocally settled—so the second funeral was arragned immediately following his coronation. And that he wished thereby to have an argument truly clinching, he ordered that the funeral be spectacular—something never before seen in the Kingdom of Poland. At any event it was a majestic, unforgettable ritual, which certainly set the standard for the later royal funeral rites of the Jagiellons. Janko z Czarnkowa (Jan of Czarnków) has described in detail the course of the second, grand funeral of Kazimierz Wielki, and it is from him that our excellent knowledge of the event comes.[41] There were four wagons at the head of the parade, each with four horses in harness, draped in black. Behind them came forty knights in armor clad in scarlet cloth, then knights carrying shields with the coats of arms of the lands of the kingdom and banners of the provinces, along with the largest, royal standard. Right after this banner rode a knight on horseback dressed in a royal cloak of gold, a personification of the dead ruler (and so it was as if poor Kazimierz had been resurrected). Then the courtiers with lit funeral tapers, the clergy, and then, at the very end of this great procession, rode Ludwik Węgierski himself. In such a fashion, with the figure of the king in armor, mounted, into whom one of the knights had been incarnated, the ritual suggested that the dead monarch accompanied his own funeral to the very last moment as the incarnation of the majesty of crown and kingdom, until he lay his earthly remains in the grave. This second funeral ceremony of Kazimierz's must truly have made a gigantic impression on our forebears, since two hundred years later, in a similar manner, but with even greater pomp, the last king of the Jagiellonian dynasty, Zygmunt August, was laid to rest in Kraków—and that despite the clear instructions left behind by him in his testament that his funeral be a modest affair. That was not to be, however: the funeral procession, which passed through Kraków from Kleparz to the Wawel Cathedral, was even more numerous and splendid than that of Kazimierz the Great, and the Royal Steward (*krajczy*) Mniszech, in the golden armor of the royal majesty, horsed, represented the deceased monarch so that once again the royal majesty could accompany his mortal remains to the very end of his last mile. The reason why the last wishes of this last of the Jagiellons were ignored in favor of an ostentatious royal funeral ceremony was, however, a very important one, perhaps even much more important than the doubts associated long before with the succession of Ludwik Węgierski. Zygmunt died in July 1572 in the castle at Knyszyn, in circumstances that must have been quite sad, due to his milieu that, as his sister Anna stated, had held him for some time in a state of physical and mental decline. But the splendid royal funeral took place only in February 1574. And thus, the dead king had to wait long until, in accord with the ritual, his mortal remains should be borne to their grave. All this on account of the free election, which signified a complete, revolutionary change in the functioning of the state—the *regnum*, the kingdom, having been transformed into the Republic.

We need to pay attention to this transformation a little longer in order to better understand its nature, since perhaps here hidden is the one and only sensible answer to the question why Zamoyski, the mightiest person in the Republic, did not reach for the crown, although he certainly dreamt of so doing, and at least some others felt that it belonged to him more than to anyone else. Like every revolution, this one, which irreversibly transformed the kingdom into the Republic, had its beginnings among the intellectuals. That's what we need to call them: intellectuals, despite the fact that this is a modern term. Although each of them is a separate case, and their views diverged, still all of them wrote tracts in which they postulated a fundamental reform of the Jagiellonian monarchy. I'm speaking here of people such as Jan Ostroróg, the voivode of Poznań, author of the *Memoriał o urządzeniu Rzeczypospolitej* (Memorial Concerning the Arrangement of the Republic), Stanisław Zaborowski, the author of the *Traktat o naturze praw i dóbr królewskich* (Tract on the Nature of the Laws and Royal Domains), and Filip Kallimach Buonaccorsi, whom I also include in this group, although he wrote neither legal nor political tracts, but rather historical texts and verse. Still, his influence on Poland as the grey eminence of the Jagiellonian rulers was gigantic. I would also certainly include here Jakub Przyłuski, the creator of a codex of laws, as well as Jan Łaski, creator of statutes; Frycz Modrzewski and his tract *O naprawie Rzeczypospolitej* (On the Emendation of the Republic), as well as, obviously, Frycz's great rival, Stanisław Orzechowski, although we need to remember that for many reasons his was a unique case. These intellectual meditations on the theme of reform all headed, more or less, in the direction of the strengthening of the effectiveness of the monarch's power, the separation of the Church from the state (which obviously is foreign to the views of Orzechowski), the strengthening of the state treasury from the point of view of public works, and the establishment of the rule of law universal to all, preferably after the fashion of systematized and unified Roman law, just as Emperor Maximilian had done in the German Empire, which in the fifteenth century he effectively reshuffled, shoring up his authority. All of these were very important and legitimate postulates from the point of view of the interests of the Polish state of the time, which also clearly expressed the political ideas of Italian Humanism currently predominating in Europe as well as of the German Reformation, preparing the ground for the strong, centralized power of the future, modern states of Europe. It is for this reason that many of our thinkers who in the last decades of the fifteenth century and at the beginning of the sixteenth sought fundamental changes in the Polish system were rightly known as "statists." (Today, we would call them "state-oriented.") For they reasoned that power in the state, its institutions and mechanisms must be decidedly strengthened, first of all and primarily to resist the growing influence of the oligarchs. These intellectuals saw the person of the monarch as a natural ally in their cause of reform, for he ought certainly to be interested in a strengthening of his own position. And here, our statists must have experienced a great disillusionment. For, unfortunately, it must be clearly stated that the last of the Jagiellons—despite their virtues and indubitable accomplishments—proved themselves to be immeasurably weak and indecisive rulers. Their inborn meekness and softness never allowed them to take the reins of government firmly in hand. The horrible humiliation of Aleksander Jagiellończyk in 1501 in Mielnik, where, as the price of his crown, he was degraded by the magnates to the rank of the *princeps senatus*, the executor of the decisions taken by the senators, was an unequivocal warning that the ruling dynasty was incapable of forcing the reform and emendation of the state through in Poland—of which our pro-statist intellectuals were dreaming. However, this open boldness, this shamelessness of the oligarchs in Mielnik, who wished to make of the king a marionette in their own hands, bore fruit in an unexpected resistance, in a reaction from the side of the now politically-experienced middle class of the nobility. In such a way, the intellectual revolution was displaced by the revolution of the noble masses demanding democratization and reform—appealing on an ideological level to the values of neo-Roman republicanism. The societal force that made such a transformation possible was the executionist movement, that political movement of the nobility that demanded the abolition of the aristocratic privileges of the oligarchs, and which over the space of several decades was to lead to fundamental changes in the political system of the state. Several decades later, in 1572, one of the leaders of the executionists and the inventor of the idea of free elections, the Sandomierz voivode Piotr Zborowski (most likely the most balanced of all that eccentric and wanton crowd of the Zborowski brothers), was to declare after the death of the last Jagiellonian king, Zygmunt August, that "it was nothing new to our forefathers that the Polish kings would die, as die they must, but they also understood that their Republic was, and ever was to be, immortal."[42] And so the systemic revolution was realized, and the immortal crown replaced by the immortal Republic.

The executionist movement fulfills all the typical traits of a revolution, and as such, I reckon, it should be understood. It gathered together the most politically conscious representatives of the middle nobility, who, in the name of the common weal, the *bonum commune*, and of the respect of common rights, came out openly against the privileges of the oligarchic caste, which battened itself on the royal estates it had usurped. One might say that, in the face of the weakness of their monarchs, they took matters into their own hands, thanks to which the democratic factor, and not any absolutist monarch, became the main force of state reform. Thus, the Republic was to constitute the incarnation of the good of all its citizens, equal and free, as a sort of reciprocal obligation, a union, a contract, as well as a universal concern. Instead of the power of a small number based upon inequitable privileges and the ancient laws of their forebears, a new power was to arise: the power of many, a democracy founded on a free citizenry, on participation, on the common legislation of rights and laws as well as an officialdom—including a king—responsible to the unified political body of territorial representatives. The executionist movement can, therefore, be acknowledged as the one serious political revolution in Poland which led *de facto* to a new system along the path of the radical transformations which had been being realized over the space of several decades in the sixteenth century. By degrees, beginning with the 1505 constitution *Nihil novi*, continuing with the Henrician Articles set before Henri Valois in 1573, the executionists forged the principles of the functioning of a new state: political and religious freedom for its citizens, control of the king by parliament (Diet, *Sejm*), the free election of the monarch by the generality of the nobles, and even the right to rebellion (*rokosz*).

Of course, the executionists eagerly adopted some of the slogans of the intellectuals' revolution, for example: the weakening of the position of the aristocrats, in other words, the Senate, or the separation of Church and clergy from public matters. Here, particular emotions were stirred, of course, by the question of the jurisdiction of ecclesiastical courts, as well as the matter of taxes in support of the Church. The executionists were also inclined to carry out some essential reforms in favor of the public treasury, at least with regard to the establishment of permanent funding for the army. They also demanded the strengthening of the Diet (parliament, *Sejm*) and the establishment of its regular convocation, while from the other side they opted for solutions that were decidedly out of sync, indeed, contrary to the expectations of our renowned statists. A true phenomenon of this our only great political revolution was, for example, its relation to Roman law, or rather, its entirely conscious rejection of the same as contrary to the fundamental principle of republican freedom. The results of this for the new system and new political culture were quite peculiar, as in the end Roman law was introduced to Poland first by Napoléon and the partitioning powers over two hundred years later. Up till that time, a universal legal system, the sentries of which would be state officials, was universally recognized as a symptom of tyranny, an instrument of enslavement in the hands of absolutist rulers. In the Republic, law was to arise from the people, that is, be legislated by the votes of participatory citizens, and was to serve the people, not be elevated somewhere above them—in accord with the republican idea that we are only subject to such laws as we, free people, should enact for our own community. If we take into account that, on the ideological level, the Roman Republic constituted the basic pattern for our political revolution, and that therefore this was a revolution of neo-Roman republicanism, then, this casting aside of Roman law, this qualification of it *in toto* as something non-republican, as a later product of the despotic Caesars of the imperial era, was an entirely courageous and somewhat arrogant procedure of political auto-creation on the part of our executionists. At any rate, it seems as if they were convinced that on the banks of the Wisła they were building their own Roman Republic, but without Roman law, basing themselves only on certain institutions, values, and legends, and above all on the legislative power of the political sovereign—the nobility. Even more—they quickly began to recognize that the realization of such an attempt, of life in freedom, had for them a great civilizational significance. Certainly they had read Livy, Cicero, and later Machiavelli well, adopting for themselves the idea that only a republic on the Roman model, and thus a republic as the community of free citizens, and not, for example, the might and power of rulers guaranteed success and greatness, and allowed people to emerge from their natural state of barbarity. Contrary to this, tyranny is the sort of government that confirms and cultivates barbarity in people. For this reason Klemens Janicki could so beautifully write of the Poles of the first decades of the sixteenth century, that "ancient barbarity has been banished from your lands, returning to its kindred Dacians. At one time, the Sarmatian only knew how to make war, how to thrust and slice with his sword; he knew only how to conquer, and to pursue those fleeing the field. Today, although he has not forgotten these arts at all, he has also learned other things, such as belong to the gentler lifestyle. How many are the languages he speaks! How many dignified arts does he cultivate! Arts that require mighty inspiration, and a clever hand."[43] In this way, the seed planted in the twelfth century by Wincenty Kadłubek bore impressive fruit in the sixteenth, although to a certain extent this was also exotic fruit: the formerly savage Sarmatian, civilized by republicanism.

Some thinkers draw attention to one more peculiarity of this of our only grand political revolution, which led to the establishment of the immortal Republic—individualism. This is a rather curious phenomenon in the case of Poland, for much seems to point to the fact that we need to look for its sources in the clash of the politically awakened mass of nobles with the liberational currents of Renaissance Humanism, although, on the other hand, a not inconsiderable role was also played here by the Reformation, especially Calvinism. Because of the later Counter-Reformation, and the significance of Catholicism in the formation of Polish political culture, and still later, the development of the modern national consciousness of the Poles, this Reformation episode—for, after all, it lasted only the brief space of several dozen years—when a portion of the nobility was inebriated with the ideas of the Reformation, is a problematical question that is perhaps underappreciated. It is, however, a fact that in the first half of the sixteenth century, there appeared in certain places in the Republic something along the order of a sudden phenomenon of conversion of the nobility to Calvinism. By the same token, this was less a religious movement, a matter of confessional conviction. The ease with which many in the Republic converted from Catholicism to Calvinism or other Protestant sects, just as frequently to return to the bosom of the true Church later, shows that it wasn't the religious ardor of faith that played first fiddle here. Zamoyski himself is a good example of this, since he went off to his studies in Padua as a freshly-baked Protestant, but returned to Poland a Catholic once more. The sudden popularity of Calvinism amongst a portion of the nobility was rather, and principally, related to the liberational ideas of republicanism, legal and fiscal antipathy to the Papacy, and that element of strong individualism contained in reformed religion. Our forefathers made of Calvinism a different use than did the inhabitants of the German-speaking lands, where the Reformation had a great influence on the centralization of government and the fostering of an inclination to obey said centralized government on the part of the citizenry. (This in accord with St. Paul's doctrine that all authority comes from God and demands obedience). Individualism was confined to the sphere of mental attitude and private life, paving the way for the foundation of bourgeois culture in the future. The nobility of the Republic, on the other hand, chose individualism for the strengthening of their political autonomy, rejecting the concept of obedience to government and state as something non-Republican. And so, the results of that Reformation episode in sixteenth-century Poland were peculiar, though all the same having far-reaching consequences. Individualism lifted autonomy and the self-determination of the democratic community of free citizens above all else. Most importantly, it did not bind them with any higher, uniform law on the Roman model. And so it lifted them above the state itself, which in no way might be considered a separate entity or value, as *raison d'état*; elevating them also above all the other constituents of the societal whole. And thus, this one of a kind great political revolution in Poland, which took place amongst us in the sixteenth century, saw to it that the most conscious and politically active segment of society proved itself ready to assume responsibility for political rule, while taking no responsibility for the state, society, or the economic life. The results of this state of things became clearly apparent in the next era, following the death of Zamoyski, when the autonomy of the political community of the nobility began to be transformed into open alienation.

There exists an impressive symbol of this very alienation as the final result of our one and only splendid revolution. To this very day, hosts of delighted tourists are attracted to the ruins of the great castle called Krzyżtopór, a *palazzo in fortezza*. As we can read in the tourist flyer: "Full of magic and mystery, the ruin is nestled amidst the fields and hillocks of the Opatowski region, far from all main roads and byways." No better description might be found for the actual symbolism of the place. The ruins of a gigantic palace "nestled" or "hidden" among fields and hills. Indeed, strolling along the palace fortifications or gazing through its windows, we see broad fields and forests stretching away from the walls, but not a single homestead, not a single other living soul. Constructed some thirty years after Zamoyski's death by the fabulously wealthy Krzysztof Ossoliński, in a place known as Ujazd, which would be difficult even to describe as a town in which nothing was to be found but a wooden church and a tavern, the gigantic palace was destined to cast all other such great residences in the country into the shadows. "It had as many windows as there are days in a year, as many rooms as there are weeks; as many great halls as there are months, and its four corner bastions corresponded to the seasons." The palace was an absolute universe unto itself, an Alpha and an Omega. Set in the wilderness, it had no need of communicating with the outside world, with its surroundings. It is worth dwelling a bit here on that alienation into which the fruit of our one splendid revolution of the sixteenth century was to develop. Zamoyski and Żółkiewski had quite a different way of looking at things. When one gazes upon Zamość or Żółkiew, which both of them had constructed earlier, one can clearly make out the completely different intention of the builders: the *città ideale*, that constantly vibrant faith in the possibility of erecting an ideal society, all the elements of which are arranged in complete accord with the function they fulfill, and the residence of the governor, the lord, has only one sense: as the head of the entire organism. In those places individualism, due to the splendid revolution taking shape as political autonomy, the natural right to legislating one's own laws, as well as the free election of the ruler, fomented by great wealth such as had never before been seen in our history, had not yet arrived at such fantastic forms of self-enclosure, the locking of oneself up in a universe of one's own laws, language, culture, and interests as it happened in the case of Krzyżtopór. Only a few dozen years separate Krzyżtopór from Zamość and Żółkiew, and this leads to a natural question: was it possible to avoid this? Could anything have been done to ensure that the tree of the splendid revolution not bear such beautiful, but poisonous fruit? I dare offer my own theory on the subject, which refers directly to the character of Jan Zamoyski and the role he might have played, but which in the end he did not assume. Our splendid revolution, as it so often happens in the case of revolutions in general, set in motion the huge potential of the mass movements, which had been growing in strength for some time and led to the transformation of *regnum* into Republic. But just like every such great political change, this one also had a potential extreme, which, in order to become fixed in the enduring forms of a new whole, had first to be questioned from within. I call this a dialectical return: the situation when a mighty political extreme, a transformation capable of tearing itself away from the *status quo*, arrives in the end at its own opposite, at resistance, a questioning which it must face. Only in this way can the extreme lead, in effect, to the establishment of a new, generally acceptable, state of things. And it is just this, just such a dialectical return, that our splendid revolution lacked, as a result of which it could only continue along the path of extremity, without sufficient resistance and without any basic opposition. No one decided to build a dam to its impetus—neither the successive, weak monarchs (with the possible exception of Batory, who died too quickly and too suddenly) nor our intellectuals, our statists, our wisemen, or their well-read comrades; nor did the armed inhabitants of the cities do this (their attempts fizzled out at the get-go), nor did the peasants scattered throughout the immense territory of the Republic. Zamoyski might have done so, not only as the man whom so many acknowledged as worthy of the Polish crown but also as one of the creators of the Republic, its founding father. But this would have meant a usurpation of a kind, the open denial of the foundational ideals of the Republic. It would have required of Zamoyski a readiness to play the role of the dictator of the Republic, a Polish Caesar. I reckon that Zamoyski himself dreamt of this, doubtlessly, but in the end he never took the risk. And thus he wasted the one chance for that necessary moment of dialectical return in our splendid revolution. Some hundred years after, the above-mentioned Piotr Zborowski stated that kings die, but the Republic is eternal; Stefan Czarnecki, defending Kraków from the Swedes, repeated a similar statement to the Swedish general Wittenberg, commenting that people are mortal, but the Republic is eternal,[44] i.e., it never dies. Contemplating all of this today, one might say that he was right after a fashion, although that Republic certainly did perish.

Gutenberg's Moment

Certainly, every revolution needs some sort of additional impulse, something to set free the forces that had been swelling for so long a while. Sometimes this can be an all-embracing tragedy, sometimes a strong moral shock. But such an unexpected impulse can also come in the form of essential technological transformations, which may not be the chief cause of great change, as the Marxists believed at one time, but something along the order of a flywheel, a new mechanism that allows for the liberation, on a grand scale, of contradictory ideas and interests that had been accumulating earlier. They are like a battering ram, which knocks down old structures, or an irrepressible, sudden cascade of new possibilities, which overthrows the order of roles, divisions, and dependencies which had heretofore obtained.

The stock market and trading companies precede the English Revolution of the seventeenth century; a true technological revolution came before the French and American Revolutions in the eighteenth; the revolution of mass production preceded the mass democracies and totalitarian societies of the twentieth, and the digital revolution is today shattering the structures of the liberal order that came about following the Cold War, which was to lead us safely into the twenty-first century. The case was no different in the sixteenth century with the neo-Roman, republican revolution and the Reformation, when it was the printing press, the technology of producing books on a mass scale, which completely transformed the conditions of the functioning of politics, public life, and government in Europe.

Supposedly, Zamoyski was to have claimed with unfeigned pride that the professors of the Academy in Zamość, which he had established, were his musicians, and his orchestra the printing press.[45] That the chancellor had intellectual ambitions is beyond doubt. He himself reached for the pen from time to time. His monumental work, *Komentarze o wojnie moskiewskiej* (Commentaries on the War with Muscovy) in six books, was written, it is true, by Reinhold Heidenstein, who had been the chancellor's personal biographer and friend since his years of study in Padua. But it is universally believed that Zamoyski had a significant role in the creation of this book in praise of the Russian expeditions of Batory. Supposedly, the Chancellor considered it the Polish equivalent of Julius Caesar's *Commentaries on the Gallic War*.[46] But such a comparison brought with it certain risks, which came to the fore at the Diet of Convocation as well as during the free election of 1587, when Zamoyski's enemies sought to use this against him. They demanded the condemnation and banning of the book as an example of the Chancellor's absolutist tendencies. The setting of Zamoyski, accused of tyrannical leanings, of the desire to destroy the noble, republican freedoms, alongside Julius Caesar—dictator and gravedigger of the Roman Republic—was not advantageous to him. To the noble brotherhood it was like a red flag waved before a bull. But that one example of the *Komentarze* proves aptly that, at the time, books and the printed word constituted a mighty instrument in politicking and political warfare.

And so his printery was his personal orchestra—aptly stated. Thanks to that printery he could play some imposing political works, which moved the masses of the noble auditory. Zamoyski was a man who, independently of his great personal intellectual ambitions as former rector of the law college in Padua, quickly understood that the printing press allowed for real political action. He sensed perfectly what great possibilities were presented by the revolution which, since the second half of the fifteenth century, had completely transformed the face of Europe. Taking into account the consequences of his invention, Gutenberg's work of genius—moveable type and the printing press—may be aptly compared to the world-changing revolution sparked by today's digital explosion. Similarly, just as the significance of the invention of the personal computer was not immediately understood, nor that of digitization and the Internet, so it was only several dozen years after Gutenberg began printing the first pages of his Bible in Mainz that people slowly began to comprehend that this was not just some slick technical invention that greatly simplified life so that, for example, one might quickly produce an unlimited number of copies of documents necessary to the administration of the Church (such as, for example, letters of indulgence). Rather, print changed literally everything in the way that public opinion was produced, communicated, and shaped, as well as changing the hierarchies of authority and dependency encoded therein. It was a real intellectual, political, and societal revolution. Earlier, ideas had circulated about Europe along well-marked, narrow paths, addressed to a select, narrow group of the initiated—experts, élite and privileged receptors.

European culture developed in waves, which tossed up on the shore the priceless treasures of ancient literature. The first of these waves broke with the Carolinian Renaissance. It began to swell in the seventh and eighth centuries, far to the north-west, in the raw climates of Scotland and England. It was from the scriptoria there in Iona and Lindisfarne and in the archdiocese of York that priceless texts, copied by hand, began their journey throughout all of Europe, through the court of Charlemagne, through the network of Benedictine, Cluniac monasteries, to reach, slowly but surely, the north-eastern boundaries of Christian Europe, down the lower reaches of the Wisła to Tyniec and Kraków. The second wave made its appearance in the twelfth and thirteenth century, but now the motive force was provided by the universities and their law professors—canonists, commentators on the rediscovered codex of Roman laws established by Emperor Justinian—their students travelling the length and breadth of Europe from one university center to another. All the same, in both cases, so crucial for the development of our European culture, the flux of ideas was very limited in space and in time, and its most important material form (the manuscript) was extraordinarily fragile, rare, and difficult to obtain. That main source of knowledge at the time, the manuscript, was also extremely clumsy, but due to this, both knowledge and opinion concerning knowledge was something specifically elitist and hierarchical. By force of nature the libraries of the time, clustered around monasteries, archdioceses, and a few monarchical courts, universities and schools could gather together several hundred books at most, no more. An exception to this rule was the Papal library in Avignon, the catalogue of which contained, most likely, two thousand one hundred titles, many of which, alas, were looted by thieves. The library of the Hungarian king Matthias Corvinus was also renowned for having amassed some thousand manuscripts.

The printery that Gutenberg established in Mainz toward the end of the 1440s opened the floodgates to an informational upheaval in Europe.[47] It is estimated that over the first fifty years of the existence of print in the world some eight million books passed through the presses, which number surpassed that of all books copied by European scribes since the days when Constantinople was founded. A mere five decades were all that was needed to double the supply of information that had been amassed over centuries. Above all, however, what changed completely was the availability of that information. Such a numerically overwhelming transformation cannot but have had an influence on the intellectual and political life of Europe. Of course, the decided majority of the first printed books touched upon theological and ecclesiastical questions. The universal Church created a universal market for the printed word. Initiated by Pope Nicholas V and then unfolding on a large scale throughout the continent, the action of revision and normalization of the Church's liturgy sparked a gigantic need for printed missals, breviaries, and agendas, to say nothing of the Holy Scriptures themselves and those letters of indulgence, which were printed on a mass scale. At the same time, in 1487, Pope Innocent III emitted a bull imposing upon the bishops the responsibility of enacting a proactive censorship concerning all printed matters. For the great force of the New, but also the force of destruction lurked in this new invention of Gutenberg's. It multiplied the reach and availability of information and ideas, immeasurably accelerating their circulation, facilitating the possibilities of authors propagating their own views and doing battle against those of others, and, what was most important, it brought into question the current structures, hierarchies, and authorities, which up till then had defined the direction and forms of dispensing knowledge and information. Up until then it had been clear what sort of concrete authority and power stood behind the written word. Now, that certainty had been completely upturned by ease of access and the universality of print. Nor was it obvious any more what sort of status and authority needed to be accorded to information and opinions multiplied exponentially—which set traditional societies and ancient structures before a problem similar to today's question of "fake news."

The invention of printing quickly spread to conquer ever more legions of advocates. Universities, their professors and students, soon queued up for the books being produced in printeries and the first publishing houses. In particular, this market was avid for new translations and editions of ancient authors, for which the Renaissance in Europe had created an ever greater appetite. Toward the end of the fifteenth century, there were some one hundred fifty print houses in Venice, which became the undisputed leader of the emerging publishing market. Above all, the city would be distinguished by a great clan of printers and publishers, the Manutius (Manuzio) family, the first printery of which had been founded by Aldus in the year 1494. The Manuzi were, however, significantly more than mere craftsmen or booksellers. They were intellectuals of a new type, humanists. They established a great, impressive critical project for the publication of many Latin and Greek manuscripts. The team of philologists, learned experts, which they established, had as its mission the location of the priceless texts of ancient authors—such as Aristotle, Theocritus, Aristophanes, and Sophocles, throughout Europe and even beyond. Their goal was the establishment of a correct, canonical version of such originals as they found, as well as the preparation of critical versions for the publishing house. Perhaps the greatest service done by the Manuzi for our culture was their publication of all the works of Cicero. Paolo, the son of Aldus, himself a renowned and valued professor of philology at the Papal court in Rome as well as a publisher, was fascinated by Cicero's legacy and set himself to the publication of all his letters and speeches. Zamoyski must have met him during his numerous visits to Venice in his role as rector from Padua and also at the occasion of the composition of his work on the Roman Senate, since Paolo sent a letter of recommendation on his behalf to Piotr Myszkowski, the great crown secretary of Zygmunt August, in which he praised the talents and virtues of the young Polish nobleman. The Manutius family was also to maintain many intensive contacts with the Republic and the Kraków Academy—with the just-mentioned Myszkowski, with Zebrzydowski, Goślicki, Dudycz, and, of course, with Zamojski himself, who sought the advice of the Venetian clan in his task of reforming the Kraków Academy during Batory's reign, and later, when he himself took in hand the reins of the academy he had established in Zamość.[48]

The lightning-fast spread of print in Poland cannot have been without meaning for the evolution of Polish political culture and that revolutionary turn in the direction of noble democracy; indeed, its impression on the political face of the democratic Republic was a profound one, although the beginnings were not auspicious. In the 1470s, and thus some twenty-five years after the upheaval effected in Mainz, a certain craftsman from Bavaria, Kasper Straube, made his appearance in Kraków. He is recognized as the first printer in Poland. From his press emerged our first printed works—the majority of which, however, are of a simple, practical character, and thus: an almanac or leaved wall calendar for 1474, made up of practical information from the fields of astronomy and medicine; a commentary on the Psalter; a tract on damages and compensation, usury and church anathemas. The most ambitious work of a literary character printed by him were the *Opuscula* (Lesser Works) of St. Augustine. And so, nothing extraordinary. Soon after him came some Szwajpolt Fiol from Franconia to try and make a career among us, printing liturgical books in Old Church Slavonic, and so with something less than precise aim, as not for our own, Latin, market but that of the eastern marches of the Republic. So far, it's difficult to speak of any sort of technological revolution, which was to transform the manner in which the political life of Poland functioned. The real movement in the business, along with the great transformations, began only with the sixteenth century, due to the efforts of the wealthy Cracovian burgher Jan Haller. He was proprietor of a paper manufactory, a printing establishment, and a bookstore—the first true monopolist, who won from King Aleksander the privilege thanks to which no title of those produced by his press could be imported from abroad or printed. Then other families of printers arrived among us: the Szarffenbergs, the Wietors, the Ungers, and all attempts at preserving a monopoly of print quickly evaporated, but not only on account of competition amongst the printing potentates. What happened was the rapid rise of the market for the printed word, and its democratization. The receptors were now no longer just the royal chancellery, the Academy, and the Church. The great political movement of the executionists as well as the numerous Protestant enclaves that began to make their appearance treated the printing press as a mighty ideological weapon which allowed for the swift and mass-scale dissemination of new ideas, points of view, and postulates. For this very reason, Gutenberg's invention provided a significant impetus to the victory of the splendid noble revolution in Poland and the establishment of a new political culture, the Poles becoming, along the way, passionate receptors of the publicly printed word.

If anyone wished to harness the power of the new democratic elements in the Republic, he had first to master the instruments of the printed public word. As has already been mentioned, Zamoyski belonged to those who perfectly understood the technical transformations of print in reference to politics in the Republic. For this reason, he treated the printing press as his own "political orchestra." Thanks to Jan Januszewski, he organized his own printery in Zamość, which provided him with a powerful instrument for the cultivation of noble opinion in the country and the promotion of his own political interests. Earlier, with the help of Mikołaj Scharffenberg, he effected the innovation, peculiar for the times, of the so called "flying press," which could be transferred from place to place, camp to camp, during Batory's Muscovy campaign, and allowed for the production of addresses, ephemeral prints, from the very battlefield, as it were. However, it was not only ephemerals that the flying press emitted but also artistic works supporting Zamoyski's politics, amongst others, the poems of Kochanowski, which were then distributed to the farthest corners of the Republic and even to foreign parts, in any numbers deemed necessary.[49] In this way then, the printery indeed functioned, as Zamoyski put it, as his own political orchestra in which he filled the role of the maestro of the printed, public word. He could in such wise tune the opinions that pertained amongst the hosts of the democratic nobility, skillfully harmonizing them or making them collide in cacophony, subduing some tones while giving others greater volume, stirring the emotions of his listeners, such as dread, anxiety, gratitude, a sense of guilt, pride, or anger. He was thus a great director of opinion and mood. Above all, however, he could realize his own political goals on a scale embracing the entire Republic, communicating directly with the democratic, noble brotherhood above the heads of the proud senators or the king himself, for that matter. And so, he did exactly what every politician worth his salt, who understands the spirit of the times, does today—communicating directly with his electorate day after day via Twitter.

Free Election

It must be stated clearly, without hesitation, that the first free election, that pillar of the new system of the Republic, ended in a horrible fiasco. The shameful escape of twenty-three-year-old Henri Valois after just a few months of simulated rule in Poland ought to have been a warning to all. This same sentiment was cried aloud by the starost of Oświęcim, who was supposed to have thrown himself into the river after the escaping king in the neighborhood of Pszczyna, helplessly calling: "Your Most Serene Majesty, why are you running away?"[50] Well, exactly. Why was the newly elected king running away from his free citizens? It was a shameful situation, a great disillusionment, which also must have had a serious influence on the rising sense of chaos and threat. The noble Republic, only just constituted following the death of Zygmunt August, was threatened with breakdown; at the very least, with turmoil. Hordes of Tatars were devastating Podolia and Ruthenia; Muscovy was threatening Courland, and the nobles were left to deliberate whether the escape of Henri meant an interregnum, whether he had abandoned the throne, and whether, in such a case, they needed to think of electing a new ruler. But if so, then whom? Should it be someone from the Imperial family of the Habsburgs (such a candidacy had strong supporters in Poland: among others, the Zborowskis), or should it be someone else, someone of their own, someone who would not run away or commit treason. With all certainty, in the face of the fiasco that came about at the escape of Valois, the position of those who opted for a home-grown candidate, a so-called "Piast," grew in influence. These were those of whom Bielski writes that they wished "to choose their lord from among their own number."[51] But was such a thing possible? Was it at all proper to raise someone of one's own above the group of nobles who, after all, were supposed to be equals? Was it not, after all, in the name of equality that the whole executionist movement had struggled, and was it not equality upon which the golden freedom of the nobility of the Republic was based? Here, amongst various electoral systems in Europe at the time the well-known example of the Republic of Venice provided the most obvious pattern of how one might solve the question of the election of a king. And it was a pattern which through his years of study in Padua, Zamoyski (and many other representatives of the Polish nobility) had observed at close quarters. The Doge, the supreme officer of the great Republic, elected by the generality of adult citizens from amongst the ranks of the most eminent clans, constituted an example of what the choice of a "Piast" might look like in practice.

The chaos unleashed by Valois lasted a whole year: until October 1575, when it was possible to call a Diet of Convocation. So as not to drag the feet any more, the election of the new monarch was set for the next month. This second interregnum was truly much shorter than the first. Yet, still and all, it seems to me that the earlier election of Henri Valois, the first free election, was little more than a bandage pasted on the systemic problem of the newly born noble Republic; the great improvisation of a new political nation; something along the order of a great experiment. It is true that it was carried out in an elevated atmosphere, with much ado and numerous debates in local assemblies (*sejmiki*, literally: "little Diets"), and gave rise to a rich ephemeral literature of appeals, poems, and agitations. Over the course of the six months stretching between the death of Zygmunt August in Knyszyn and the Diet of Convocation in Warsaw, some thirty gatherings of nobility took place in the Republic, at which the choice of the monarch as well as the systemic guarantees accorded the nobility were deliberated. This gives us an average of five such gatherings per month! So, the hubbub surrounding the first election in the Republic must have been great. Still, I cannot get rid of the sense that in the end, the nobility wanted, above all, to have the problem settled, to choose a new king and to go back home. For a decision was not even taken as to whether the principles of election of this systemic pillar of noble freedom ought to be written up good and properly in one document so that the whats and hows should be known once and for all. As some cynics stated, this was most likely because the very inscription of the principles of free election as a systemic law would unnecessarily bind the fundamental liberty of the political nation. So, truly, the escape of Valois might have been seen as a punishment from God for such an obvious omission, for too light an approach to so crucial a matter. These days, it is difficult to reconstruct with precision the moods that accompanied the second election, following the escape of the king elected by his free citizens, but the numbers here might provide some testimony. It is accepted that the first election gathered as many as fifty thousand nobles at the Kamionek fields on the banks of the Wisła. The second, called to Wola, brought together only twelve thousand. Now, these numbers are mere estimates and none too certain. Indeed, generally speaking, not much should be made of them. Perhaps, quite simply, when the nobility reflected upon themselves for the first time in their political act of election and totted up the numbers, the scene was so exceptional, so breathtaking, that the number "fifty thousand" was rather hyperbolic. From the election of Władysław IV on, it is easier to make a confident count, due to the so-called "suffragia," or lists of attendance signed by the electors physically present. These numbers vacillate in the several thousands, reaching a maximum of ten thousand or so. This indicates that, in the case of the first election, even if we were to take into consideration the effect of novelty, curiosity, and mobilization, we are speaking rather of a "sense" experienced, and most likely greatly exaggerated. Although those twelve thousand from the second election surely have the same orientational value, still and all, it is a much smaller number. And so it seems to me—even if a significant role might have been played by the late season in which the second election took place (although, on the other hand, the Polish climate never really guarantees reliably seasonable weather)—that in this case we can clearly see the symptoms of some sort of demobilization, of disillusionment among the nobles. And perhaps it was this that perforce led to an attempt to revisit and think carefully through the concept of a Republic that elects its own king, and to state expressly what it all means: what the stakes of so great a political act of freedom are.

And so, when, after the months of chaos and uncertainty caused by the escape of Henri Valois, the Diet of Election assembled in November 1575, it was quickly transformed into a grand political *theatrum*, a spectacle of the political nation, in which some basic truths were enunciated by the nobles concerning themselves and to themselves—the *principia*. This second Diet of Election was therefore transformed into a momentous and elevated systemic debate, completely different to what it was to be twelve years later, following Batory's death, when beneath the walls of Warsaw it became more of an armed settling of reciprocal accounts, which almost led to a horrible, bloody shambles. But the Republic behaved in just such a peculiar, unpredictable way. Spread over immense territories, lacking a convenient infrastructure, roads and bridges such as would permit its inhabitants convenient passage from one part of the grand state to another, it preserved its political wholeness, its cohesion, its self-knowledge above all thanks to the word registered in hundreds of appeals, memorials, verses, and letters—but even more due to the spoken word delivered at the forums of those fifty-four regional Diets (*sejmiki*) that made up the political body of the Republic, and especially at the Crown Diets or Diets of Election. Here, however, in Warsaw in November 1575, the situation was peculiar as the nation was speaking to itself of itself without a king, without a ruler, who had abandoned it, and so a ruler who didn't even die, could not even be buried, which made the whole situation all the more exceptional. The nation spoke of how it understood itself, ashamed at the unexpected results of the first free election, but it also addressed its deep divisions. The speeches from those events that have survived to our times again show how beautifully the noble nation was able to speak of itself and to itself! Eventually, it is worthwhile remembering that the Republic was, above all, an oratorical culture, which had developed from the best classical patterns, from lessons taken from Cicero, Demosthenes, and Quintilian, as well as from the deductions of the most talented Italian humanists. And there was no way of conducting politics amongst us without having the best oratorical capabilities—something diametrically different from our situation today. I reckon that one may quite boldly state that, in those days, the art of speaking, of rhetoric, was for the Pole what music and opera was for the Italian, or what the theatre was to become for the French. And this to such an extent that later, Szymon Starowolski, who in his youth had been a courtier of Zamoyski's, was to state that "in Poland he cannot be called a citizen, or even, I will be so bold as to suggest, a Pole, who is unable to eloquently and decoratively speak on any subject, and this not only in Latin, but also in his mother tongue, which easily adopts whatever oratorical or poetical graces the Greek or Roman is capable of inventing."[52] And it is for this reason that, during that November election, the Poles were able not only so much, or so wisely, but also so beautifully to speak of themselves that we Poles of today, given the rough, vulgar language that we make use of in contemporary politics—and even when we speak of the most common things—can only envy, blushing with shame.

Before it was possible to gather for the election of the king, the field of election required much detailed preparation. Above all, it was necessary to prepare the embankments and trenches surrounding a square of considerable size: the field upon which the senators and territorial representatives would meet. Three gateways led into this place through the raised earthen embankments, symbolizing the three main provinces of the Republic: Greater Poland (*Wielkopolska*) from the west, Lesser Poland (*Małopolska*) from the south, and from the east, the gate for Lithuania and White Ruthenia, since Podole, Volhynia and Ukraine caucused with Lesser Poland. The symbolism and compass-directions were no coincidence. In this manner, on this piece of land set apart near Warsaw, there uprose something along the lines of the *axis mundi*, the center point of the community. It was a sacred sort of omphalos, the political navel of the Republic, in which our forefathers celebrated their mysteries of liberty. According to the political order, the square was divided in two. The smaller area was reserved for the senators, bishops, voivodes, castellans and ministers meeting under the leadership of the primate as *interrex*, that is, the regent in the absence of the king. They gathered in a special senatorial shack built for the occasion as well as a larger one intended for the equestrian caste, that is, the territorial representatives, whose consultations *sub Iove* were presided over by an elected marshal of the Diet. On the other hand, around the embankments, in military order of voivodeships, their standards flying, the rest of the noble brotherhood pitched their tents. As various descriptions inform us (left us mainly by foreign arrivals), such electoral gatherings of the Republic took one's breath away, having no rival, as spectacle, anywhere else in all of Europe.

Since we're speaking of places, the Republic actually had two navels, for it was clear from the start that there was no complete agreement or conviction as to where exactly the political nation should indulge itself in the great holiday of choosing its own ruler. The first free election of Henri Valois took place on the right bank of the Wisła, in the village of Kamionek, from which the view gave onto the river and Warsaw, situated on the opposite high bank. The second, and all the other following elections too, with the one exception of the election of August III the Saxon exactly one hundred and sixty years later, took place in Wola, much farther from the walls of the city. Certainly various practical matters determined such a shift in the place of election, although it cannot be completely discounted that Kamionek had some bad connotations, as it reminded everyone of the fatal results of the election of Valois and the later disgraceful situation of his abandonment. So, in order to erase all memory of these bitter events and provide this most important systemic institution of the Republic with a new beginning, as it were, it was decided in 1575 to move to the new spot in Wola. However, I cannot restrain myself from a certain bitter comment on the manner in which today we treat that old omphalos of our freedom. Kamionek has vanished entirely from the map, leaving nothing behind save the name of the little Kamionkowskie Lake in Skaryszewski Park. Over the square where the first free election took place, at the confluence of the busy Targowa and Grochowska Streets, trams and cars pass, while buses jam the parking lot of the National Stadium. Only nearby Jagiellońska

Street, and the short and ratty Zamoyski St., completely unfitting as a memorial to the great Chancellor, signal that some distant and completely forgotten history once happened nearby. It's a little different in the case of the election fields in Wola, where at least, in a key location, between a petrol station, the walls of the Protestant Cemetery, the Jewish Cemetery, and Obozowa St., a pedestal has been raised as a memorial—a modest column graced with a crown, having the resonant name of the Obelisk Electio Viritim, which is perhaps the only such extant memorial of that largest pearl in the crown of the Republic's system—that crowning moment of political and civic freedom, which our forefathers established for themselves as a result of that splendid revolution, so exceptional in our history.

And nonetheless, it was exactly there, somewhere between the gas station, Obozowa St. over which trams clatter, and the brick wall of the cemetery that the impressive political spectacle of the second Diet of Election took place, that political theatre of the nation, of the Republic where the nobles were both audience and actor, and where the chief persons, the *dramatis personae*, making use of well-practiced oratorical weaponry, faced one another in solemn, dignified poses in order to express just what that newly arisen political nation, which was to choose itself a king, was and how it was to understand itself. Did they stand opposite one another in the hastily built senatorial shack on the trenched fields of Wola, or perhaps rather on account of the cold November weather, did they decide to gather in the new halls of the Warsaw Palace, glamorously extended by Zygmunt August? I do not know. Both here and there the scene would look the same: a long, extensive area marked by the rows of senatorial chairs as well as the benches set behind them for the representatives of the equestrians; on one side, on his chair, the *interrex*, the regent, and on the other the marshal of the Diet. From the speeches that have survived to our days from this gathering of electors, we can derive a very interesting and instructive image of what the political nation of the Republic thought of themselves and the world, from the mouths of its most worthy and wise representatives. It is not an image that would differ greatly from our contemporary views—except for the fact that we are incapable of so beautiful and wise eloquence. Also, at the time, at that very election, Zamoyski delivered his great political speech which still today makes a colossal impression—a speech worthy of a Pericles. In it, he laid out his decided views on the system of the Republic, its values guarded by its citizens, and also openly stated his support for the election of a Pole to the throne. It is a moving speech for another reason too. For in it, undisguisedly, Zamoyski makes a complete break with the conception of the divine majesty of the royal power, obliterating the idea of the sacred significance of the crown, and placing it in the hands of the citizens. He is a revolutionary republican.

"I state openly, that just as is the case with others, my eyes and my mind have been so blinded by the flash of royal majesty, that I too thought that it would go against the honor of our nation should we not choose as king someone who descends from a kingly, or at least a princely house."[53] Zamoyski strikes his breast in penitence, placing himself in one line along with all the other guilty parties who led the assembly to its fatal choice of Valois in that first free election. For everyone knew now that that splendid flash of the kingly, royal line of France proved to be the splendor of fool's gold, which merely blinded the wisdom of the common political reason at the very moment it was to take so fundamental a decision; that it was derived from a sincere yearning, shared by many, for the brilliant shine of the extinct Jagiellonian dynasty. However, that majesty of the Polish kings had truly died, and no foreigner, imported from abroad, could resurrect it. But there was no need to! Was it for this that the nobility had created their Republic, winning for themselves those fundamental freedoms, just to hand over the crown, that symbol of supreme and immortal power, to someone else? To some foreigner?

For this reason, "now, after having meditated on both the beginnings of royalty and the duties of the king, I see nothing illogical in it, were one from the equestrian caste to be elevated above the rest as king, as long as he possessed the virtues worthy of that knightly group."[54] What sublime theatre! Our forefathers didn't stammer their speeches, fumbling with index cards, mumbling and twisting words every few sentences, nor did they engage in empty academic disputes. They were the grand actors of a public theatre, and Zamoyski, most likely, belonged amongst the most talented of them. The intentions of the speaker were already more than clear to those gathered in the hall when he stated that all citizens, the nobility of the Republic, are equal in their virtues and thus any one of their number might be elected king. A tumult grew in the assembly, with loud cries of approval mixing with outbursts of opposition and indignation. Zamoyski had to strain his voice quite a bit in order to pose the rhetorical question over the hubbub. He said in sonorous tones: "For what are they worth, those names of princes, counts, margraves? What do you think? Are they inherited merely by birth, or rather are they titles of worthy office? Those who at first received them were simply of the knightly caste and hence have not exceeded the level of that caste. If these titles were handed down to their posterity, they ought to be blamed for so usurping in that fashion what belonged to the caste entire."[55] And if that be the case, as Zamoyski says, if there is no longer any inherited throne in Poland, if there is no natural heir, then all of us are equal, and we may choose a citizen king. "How have these our intellects become blinded, that we not only search elsewhere for that which can be found in our own home, but that with such great prejudice and harm to the Republic we set a foreigner above our countrymen? [...] Who would be so imprudent as not to grasp immediately how much good would be found in a citizen king, and how much evil in a foreign monarch?"[56]

For many there gathered, these words, so courageous and consciously uttered, must have seemed too much. For that reason, many in the senators' chamber were outraged; many expressed their opposition loudly against so radically enunciated an idea. In the name of many senators there gathered, Archbishop Uchański, the regent, presented a clear opposition to the viewpoints which found their reflection in the ardent appeal of Zamoyski for the election of a homegrown, citizen king. From the start, he adopted the tones of a Jeremiah, describing the effects of a sudden interregnum, cleverly reminding all that he, as primate, had never been a great advocate of the election of Henri Valois; that in 1573 he had decidedly been in favor of the Habsburg Archduke Ernest, the Emperor's son, rather than the flighty-minded Frenchman. In dramatically mournful tones, he stated: "Chaos and laxity within, for there was neither fear of the king nor fear of the law; violence, wrong, and reciprocal murder, and all order completely overturned. Certainly, by these catastrophes the Lord God clearly wished to teach us that He will send even greater ruin upon us, if we persist in tempting Him, and if this ship of Parliament, which the Lord in His mercy has deigned to send us for our rescue, we do not steer safely clear of the anarchy of complete shipwreck with which we are threatened. We need a king! And such a king as would be king not in name only, but who should be possessed of the royal attributes necessary to rule us, and royalty in abundance for the defense of this our realm."[57] To put it simply, unlike Zamoyski, he was not at all responsible for the scandal ensuing upon the flight of the first choice of the Republic, and for that reason it is his advice that most needs to be heeded today. Uchański was a great advocate for the election of a Habsburg to the Polish throne—at that moment, Emperor Maximilian would be the best choice. He belonged to the chief leaders of the pro-Habsburg party amongst the nobility, which was quite numerous. And the Habsburgs were in a position to generously reward their Polish supporters, whether in cash, or in ducal and princely titles. For this reason, no one had any doubt whom he had in mind when he cried out "We need a king! A real king!"

I don't know exactly when these speeches of Uchański and Zamoyski occurred in time and in what relation to one another; which was first, and which followed, and at what interval of time, long or short. But when one reads them together, it seems obvious that they are a polemic, a locking of horns. According to Uchański, the future monarch of Poland should be illustrious in royal majesty and possess numerous ties of blood with the other Christian monarchs of Europe.[58] In this way, Poland would become politically united with *Europa Christiana*, or, as we might put it: integrated into the western system of European monarchies and rulers, becoming, as in the case of the Czechs or western Hungarians, a part of the chief European current, the European political trunk. There is no one who might better fulfill the conditions of that plan than the Roman Habsburg Emperor, who, anyway, ruled the whole Christian world. Here, the skeptical view of our *interrex* on the topic of Rome is clearly displayed. He was well known for his Renaissance, sectarian sympathies as well as his devotion to the idea of an autonomous Polish Church. Perhaps his thinking went as follows: On the one hand, the Habsburgs would ensure the predominance of the Catholic Faith in Poland in the face of Protestant movements, but on the other, they would allow us to keep our distance from the Pope, as a national Church, in such questions as religious freedom or the use of the vulgar tongue in the liturgy. Besides these calculations, he was after something more. A struggle was going on concerning the fundamental principles of the new Republican system; to be more precise, which of the proposed foundations would get the upper hand? For if one were to take seriously the principle that all are equal in the Republic, was it possible to raise one above all others? Practically speaking, this would negate the possibility of electing a citizen king, which Uchański, intentionally, speaks of in his speech as a "private" king.[59]

"The very equality which we have introduced amongst ourselves will not permit such a choice. For who would ever wish to set his peer above him as king? Who would not prefer to set himself forth as king, rather than any other?"[60] On the basis of this very same thesis of equality, Zamoyski had moments before introduced his deduction of a citizen king. And it is certainly for this reason that Uchański must underpin his own deduction with a sober, universally comprehensible evaluation: "In this our free realm all of us are mixed up in some partisanship, in quarrels and misunderstandings with our neighbors. And everyone is going to fear, lest his troublesome neighbor and opponent become even more nettlesome and harmful, when elected king."[61] With this particular argument, many of those gathered there would certainly be ready to agree. And yet the idea of a Habsburg on the Polish throne was something that the great majority of the nobility were not able to swallow, and Zamoyski, it seems, was always adroit in exploiting the anti-German resentment of his co-citizens to excellent advantage. It is therefore no coincidence that Uchański should make direct reference to this universal antipathy. "I see that many are displeased at the fact that he is a German. [...] It is true that amongst children and the vulgar sort—so quick to rebel and quarrelsome—a certain type of hatred toward the Germans can be found, despite the fact that, supposedly, there is no other nation with whom we should be bound with tighter bonds of friendship and interest as they; I even dare say that there is no nation set beneath the same heavens who are more similar to us by character traits, uprightness, and simplicity of customs. The first reason for such friendship is our close proximity to one another. [...] With no other nation have we such solemn pacts; with no other nation have we so many public and private bonds; with no other such great and far-reaching, important relations, amongst which there is hardly a single item which we have not tried out. We have only been lacking in one thing: that we should live under one monarch. And that, I expect, this current election will rectify."[62] It must be admitted that the manner in which the archbishop stifles the anti-German argument of the opponents to the

Habsburgs fills one with wonder. Such a passion in confessing to the nearness and friendship between the Poles and the Germans was perhaps never much in line with the generally accepted opinions derived from the history of the Republic, which Uchański sets at the feet of simple and undeveloped people—children and simpletons. This argument of his has a very familiar ring to it: Listen, maybe we have had a lot of problems throughout our history with these Germans, but now the main thing is for the Republic to become a strong constituent element of the whole European, Christian organism, under the rule of a German emperor. We are neighbors; the border between us has long been a peaceful one; we enjoy reciprocal advantages in trade and, in many ways, we are very similar to one other. But such political prudence, as usual, covers a rather shallow practicality: it is all about money and comfort. Uchański would never suggest such a thing, so baldly; he was too wise and elegant for that. But a less polished and more incendiary speaker at the Diet of Election as Stanisław Sędziwój Czarnkowski, the mortal enemy of the Chancellor at the next, third election, quite openly stated why the German Emperor of Austrian blood would be the best Polish king: "After all, only from us could a countryman-king obtain an army and funds. And so at the slightest rumor or anxiety of war, he would enact taxes and call forth a *levée en masse*. This would work once or twice, but in the end it would become irksome, especially when we should ourselves derive nothing, or very little, from such a king, but would have to constantly pay taxes and frequently take up the sword."[63] Here Czarnkowski could certainly count on much murmured approbation; emboldened, he continued: "The Austrian, on the contrary, backed by his own might, and that of nearly all the Christian monarchs and all of Europe, surfeited with his own abundance and income, is able not only to lighten our loads, but also to broaden our kingdom and increase its splendor."[64] Following this, the fiery Czarnkowski entirely loosed the reins of his fantasy to unroll before the gathering such a lyrical image of a Habsburg reign: "He shall establish cities and castle-towns with colonists, granting them laws; he shall rebuild the whole kingdom and fine-tune its apparatus. Who among us is unaware of how other nations are already blooming beautifully? How many castles there are there, and splendid cities? How many masterpieces of art? How everywhere one finds splendor and elegance in city and in village? I will adduce but one example. In our largest cities one rarely comes across a clock. There, in just about every little village, besides other ornaments, one finds a clock tower. It is nothing strange, then, that as far as memory reaches, most of us have sent our children to Germany for education, and from thence they return with all things necessary for comfort and luxury. It is true that, since the days of Bona, we have been going more frequently to Italy than Germany, but we are indebted to the Germans for all the fruits of art and wealth, for it is they who have them in abundance there."[65]

All of this delight, all of these *oohs!* and *ahhs!* over the might and wealth of the Germans, of which the Poles might have their own share, if only both countries were to unite beneath the scepter of one emperor, are, all the same, fairly humiliating and speak as it were of the growing civilizational complexes arising in the Republic, at least among a portion of the noble brotherhood. Still, they certainly resonated in the imaginations of those who counted upon the might of the Habsburgs redounding not only to the glory of the Poles, but also ensuring their security and comfort. This was facilitated all the more by the fact that Vienna was not stinting in material rewards to its partisans in the Republic—such as, for example, Czarnkowski. Yet a deeper systemic thought was also contained in the Habsburg option which cannot be reduced merely to comfort or complex. This was a certain perspective on the essence of the inner political relations in the Republic, shared above all by a portion of the mightier, anti-democratic nobility: namely, that there is too much freedom in a noble state that elects its own king; that this should be somehow reined in, subjected to control from above. The material arguments of Czarnkowski could certainly seem too vulgar to Uchański, although they were an aid to the establishment of a party. For he himself had no complexes; nothing was lacking him for a life in comfort; he was, however, convinced of the fact that a strong Habsburg government in Poland would not only create a better geopolitical perspective for the country, but would also constitute a balance to the excessively tempestuous democratic nobility. For this reason, after hedging his bets with numerous reservations, he sets forth his basic point at the end of his speech: "While it is true that I do not wish that freedom or justice be constrained by excessive severity, still, if I were made to choose between two evils, I dare state that I would rather live under such a government where nothing is allowed than one where everything is allowed everyone. For our liberty has developed so that we have become libertines such as pay no attention to any direction, whether human or divine, and who are in need of some swift and salvific restraint. No one is better set to provide this than the emperor."[66]

I get the sense that, with these very words, Uchański finally torpedoed any chance the Habsburgs might have had of obtaining the Polish crown. His thought was clear and not completely devoid of reason. But this was 1575. Two whole generations of executionists had completely changed the face of the state, bestowing upon it the character of the immortal Republic—immortal above all because of its liberty. It was an improbable thing, to say the least, that those freedoms should now be limited by the election of a German emperor. Perhaps the anti-German attitudes of the larger portion of the nobility were indeed an expression of childish immaturity or folk prejudices, as our regent would have it, but the new political reality had crystallized so solidly that it would no longer be too easily subject to limits. Zamoyski would not be himself if he did not exploit this weakness in the primate's argument, and so, unrestrainedly, he unfurled the *principia* of the new system before the eyes of his adversary: "Our freedom rests upon three chief principles, which are so peculiar to us that they can only be found here. Other peoples who consider them, either partially adopt them, or praise them to the heavens. Firstly, each of us has a voice in the election of our kings. None of us acknowledges any government to which he has not voluntarily subjected himself; or has not, at the very least, cast his vote, even if the majority chooses another king. We possess not only absolute law over those subject to us, without possibility of appeal, but also the power of life and death, whereas only we are so free that no king, no official, has power over us save that which we have given them, according to legislated public law. Finally, no king is able to deprive any one of us of our honor, our wealth, or our life, nor may he imprison anyone, unless he has first been convincingly convicted, according to the law. [...] This all happens differently abroad. First of all, government has long been hereditary there [... Their kings] rule their peoples arbitrarily, denying their nobles the same sort of power over their subjects, so that the noble is for all intents and purposes levelled amongst the commoners [...]. According to our laws no person who is not noble-born may possess any office or dignity in the state; with them, the nobility has reserved to themselves only the military dignity, while entrusting other portions of the interior administration, such as government and nearly all public offices, to the plebeians [...]. They call our freedom anarchy, but whether or not they do so justly, each of us sees clearly for himself. If the nation is an assembly of people united to one another by law, our Republic is not a sweeping of castoffs, a mere mob, but a unity of noble men. Its administration is even more moderate than that of Rome, and indeed better for two reasons: in that its rulers are not elected annually, but for life, and that following the death of one of them, it opens the road to others to contest for that honor. In this way, it prohibits the Varros of the world and all other turbulent conspirators from usurping the throne. All of the nobility bear arms, and so all should vote. Each well-born noble has a right to each and every honor [... In foreign parts] villages and cities bloom because the city-dwellers have all the power. But because such splendor is the result of damage done to noble freedom, I'd rather not have such splendor at all—not at such a price! It is not according to the products of craftsmen, not to walls and imposing structures—in which we ourselves are not lacking—that the good fortune of a people is measured, but according to their freedoms, virtues, and good manners. And I reckon that we cede place to no one in this regard. I hear some of you raising to the heavens words of praise for the abundance and power of the Austrian house. But that which attracts their yearning eyes fills me with fear, and for this reason chiefly I fear for the our public freedom and honor. I fear lest the same thing happen to us that always happens to small items that tumble into a great river: all trace of them is lost forever."[67]

Just as Zamoyski said, the election of 1575 saw to it that Poland should flow along its own great riverbed, not as the tributary to another. It is true that the choice of a "Piast" to the throne did not prove possible, and the vision of a similar system to that of the Venetian doge—of which Andrzej Tęczyński spoke at that Diet of Election: "when one dies, immediately, another who had yesterday been but a private person, today becomes the new doge, that is, the great ruler of a great republic, and receives the honors of his own people and that of strangers as well, for he represents not only himself, but the entire republic in his person"[68]—was not realized, as no one of those many free and equal nobles was lifted to the throne of the Republic. But for all that, an interesting ploy was effected, which finally closed the doors leading to the Polish crown before Maximilian II Habsburg. A portion of the nobility chose as king Anna, the sister of the last Jagiellonian, Zygmunt August, under the condition that she marry Stefan Batory, the Prince of Transylvania, who in that way became ruler. And so, instead of a "Piast" it was a "Jagiellonka," with a Hungarian husband, who became king. Uchański strove once more to rescue his plan of attaching Poland, through the Habsburgs, to the great system of European rulers. His followers acclaimed Maximilian King of Poland on the meadows of Wola. When Anna and Batory hurried down to Kraków to effect the coronation, the primate forbade the treasury be opened and the royal insignia retrieved, stating that Habsburg was the new, legal ruler of Poland. At this, Anna proved a worthy sparring partner. Being in possession of the so-called Hungarian crown, which her brother Zygmunt August once received in gift from the Zapolya family, she produced it from her private treasury and used it for the coronation of Batory.

An Italian Digression

This great systemic debate of the Poles, which took place in 1575 in Warsaw, had for me an interesting epilogue on a certain August day, just a few years ago. I was driving along the broad A1 from Florence in a rental car, passing by sun-drenched Arezzo and Orvieto in the direction of Rome. The goal of this journey was a certain little town set just a bit south of the Italian capital, somewhere in the area of the ancient Pontic marshes, to which I was invited by a certain pleasant host. At one time, he had been an ambitious politician, and I reckon that he had some grand plans for ruling Poland in such a way as to accommodate our tradition to the challenges of the contemporary world. Something on the order of "tugging at the reins". There had been some great hopes for the realization of just such an accommodation, which would enable the liberation of the potential dormant in the Poles—a dream to which many succumbed in 2005. Of course, nothing came of these plans. My host abandoned both politics and great plans, became a commentator on public events, and in his free time gave himself up to his passion: visiting various corners of Italy, as fascinated as he was by all forms of Italian culture, not excepting, of course, cuisine. After having spent an entire day in a garden with a view of the Tyrrhenian Sea, I became convinced that my host was not only an interesting person to talk with but an excellent cook as well. The dishes that he prepared by himself, which landed one after another on our table, were so delicious that to this very day I'm not sure whether it was his taste for simple and marvelously tasty foods or the conversation, which exhilarated me more. He spoke in colorful terms of his travels through the surrounding villages scattered over the Alban Hills, narrating their history with an expertise that extended all the way back to Volscian prehistory, and of the great preserved works of Italian art, sculpture, painting, and architecture. He was a walking compendium of knowledge on these topics. While listening to all this, I couldn't restrain myself from commenting that his fascination with Italy and the South was a very Polish thing. Throughout the entire sixteenth and seventeenth centuries, Poles, the sons of wealthy, but also less-wealthy, noble clans would travel here in great numbers to be educated; to visit and to accumulate aesthetic impressions and the usual adventures of youth, but also in order to *naumić się*—to "wisen up," to come to know the world, to make contacts and friendships, to win some practical knowledge of the arcane functioning of modern administration, diplomacy, and finance. I stated that we cannot understand the phenomenon of that Republic stretching far to the North and East—nearly to Moscow itself—without this strong, Italian, and Latin offshoot that reaches deep into the Mediterranean world. Certainly thanks to the papacy and Catholicism, but above all due to a conscious cultural choice taken by our forefathers, Poland became enduringly united to the Mediterranean, Latin form, of which in the twentieth century Iwaszkiewicz, Parnicki, Wat, Herbert, Hertz, Kubiak, and many others wrote—something for which the Russians never forgave us, and the Germans were never able to understand. And so it remains today. For Polishness, as a culture, will either be able to preserve its Latin form, or it will cease to exist altogether.

I was, of course, seduced by the gorgeous scenery amidst which this conversation took place, the picturesque Italian vistas. But above all it was my host's erudition in matters touching upon southern, Latin culture, his authentic love of the same, which gripped me. The devotion with which I had given myself over to my own arguments of the Latin offshoot of the Republic and the truth that our national identity has been constituted thereby allowed me to completely forget that my conversant was, primarily, a faithful advocate of the Gallic understanding of Europe, a scion of the subjects of the Austrian ruling house, and also a true adept of the Kraków historical school. The portraits of Franz Joseph that you see in some cafés in Kraków always seemed to me a local quirk of the inhabitants of that city. I was wrong of course, for one mustn't belittle a devotion to a certain deeper idea that may be found there. And so my conversant decidedly held forth in a similar manner. His fascination with the Latin South in contemporary Poland was now the mere expression of a private interest, an exception to the rule. In the sixteenth and seventeenth centuries the Latin offshoot truly formed Polish culture; today, it is an anachronism. The pulse of contemporary Europe beats not in the south, but in the north-western quadrant of our continent, in Germany, which has become the cultural and political pattern for the majority of contemporary Poles. It is only the Germans who are capable of providing contemporary Europe with a form. "Sometimes I speak with the owner of this house and garden, who is renting it to me for the summer," my host said to me. "He is a renowned Roman lawyer. He once told me what today's Italians, Romans, think of the present crisis, the relations that have got the upper hand in the capital, the center of Italian politics, and also here, in the provinces. And from what he says only one image comes into focus: that of a country deeply corrupt, and politically speaking, entirely lost. No, today, neither the Italians nor the South in general can be any source of inspiration for Europe. The only sensible inspiration today is that coming from Berlin." I answered that if this last statement of his were true, I simply wouldn't be able to bear it. For we are not only speaking of politics here, but of culture as well, from which politicians must not abstract themselves, for when they do, it usually leads to fatal consequences. The roots of European culture have always reached deep into the South; without them, Europe would not exist today. I supported myself with the arguments of Kojeve and Agamben concerning Latin Europe, and stressed that the present crisis is not only of an economic and political character, but also possesses a cultural dimension, and that of great significance for European geopolitics. For this reason its solution will have a fundamental significance for Poland's place in Europe, too. I dare not state, after all, that we are to engage in political belligerence toward Germany, but an orientation directed at Berlin would reopen that division into East and West, so fatal to us, according to which we would be condemned to a second-rate position with no place for our cultural and political subjectivity. To put it another way, for us, Europeanism—yes, but one regulated and accepted only under certain conditions. For in that East-West division the stakes are always an oppressive modernization, not identity. However, none of this made any impression on my conversant. "Please just consider the sixteenth century, which so interests you, sir," he continued. "Charles V was the last emperor who attempted the creation of a pan-European order, and that on the basis of Catholicism. At the time, Poland had a unique chance to become an integral part of the system, and to win an influence on its future form along with the Habsburgs. But then we took another decision. We couldn't forgive Charles' antecedent, Maximilian I, for depriving the Jagiellonians of their primacy in Central Europe and of the crowns of the Czech lands and Hungary, or for his conniving with Muscovy against the Republic. That was a mistake. For instead of seeking allies in Italy, above all in Venice, against the Habsburgs, and also in France, and instead of waging exhaustive wars with Muscovy in the east, we should have taken advantage of our chance and entered the European system of the Habsburgs, which Charles left behind him." While listening to my partner in that conversation, I couldn't help but recall Uchański's arguments, formulated during the second election in 1575 and directed against Zamoyski. They sounded very similar. Certainly, at the time, the future Chancellor and his partisans erected a dam blocking the Habsburgs from the Polish crown, which my host recognized to be a mistake of historical, geopolitical significance. And yet the Habsburg option had a long future life in Polish politics throughout the subsequent ages. It was present in the nineteenth century, when along with the idea of the resurrection of Poland the concept arose of recuperating that chance once lost in the sixteenth century by setting the Austrian emperor, or at least one of his numerous archdukes, on the throne of a Polish kingdom rebuilt around Galicia. In this way, Poles as Catholic subjects might become once more united under the scepter of a Catholic, and also liberal, ruler, creating in Central Europe a cultural and political counterweight to the two imperial powers: Russian Orthodoxy and German Protestantism. In his book on Piłsudski, when describing the significance of Polish Catholicism during the period of the Partitions, Cat-Mackiewicz recalls a symptomatic event, which took place during a certain meeting in Vilnius between a bishop and a tsarist general. During the exchange of introductory pleasantries, the bishop asked after the health of the Russian Tsar. The general replied with thanks and, as a gesture of reciprocal courtesy, asked after the health of Emperor Franz Josef.[69] There was nothing strange about this, as in those times, in a political sense, Catholicism was naturally identified with the reign of the Habsburgs. Well sure, but in the twentieth century, the situation changed diametrically. Catholicism ceased to be a political point of reference in Europe, and the Habsburg state completely disappeared from the map. It is for this reason that I wonder now, recalling that conversation held in the charming Italian village near

Rome, whether—just as my host was doing—was it really possible to exchange the old Habsburg option, which no longer exists, for the new German one? Exchanging the Catholic Vienna of the Habsburg Emperors for contemporary Berlin, that capital of secularized and Europeanized Protestantism? For if that were possible, were we to do so, we would be allowing ourselves to be directed by the only motive that remained us, and which in the systemic debate of the second election Uchański expressed in his sincere confession that "I dare state that I would rather live under such a government where nothing is allowed, rather than one where everything is allowed everyone."[70] However, for Zamoyski, for the executionists, and for many later generations of Poles, such a thing—the loss of liberty—would be an unacceptable price to pay.

The Bridge of the Republic

It is often forgotten that the inception of the noble, democratic Republic was closely united to the development of the significance of Warsaw as capital of the nation—that city spread out upon the high Wisła riverside cliff. What is more, one usually repeats the tried and true opinion that it was Zygmunt III Waza (Vasa) who transferred the capital of our country from Kraków to Warsaw, which is not true. Of course, during the Jagiellonian years, Kraków was the permanent royal city, the seat of the royal court, where coronations took place, and where the royal necropolis was located. There was also Vilnius, the capital of the Grand Duchy of Lithuania, but Lwów was also a sort of second, extra capital of the Polish-Lithuanian commonwealth, as was Piotrków. There were royal seats also in Knyszyn, Tykocin, and Grodno. But beginning with Zygmunt August, Warsaw begins to become, by degrees, the most important political city of the Republic, the parliamentary city, which attracts to itself the nobility of the entire country, and following the death of the last of the Jagiellonians, it becomes the place where the kings of Poland are elected up until the Partition period. This endowed Warsaw with a completely unique status on the political map of the democratic, noble republic. Zygmunt August understood this; he sensed the new significance of the location, and it is to him indeed that credit is due for Warsaw becoming, by degrees, the chief place of assembly for the entire noble caste—the political capital of the Republic. Alongside the political motives, a role was played here by a more practical consideration: that the monarch, travelling from Kraków through Piotrków Trybunalski to his beloved Knyszyn or Tykocin in the Podlasie region, would cross the Wisła in Warsaw. The history of the first permanent bridge over the Wisła is directly related to the growing significance of the city on the high bank, and to Zygmunt August—which says a lot about what the Republic was, in practice, and what it was not. I do not know whether it is true in fact, what some suggest, that there was only one public (for built with public funds) bridge of stone in the entire, mighty Republic: that which united the fortress of Kamieniec with the city thereof. It is, however, a fact that bridges and roads were the evident Achilles' heel of the Republic, as was, in general, public infrastructure. In the report of Pietro Duodo, that Venetian representative who was planning to open a new business corridor for the sale of wine through Central Europe to Poland, there can be found one statement, full of wonder, concerning the fact that Poland is a huge country with access to the sea and many ports, yet it hardly has its own fleet, although there is a superabundance of construction materials at hand.[71] For the Venetian, whose republic was founded on its robust fleet, this was something of an unsolvable paradox. But the matter was actually simple: There was no great fleet in the Republic, because no one wanted to pay for its construction, just like there were no stone bridges or wide and well-paved roads. In other words, the timeless Polish problem: wealthy Poles inhabiting a poor state.

It was no different with the bridge thrown over the Wisła in Warsaw. When it was settled under Zygmunt August that Warsaw was to be the chief city for the parliamentary gatherings of the united Republic, and crowds of nobility began ever more frequently to throng to the city from the farthest corners of the state, the king decided to build, with his own money, a permanent crossing over the Wisła. This was a decision that was both practical and courageous. The idea was, of course, to provide the nobles with a safe and swift passage to the western bank of the mighty river, especially during the sittings of Parliament. Jan Kochanowski was later to praise the ingenuity and generosity of His Majesty the King in one of his poems as follows: we should be grateful to him not only for permitting us to cross the Wisła to Warsaw dry-shod, but because by saving on the cost of a boatman's fee we might use that money to raise a long draught to the royal health.[72] The advantages were self-evident, and, indeed, the nobility truly praised Zygmunt August's ingenuity and generosity. A good king! All the more so, because it was no easy task at the time to construct such a bridge. As a matter of fact, it was an insane task, taking into consideration both the thick, sticky mud-flats of the shore on the western Powiśle, under the embankment, and those on the Praga side, as well as the capricious River Wisła itself, which flooded its banks frequently, and finally the severe conditions that prevailed in the winter-time, which threatened every wooden structure with destruction by racing, heavy ice-floes during thaws. Yet, Zygmunt must have been very determined to implement his courageous idea; this must have been something of a state interest to him, to fasten both shores of the Republic together with that great clasp. The commission for the implementation of the project went to the German engineer Erasmus of Zakroczym. It's evident that as early as that, German constructions were associated with solidity if the king made such a choice. And it's true that Erasmus accomplished his task perfectly, even though the final effect of his work was a little strange. For the bridge did not cross the river in a perfect perpendicular, but rather on an angle, which made the bridge very long—almost half a kilometer! It was constituted of twenty-two spans, the majority of which rested on gigantic pillars driven deep into the riverbed and held in place by mighty gable trusses of wood and iron. The whole construction was protected from billows and ice flows by fifteen breakers constructed of solid Hungarian iron. What is more, the central portion of the bridge was to rest on five floating supports, thanks to which it might be opened to facilitate the free passage of ships. As early as the reign of Stefan Batory, Anna Jagiellonka ordered the bridge to be fortified from the city-side by a brick and mortar defensive bastion, located near today's Mostowa (Bridge) Street. It still stands today, completely unnoticed, as a portion of the building known as the "old powder-house" (*Stara Prochownia*). The bridge-wards were stationed in this bastion: fifty armed men, who kept order on the bridge as an object of strategic importance not only for the city, but for the whole Republic as well. For on account of its dimensions, but also because of its public, state function, this Warsaw bridge became a symbol of the might and unity of the Republic, admired by one and all. Georg Braun, a German traveler and geographer, the author of a famous atlas of the cities of the world, wrote of it that "both in length, and in its splendid appearance, this bridge has hardly an equal anywhere in Europe. It arouses universal awe."[73] The nobility of the Republic as well, always eager for exaggeration, were inclined to see in the bridge the eighth wonder of the world. It was a great object of their pride. Of course, there was some exaggeration in all this. Yet their feelings of pride must have been authentic, since no one really made much of a fuss when Stefan Batory demanded that everyone, including the nobles, have to pay to cross the bridge—the so-called *mostowe* or bridge toll, which was collected for upkeep and repairs.

Zygmunt's bridge was not only a strategic object linking the west of the Republic with its east. It was also the mute witness of numerous political events, including some very dramatic ones, that took place in the capital of the new, democratic, noble state on the occasion of the diets and first three elections. Perhaps the most ominous of these, directly touching upon the bridge itself, took place in connection with the third, fatal (for Zamoyski), armed election following the sudden and unexpected death of Batory. For as soon as the Diet of Convocation was summoned to Warsaw in February, 1587, it became immediately apparent that the Zborowski family, above all Krzysztof, that "villainous rabble-rouser," and Andrzej, the Court Crown Marshal, would not give up, but rather determined to seize upon every possible occasion to exploit the interregnum in order to attack their mortal enemy, Zamoyski. The situation must have been truly threatening, since the *interrex*, Archbishop Karnkowski, even suggested to the Chancellor that, for his own safety, he not come to Warsaw for the convocation. It was then that Zamoyski was supposed to have pronounced that opinion of his concerning the noble caste: that the whole affair was like beer brewed of chaff, which soon enough would find itself among Miechowita's mushrooms, that is, tossed out the window. All the same, just to be safe he didn't go to Warsaw, sending to the Diet of Convocation instead his most trusted confidant and relative: Stanisław Żółkiewski. He preferred to see how things should develop. Meanwhile, in Warsaw, it was the Zborowskis who played first fiddle. At the Diet of Convocation they demanded that Zamoyski be deprived of the office of hetman for the duration of the elections. They also wished that the work of Heidenstein, the Chancellor's personal biographer, who glorified King Batory in his *Memoirs of the War Against Muscovy* (Pamiętnik wojny moskiewskiej), and which, it was suggested with some reason, had been dictated by Zamoyski himself, chiefly in order to boast of his own martial deeds, be condemned. Above all, however, they were after a settling of accounts for the wrongs that the Zborowski family, and the nobles who supported them, had suffered at the hands of the Chancellor.

Żółkiewski tried to hold forth at the Diet, to explain matters, but all he succeeded in doing was to arouse a great tumult against himself. During the tussle, some feisty servant of the Zborowskis threw a pickaxe in his direction. "Was that at me?" cried out the insulted voivode, who heard in reply a thunderous "right at you, you son of a whore!"[74] Nothing could be done to calm the fracas, and on the next day Żółkiewski himself had to take to his heels for safety. He was racing across the Zygmuntowski Bridge to the other side of the Wisła when, from the side of the tower, a posse of the Zborowskis' supporters appeared with the clear intention of pushing Żółkiewski and his companions, retainers of the Chancellor, into the river. While it is true that the bridge was wide—a full six meters across—the wooden pavement was slippery in winter, and still incomplete on the eastern side, lacking the proper guardrails. Accidents and drownings were not uncommon. If it had come to a regular battle on the bridge, Żółkiewski wouldn't have had a chance—he would have gone under with all his companions. Supposedly, only the intervention of the queen, Anna Jagiellonka, averted the tragedy. Catching sight of what was about to happen—that a regular battle was about to take place on the bridge—she ordered that the Zborowski side be stopped at all costs. At the time, when the banks of the Wisła were linked by the powerful, wooden bridge built by her deceased brother Zygmunt August, the royal castle, the seat of the old queen Anna, looked entirely different than it does today. Actually, it was a lofty little group of various buildings cobbled together high on the embankment. There was the regional law court of Warsaw, also known as the "shed" (*szopa*), baths, and a cook-house. The Great Court (*Dwór Wielki*), its three-storey representational portion, was built in the Renaissance style with a spiral staircase as well as a great hall for spectacles and performances—the altana, or "gazebo" on the second floor, and was attached to the so-called Lesser Court (*Dwór Mniejszy*), where the queen resided, by a porch. In 1587 Anna was sixty-four years old. So she was up in age, but all the same was a very energetic lady. I can imagine how, alerted by her courtiers to the events playing out on the bridge, she ran through the porch and into the Great Court in order to quickly assess the critical situation from the open "gazebo." When she saw just what a shambles was brewing on the bridge, she immediately commanded the guards at the bridge tower to rush out and restrain the Zborowski troops from attacking Żółkiewski. That is how I imagine the scene, although, of course, it could have looked completely otherwise. Still and all, on that freezing day, it was the old queen Anna who saved the life of the future grand hetman and scourge of the Muscovites.

Only a few months after this, some new events happened on the bridge which might be taken for an evil omen, a portent of the misfortunes and catastrophes that were on the way. It was just as if the mighty wooden construction of the bridge linking both banks of the united Republic sensed the thickening, evil atmosphere surrounding the third, armed election of the king in 1587 and wished to send a clear warning to the Poles. For in June, after Zamoyski had already led his entire army onto the Field of Election at Warsaw, a catastrophe described by Joachim Bielski took place: "The Chancellor had entered Warsaw at the head of more than three thousand men. As soon as he had passed over the bridge, it broke down under the weight of the people, augmented by a wagon drawn by six horses, but no one drowned."[75] So, quite an accident accompanied the entrance of the Chancellor to Warsaw over the bridge. It must have drawn the attention of everyone, and surely a lot was said about it, since in his letter to the pope the nuncio Annibale di Capua mentions it, although in a little different light, stating that the Warsaw bridge was washed away: "And on the very same day of my Lord the Chancellor's entry the bridge was washed away; and shortly thereafter, while my Lord the Voivode of Kraków was passing this way to visit the Lithuanians, three court carriages of the Voivode fell into the water, but without great loss amongst the Courtiers; indeed, no one perished."[76] And so it looks as if Zamoyski's entrance to Warsaw seriously damaged the bridge, as a result of which the entourage of the Kraków Voivode suffered their accident. At any rate, it was an evil omen, a bad sign indeed, the rupture of the bridge of the Republic in the days preceding the election of the king. It was as if the Republic herself, her solidity in unity, had been ruptured at that key moment.

The Kraków Massacre and the Dream of the Crown

Well, all right then, but how, in the end, were the dramatic events around the third, armed election of the Polish king brought to a conclusion? How, following that mortal conflict of the Zborowskis and Górka on the one hand, and Zamoyski on the other? And the dashing of the Chancellor's hopes to obtain the crown on account of the fraternal broil beneath the walls of Warsaw, and his subsequent strange, mysterious nervous breakdown? In 1587, on the field of election at Wola, Zamoyski tasted the bitterness of an exceptional catastrophe. Under the dramatic clouds of smoke billowing upward from the senatorial shack set aflame, on 19 August Primate Karnkowski declared Zygmunt Waza (Vasa) the new King of Poland. This he did under the cover of the armies of Zamoyski, since the supporters of Zborowski and Górka, and the Lithuanians as well (as stubborn as Lithuanians are, refusing all the while to cross over the Wisła and come to Wola) had no intention of stepping away from their Habsburg choice, Maximilian, the Emperor's brother. Zamoyski did not mix his voice in among the loud *vivats* in honor of the new king, nor did he sign the act of election. He sat in his tent, certainly furious at such a turn of events. Throughout the entire election period, he wavered between the candidacy of Vasa and that of Habsburg, conducting secret negotiations, because up until the moment of that final misfortune, the Battle of Warsaw (which, fortunately, did not actually occur), he could count upon the possibility that, because of the lack of agreement as to one of the two chief candidates, he might slip in his own name at the proper moment. Was it not in this very way that, so many years ago, he had finagled his election as rector at the University of Padua?

Where two are fighting, the third wins the day. But in this struggle, Zamoyski underestimated his most important opponent: Anna Jagiellonka, Stefan Batory's widow. Nor was he the only one; none of us have ever been able to properly evaluate her place in our history, treating her as we often do as somewhat of a secondary character. Meanwhile, the blood of the Jagiellonians and Sforzas coursed through her veins. Perhaps it is true that she was not a beautiful woman. However, she certainly inherited a talent for politics from her mother Bona. Chosen queen of Poland after Valois' escape, only in order to marry her off immediately to Batory, who was to be the real lord and ruler of Poland, she must have felt objectified by the nobles and the magnates. And yet she was as proud as any Jagiellonian. Following her husband's death (and that marriage was merely one more public humiliation for her—Batory ostentatiously avoided his wife, and even, under the influence and at the urging of Zamoyski, was thought to be considering divorce), she wished at last to get her own back, taking out her revenge upon those whom she considered to be behind her numerous humiliations. Zamoyski, to be sure, headed the list of the old queen's enemies. For this reason, she intrigued intensely on behalf of her nephew Zygmunt Waza, over whom, in the absence of children of her own, the old aunt gushed, calling him her darling "Zysio" and "mister sonny" (*pan synaczek*). The Jagiellonian aunties are an interesting bunch; indeed, they deserve a history of their own. Bona had four daughters: Izabela, the eldest, wife of the king of Hungary Jan Zapolya (János Szapolyai), who was later to become ruler of Transylvania in her own right; and her younger sisters: Zofia, who married the Prince of Brunswick, Anna, "queen" of Poland and wife of Batory, and finally Katarzyna, who became queen of Sweden and mother of "Zysio" and "Janusia" (Anna, the younger sister of Zygmunt Waza). Following the death of Zygmunt Stary (the Old), when Zygmunt August took over the fulness of royal authority from his father, his relations with his mother Bona grew chilly. It was then that Sforza decided to move, with her three younger daughters Zofia, Anna, and Katarzyna, to Mazovia. Following Izabela's banishment from Transylvania, her eldest daughter as well rejoined the family along with her son, Jan junior. Parenthetically speaking, would this not be prime material for a fascinating novel or film? Bona and her daughters living for several years together in the palace at Warsaw set on the Wisła embankment? But this does not bring the Jagiellonian connection to an end. Zygmunt Waza, or rather "Zysio," whose election his widowed royal auntie Anna Jagiellonka was able to realize only in 1587, enjoyed a popularity amongst the nobles not only because he spoke Polish well (which his mother Katarzyna ensured), but also because through his mother he might be viewed as a near descendent of the Jagiellonians. However, his rival, Archduke Maximilian, favored by the Zborowskis and Górka, was also of Jagiellonian blood, although he didn't speak Polish that well—for his grandmother was another Anna Jagiellonka: the daughter of Władysław Jagiellończyk, the king of the Czechs and the Hungarians, the brother of Zygmunt Stary. The dynastic relations and affinities of the Jagiellonians were, therefore, quite mighty and wide-reaching. As the choice of Zygmunt Waza shows, these still pulled a lot of weight in the Republic. I think then that Zamoyski, although a convinced republican, a Ciceronian, who believed that the Republic, and not any royal dynasty, was eternal, and that in these brave new days of republican freedom the nobility might well choose a king from amongst themselves, obviously underestimated the strength of the dynastic influences of the Jagiellonian aunties, that of Anna, Batory's widow, above all. He recognized that the rights of the Jagiellonians had expired along with the first and second free elections. Yet in 1587, it turned out that the long shadow of the dynasty cast far, far into the future of the Republic, and that thanks to the Wazas it would last long indeed, up until the abdication of Jan Kazimierz, and so surviving Zamoyski by many decades.

Such a turn of events must have been a great disappointment to the Chancellor. What is more, he might have sensed the earth beginning to give way under his feet. A king had been elected—actually, two kings had been elected. Until the coronation of Zygmunt had been accomplished in the Wawel Cathedral, Zamoyski, as Grand Hetman, still held the greatest sway in the Republic. Furthermore, he was responsible for its security. In contrast to his father, who in 1576 did not decide upon an open war with Batory over the Polish crown, Archduke Maximilian had no intent of resigning his rights on behalf of his distant Swedish cousin. No, he gathered an army and set off for Kraków. It was up to Zamoyski to stop him and—what bitter irony of fate!—defend the city where the coronation of Waza was to take place, and the royal treasury at Wawel Castle, where the crown jewels were kept, the insignias of the authority of the Polish kings—and this in circumstances none too favorable. A portion of the nobles, incited by the Zborowskis and Górka, continued to support Maximilian as the rightful King of Poland. There were no resources for the defense of the country. Further, Kraków was defended by old, mediaeval walls which were practically no obstacle at all to the artillery of the time. Much debate went on in the Republic concerning the necessity of securing the capital with modern fortifications, at least such as the *mura veneziane* in Padua, or like those with which the Chancellor had ringed his Zamość. But the requisite money was never found. Obviously, it was thought that, just as in the case of the Warsaw bridge, it was rather the King's duty to finance them out of his own pocket. And now, in haste, Zamoyski was obliged to raise provisional battlements on the outskirts of Kraków so as to defend the royal city from the advancing Maximilian. The Chancellor's nerves must have been strained to snapping at the time, because as much as beneath the walls of Warsaw, on the fields of Wola, the crown was in play, perhaps here, in Kraków, quite everything was at stake: Zamoyski's reputation and his position in the Republic. If he were to lose, he would be covered in infamy, and the Zborowskis and Górka—with the approbation of the new Habsburg king—would leap at his throat. If he were to win, Waza would become king—a twenty-year-old youth, which for the forty-something Chancellor meant that in all probability he would not live to see the next election.

The defence of Kraków and the Battle of Byczyna a few months later are amongst the most heroic but also most dramatic moments in Zamoyski's career. The hastily organized defense of the capital city allowed him to face Maximilian's army effectively. His opponents, among the ranks of whom were also to be found Polish supporters of Habsburg as well as the Zborowskis, with Krzysztof, that "villainous rabble-rouser" at their head, had to resort to deceit. Taking advantage of the treason of the German citizens of Garbary, the defensive abutment of Kraków pushed furthest forward, they strove to penetrate the fortifications and take the city. The Chancellor, in his black armor, personally led his black-clad infantry into the fray. The enemy was repulsed—at the sight of the Chancellor, Zborowski had to take to his heels—the capital was successfully defended, and yet the battles were to exact a high toll in victims: the enemy dead alone was reckoned at two thousand, while Bielski (with the emphasis characteristic of this historian) noted that the nearby small River Rudawa "was choked with corpses, and water mixed with blood so that the fish, drunk on blood, perished. Everywhere, corpse lay upon corpse."[77] From the get-go, the treasonous German burghers of Garbary became objects of such ferocious vengeance that the Chancellor himself had to order an end to the shambles. In order to satisfy the riled citizenry of Kraków, he had several dozen Germans beheaded.

So one might say that, in this very manner, the fraternal slaughter which almost occured on the fields of Wola beneath the walls of Warsaw, was realized fully later, here, beneath the walls of Kraków. But this was only the beginning of the bloody events. Maximilian did not give up. He gathered his army, safe beyond the southern border of the Republic. It must be mentioned that there were still quite a few Poles in his ranks, who acknowledged him as their rightful ruler. In this sense, this was still a Polish civil war. Meanwhile, the king-elect Zygmunt arrived in Kraków with his sister Anna, his old aunt Anna Jagiellonka, his courtiers, and the magnates who, from the moment that young Waza first set foot upon Polish soil, began intensively to chat him up, pursuing their own interests and agendas, complaining frequently in so doing about the omnipotence of the powerful Chancellor. Zamoyski must have known all about this through his spies. And yet, simultaneously, he was so entirely engaged in the defense of the capital at Kraków that there was not much he could do. His position was weakening. It is for this reason that he greeted the king-elect and his entourage in Kraków as a great conquering hero, the defender of the capital, the one who, practically speaking, had cleared the road to his coronation. At the same time many of the eyewitness accounts of those days allow us to assume that, beneath the surface pleasantries and all the courtesy that the Chancellor directed at the young king during the coronation itself and the Coronation Diet, a whole storm of emotions, antipathies, dread, disdain, and contempt was raging. During the welcoming ceremonies, Zamoyski was supposed to have uttered the following unflattering statement concerning the king to Leśniowolski, who was standing beside him: "And so what sort of mute specter (*niema mara*) have you brought us here from Sweden?"[78] The dangerous game played on. The magnates and nobles gathered at the Coronation Diet strongly pressured Zamoyski, as the defender of the Republic, the mighty hetman, to pass beyond the southern border with his men and put paid to Maximilian and his Polish supporters once and for all. The Chancellor smelt a trap: he would not be able to oppose the archduke in the open field with properly prepared and outfitted forces, as despite the urging of senators and nobles to set off for battle as soon as possible—they were not so quick to vote new funds for the army. Zamoyski suspected that, taking advantage of the opportunity, his opponents within Poland, rivals for the ear of the new king, were wishing to dispatch him on a suicide mission so that he would finally and completely founder in a catastrophic battle with Maximilian. For this reason he squirmed to beat the band, thinking up ever new reasons to put off the expedition for a later time, something that is beautifully recorded in the diaries of the Coronation Diet from the turn of 1588.[79] At last, the breakdown came. Stanisław Grzybowski was later to describe this dramatic situation in such a way: as if finding himself in a situation with no exit, Zamoyski departed Kraków with his army, heading toward Maximilian "as his contemporaries noted: 'with fear and dread.' Bidding farewell to the senate in pathetic fashion, he cried out, with tears, that having lost his entire fortune, now he was risking the last thing that remained him—his glory. There was in this mental breakdown the disappointment of an ambitious politician, of a man who dreamed of a crown, but now has lost all hope of it entirely; one who later reckoned that he would be able to direct the young king, but found in him an independent and a stubborn individual."[80]

Indeed, strange things must have been going on in the head and heart of the Chancellor during the course of those dramatic events. In his history of the life of Zamoyski, Heidenstein has left us an eloquent story of a dream which visited the Chancellor in the night before to his defense of Kraków. The historian Wacław Sobieski, following Heidenstein, describes the dream thus: "Zamoyski spent the night before the assault at the most extended line of defence. While asleep, he had a strange dream. It seemed to him that Maximilian lifted up from the ground a diadem flashing with the most valuable jewels, which Marek Sobieski, the crown ensign and grandfather of the future king, then set on the brows of Hetman Zamoyski."[81] Now, it seems to me that this story of a dream offered by Heidenstein concerning the flashing diadem, or, rather, we should say crown, does not seem strange at all. On the contrary, it is very understandable and fits the circumstances of the third, armed election of 1587 quite well. Zamoyski dreamed exactly of what he had been wishing for, and which had occupied his thought so intensively for some time. But something else catches my attention here. For I thought: exactly what sort of flashing bejeweled diadem would Maximilian lift from the earth only for it to rest, at last, on Zamoyski's brow? The answer to that question is not as simple as it may seem.

Five Polish Crowns—and One More

When visiting the Oriental-Westminsteresque House of Parliament in Budapest, where, beneath a great dome the Crown of St. Stephen—that relic of the nation and symbol of its statehood—can be seen in its armored glass display case, one may understand perfectly why, in the matter of royal insignias, the Hungarians had much greater good fortune than we, the Poles—and that from the very dawn of our Polish and Hungarian statehood. As far as coronation is concerned, St. Stephen I beat our Bolesław Chrobry (the Brave) to the punch by some twenty five years (of course, Bolesław was far from sainthood). Later on, the Crown of St. Stephen finally rested on Jagiellonian brows when Władysław Jagiellończyk, also known, spitefully, as the "well-well king" (*król dobrze*), became the ruler of Hungary. He subsequently set it on the head of his son, that misfortunate Ludwik II, who fell at Mohács, slain by the Turks, at which Hungarian statehood vanished for long years. As a result of various events, the Crown of St. Stephen at some point came into the hands of Izabela Jagiellonka, the eldest daughter of Bona and Zygmunt Stary (the Old). However, when she was banished from Transylvania, she had to relinquish the insignia to the Habsburg Emperor Ferdinand. Throughout the stormy history of Hungary, the crown passed from hand to hand, wandering all over Central Europe. Following the Second World War, it was even carted off to the United States, where it rested in the famed Fort Knox, from which it once more returned to Budapest thanks to President Jimmy Carter. We haven't had such good luck with our crown, or rather, our crowns.

Our first crown—that most important crown of Bolesław Chrobry—was lost, and thus, in his dream, Zamoyski could not be crowned king with it. There is, of course, one path leading to the assumption that it was this very crown that Zamoyski had in mind. For in his dream it is a diadem flashing with valuable jewels, which brings our thoughts round to that old story, still related by Gallus Anonymous, according to which the first Polish crown was the imperial diadem, which Otto III was supposed to have set upon Bolesław's brows.[82] The first truly Polish crown, the one which Bolesław actually used in his coronation twenty-five years later, was carted off to Germany following the death of Mieszko II by Rycheza, where it vanished. We don't even know what it might have looked like—whether, for example, it contained a portion of that imperial diadem? Also, the second Polish crown, that which Bolesław Śmiały (the Bold) had fashioned for his coronation in 1076, although surviving for over two centuries and being used for two further coronations (those of Przemysław II and Wacław II), was taken off to Bohemia, where it also vanished without a trace. And so, in such dramatic circumstances, defending Kraków and the royal seat on Wawel from Maximilian, when Zamoyski dreamt of his crown, the one preserved in the royal treasury behind thick, iron-clad doors was a completely different symbol of royal authority. It was, above all, a privileged crown, a *corona privilegiata*, which Władysław Łokietek (the Short) had fashioned, though in order to underscore the reacquired continuity of kingship, it was vulgarly known as the "crown of Chrobry" though it was nothing of the sort. We know exactly what it looked like because, with only a few exceptions, it was the crown used by nearly all Polish rulers up to the period of the Partitions, and is preserved on many different portraits and drawings. It was made up of two arched loops of pure gold, with ten segments finished in the characteristic lily motif, richly encrusted with valuable jewels. If, therefore, Zamoyski's dream had become reality in 1587, if he had not underestimated the dynastic relations of Anna Jagiellonka and her political savvy, and if he had not permitted the shameful scenes under the walls of Warsaw, on the field of election at Wola, including the firing of the senatorial shed; if he had decided after all to become a Polish Julius Caesar, a dictator with all the trimmings, who would use his own army to bring about the death of his enemies as the inciters of a civil war and the downfall of the Republic, certainly, in the Wawel Cathedral, it would have been this very crown that the primate would have placed upon his head. Or maybe not. For there have been exceptions to this rule, and in the crown treasury, which Zamoyski so courageously defended from the Habsburg archduke, there were at least two other crowns. One of these belonged to Władysław Jagiełło, who was unable to be crowned with Chrobry's diadem since from the days of Ludwik Węgierski (Louis the Hungarian), who arranged the double funeral of Kazimierz Wielki (the Great), that was to be found in Hungary. Following that affair with Janko z Czarnkowa (Jan of Czarnków), Ludwik was terrified that during his absence from Poland, some other conspiracy might deprive him of his throne, for which reason he preferred to have the Polish crown within reach of his hand in Buda. And so Władysław had to order the creation of a new crown, similar in style and shape to the crown of Chrobry. It was also ringed with lilies and encrusted with many valuable stones: sapphires, rubies, and pearls. When Zygmunt of Luxembourg, the king of Bohemia, Hungary, Germany, and later emperor, decided to return the crown of Chrobry to

Poland, Władysław's crown, obviously, ceased being privileged and was often used thereafter during the ceremonies of tribute received by the kings of Poland from their lieges. It seems that on Matejko's famous canvas showing the Prussian Homage (*Hołd pruski*), Zygmunt Stary has that very crown of his grandfather, Władysław, on his head. There was also one other crown in the Wawel treasury, just as beautiful, although different in appearance from the other two. This was the so-called Hungarian crown, with which in 1576 Stefan Batory was crowned. It had earlier belonged to the Hungarian king Jan Zapolya, the husband of Izabela Jagiellonka, as his private insignia. In shape and motif it was very similar to the original crown of St. Stephen, which we can inspect today at the Hungarian Parliament. It arrived in Poland along with Izabela and her son Jan Zygmunt Zapolya, and after his death, it became the property of his uncle, Izabela's brother, the Polish king Zygmunt August. And so alongside many other insignias, three royal crowns were to be found in the treasury, which were used at the coronation of Polish kings. However, I reckon that on that night before Maximilian's attack on Kraków, Zamoyski was dreaming of the most important one of them: Chrobry's crown, imagining himself on the throne as a Piast chosen by the Republic as her ruler. This seems most logical and proper to me.

Now, since we have begun to seriously muse upon the question of royal insignias in Poland, it's worth our while to consider it to the very end. For there were even more crowns, and we ought at least to speak of two others. Zygmunt Waza (Vasa) had himself crowned with a new one, which he treated as his private crown. In the records of the crown treasury at Wawel it figured as the "Swedish crown." This is the crown that the king is wearing today on his column in Warsaw. It is certainly significant that Zygmunt made such eager use of a new crown, which might be taken as indicative of his intent to underscore the dynastic line of the Wazas, distinguishing it from earlier dynasties, as well as emphasizing his pretensions to the

Swedish throne. Or perhaps in this way he wanted to underscore his autonomy from the Republic and give expression to his absolutist tendencies, accusations of which were often cast in his face. In his testament, Zygmunt willed that crown to the Republic—a beautiful gesture testifying to the fact that, at least toward the end of his life, he acknowledged the Republic as his natural kingdom. During his funeral ceremonies it was this very Swedish crown that was used as the crown of exequy, but later, despite the will of the departed king, it was coopted by his sons Władysław and Jan Kazimierz, and returned to the Wawel treasury only years later, following the abdication of the latter. On an old painting by Christian Melich dating from 1633, which shows Zygmunt's body lying in state, we see the Swedish crown on his head. But our attention is also drawn to another detail: just next to it, at the head of the bier, we can see another royal insignia which neither resembles the most important crown of Chrobry, nor the Hungarian crown—the so-called "Muscovite crown." Zygmunt had it made especially for his son Władysław, for the planned coronation of the prince in Moscow as the new Tsar. Some descriptions state, however, that during the funeral of Zygmunt it was just the other way round: that it was the Muscovite crown that was set upon the corpse's brows, while the Swedish crown was placed nearby. But that would be quite strange. Besides, if we study Melich's painting with attention, it would seem that either the painter was mistaken, or the reports that have come down to our times are imprecise, for it is clear that the dead ruler is wearing the Swedish crown, with its characteristic small cross fashioned of gold. The identification of the Muscovite crown here is made more difficult by the fact that its exact iconography has not survived. Without the acquiescence of the Diet, Jan Kazimierz had this crown melted down for coin, which caused a great political scandal at the time. For he was treating the Muscovite insignia as his personal property and making use of it, so unceremoniously, to repair his own private budget. But at the time in Poland, the royal insignia no longer belonged to the rulers; they were neither private nor dynastic property. At least since the times when the Republic had begun to choose her kings by herself, the insignia became her property and could only be disposed of according to her will. For this reason too, the royal treasury on Wawel, where the insignia of the Polish kings were kept, could only be opened by a unique decree of Parliament. Despite this, Jan Kazimierz treated the question of the Muscovite crown as his own private matter, which aroused a universal uproar amongst the nobility. The question dragged on for years, until the very abdication of the king, who, wishing to secure income for his political retirement in France, decided to come to mutually acceptable terms with the Republic and had a copy of the earlier destroyed Muscovite crown created. This was said to have been entirely dissimilar to the original, but in the end, in 1674, it took its place in the crown treasury alongside five other royal crowns of the Republic—the crown of Chrobry, the Hungarian crown, the Swedish crown, and the crown of homage (most likely belonging to Władysław Jagiełło) and the one known as the "queens' crown," which we can inspect today on Marcello Bacciarelli's painting depicting Jadwiga of Anjou. However, the destiny of this duplicate of the Muscovite crown wasn't fortunate, as in 1700 it became a portion of the Republic's pledge set in the hands of the Elector of Brandenburg, Frederick III, on the strength of his agreement with August II Mocny (the Strong) to find itself, at last, in the Hohenzollern treasury in Berlin. The fate of that crown was something of a bad omen for the Republic. When, toward the end of the eighteenth century, on account of the Kościuszko Uprising, the Prussians occupied Kraków and Wawel without much of a struggle, the Prussian king Frederick William II decided to rifle the Republic's coronation insignia. This was to happen on the night of 3 and 4 October 1795, when the locks were broken, the bolts and padlocks burst, after which the five Polish crowns were carted off to Berlin through Wrocław. All of this took place in the greatest secrecy; it was a clandestine action of the Prussian ruler, of which even his own cabinet members were unaware. The later fate of the Polish crowns, which in 1795 were held captive in the treasury of the Hohenzollerns in Berlin next to the copy of the Muscovite crown, was kept in such strict secrecy that, when following the Congress of Vienna, Tsar Alexander I decided to have himself crowned King of Poland and demanded the location of the Polish coronation insignia, the Prussians insisted, stubbornly and with conviction, that they had no idea what had happened to them. An identical situation was repeated in 1829 in connection with the coronation of Nicholas I in Warsaw. Only in the 1830s, after a thorough investigation by the Prussian government, the shocking truth was uncovered. Following the unsuccessful conclusion of his war with Napoléon in 1806, fearing for his own survival, Frederick William III personally ordered the destruction of all the Polish crowns gathered in Berlin. This took place in 1809; his intent was that they should not fall into the hands of the French or the Poles. All of the dispositions touching upon this final, symbolic execution of the Republic were delivered verbally so that no written record of this act of barbarism should remain. On the basis of this verbal order, on 27 July 1811, the previously disassembled royal insignias were melted down in Königsberg into gold and silver coin. The valuable stones and pearls were delivered to the Directorate of Maritime Trade, which was to sell them. For me, this decision of the Prussian king swells to the rank of a significant historical symbol. Frederick William III proved himself to be capable of a barbarian act of symbolic execution of all of us Poles—which can be seen as an early omen of the acts of physical extermination which were to be carried out a hundred and some dozens of years later. At any rate, in the light of this act—the destruction of the six Polish crowns—and from the perspective of the real threat of the final slaughtering of the defeated Republic, the words that Józef Wybicki wrote a few years earlier in Reggio nell'Emilia, and which we repeat at all important functions, that "Poland has not yet perished, as long as we still live," take on, indubitably, a more profound significance.

* * *

Zamoyski did not fulfill his dream; he never set the crown of Chrobry upon his head. He must have been very sensitive on this point, as anyone would be, who by his own efforts and abilities had pulled himself up from a humble position to the very heights of authority and wealth. After all, he had the following legend carved upon his headstone: "Here lies Jan Zamoyski, who suffered much for his fatherland, and even more at the hands of his fatherland."[83] What sort of wrong did he receive at the hands of the Republic, which he so faithfully served as chancellor and hetman? Zygmunt, that beloved "sonny" of Anna Jagiellonka, that mute specter carted to Poland from Sweden, quickly proved himself to be quite a clever and effective politician. He built around himself a strong court party, thanks to which he was able to free himself, by degrees, from the powerful influence of the Chancellor. After all, in 1588, Zamoyski had returned from Byczyna in the aura of a great conqueror, having vanquished Maximilian. His fears upon leaving Kraków, which bordered upon a nervous breakdown, did not come true. Maximilian was not only defeated, he was humiliated, taken captive. And so while the Chancellor did not acquire the crown, he did have in his power an exceptional captive: the brother of the Emperor, whom after the battle he transported to the well-defended Krasnystaw, his own seat, avoiding by a wide arc Kraków in which freshly-crowned Zygmunt was waiting. Can one imagine a greater act of disrespect offered to the young king? After all, Maximilian was the prisoner of the Republic, and in making of him his own prisoner, Zamoyski was declaring, no more and no less, that HE was the Republic. For the next twenty years or so, Zamoyski would continue to shape Polish politics, but fortune turned out to be less than gracious to him. In 1589, at the Diet of Pacification in Warsaw, to which he arrived as the Victor of the Battle of Byczyna—and thus in diametrically different circumstances than in 1587—Zamoyski would yet again seek to influence the system of the state. As if under the influence of the lessons learned from the third, armed election, he submitted for discussion a written project for the fresh establishment of the principles of the universal election of the monarch by the Republic. The free election was to take place at an expedited tempo, according to accepted terms, guaranteeing the continuity of the state institutions during the interregnum period, without influence or bribery on the part of foreign ambassadors, and, most importantly, with the understanding that only a citizen of the Republic as well as people "of Slavic blood and language"[84] might be considered as candidates for the throne. At this time, Zamoyski, just like a large portion of the nobility, were seriously wondering whether or not Zygmunt was secretly negotiating with the Habsburgs, or with his father, the Swedish king Johan, for his return to Stockholm. The fact that a king might abandon his beloved subjects was certainly not unthinkable, given the whole shameful history of Henri Valois. Thus, the reform of elections proposed by Zamoyski gives one the impression of having been cut to his measure, which testifies to the fact that he had not yet thrown his dreams away. However, the suspicions concerning Zygmunt and his eventual abdication, even if they were not devoid of a basis in probability, did not come to be realized, and he was to remain on the Polish throne as most likely the longest-reigning Polish monarch, for he was king for nearly half a century. The project for the reform of the election fell to nothing, and the relations between Zygmunt and the Chancellor grew worse and worse with each passing year. The king valued Zamoyski's position and talents, taking eager advantage of them (when it was in his interest to do so), but he had no intention of tolerating his monarchic pretensions. There can be only one king, whatever Matejko thought to the contrary.

In 1592, during a sitting of parliament, what was inevitable came to a head. Zygmunt, driven to white fury by Zamoyski, was haughtily to declare: "I am the Polish king, and have neither the desire nor the ability to share the royal power with anyone." Reflexively, the Chancellor parried: "You are a king elected by the Poles, not a tyrant." At that, Zygmunt lost control of himself entirely. He leapt from his seat, crying "I have no intention of bearing the insolence of that man any further," after which he left the senate chamber.[85] This open conflict eventually led to a proper recalibration of the balance. The Chancellor was made to apologize to the king, which settled the tense situation. The Chancellor continued to play a gigantic role in the Republic until his death in 1605, but in more or less open opposition to the court. In the end, he did not obtain the crown of Chrobry, he did not become the king of the Republic, yet, in a certain sense, he recompensed that failure in his own unique way, founding a state within a state with its capital in Zamość, fortified in the style of the *mura veneziane* of Padua. This was the Zamoyski entail: indivisible and hereditary, a law unto itself without regard to the Republic, and founded upon its own statute. And this very state, the Zamoyski entail, survived the Republic, as a matter of fact, by one hundred and fifty years.

I'd like to bring the story of the Black Chancellor to an end by returning to a certain late evening in 1603, which the inhabitants of Warsaw were to recall with unfeigned emotion for long years. A harsh winter was coming to an end, and the first thaws were on the way. The windows of one of the palace halls on the high embankment above the Wisła in Warsaw were lit up with candles, despite the late hour. In his satin dressing gown with fur collar, King Zygmunt was sitting at his beloved clavichord, abandoning himself to music. He had just finished playing a work that he had composed for his own pleasure. Music, and the construction of watches, were his two great passions. The final chords of the work resounded, echoing from the palace walls, until they completely died out. Zygmunt sat on, unmoving, in the flickering glare of the candles, absent, pale, with eyes closed—just like in the painting by Matejko. He didn't even lift his hands from the keyboard, as if he were still contemplating in his head the music that had so recently resounded in the room. Round about a complete silence reigned when, suddenly, unexpectedly, a powerful boom was heard as if the sky had been split, the earth shaken; it was a gigantic sound, which struck the city on the embankment with all its might, and then moved on like a wave through the whole river valley sunken in darkness before dying out in the nearby woods. This was the sound of twenty-two spans of oaken balks and Hungarian iron of the Warsaw bridge, which thirty years earlier, Zygmunt August had built, bursting under the pressure of ice floes—gone was the bridge uniting the two shores in one Republican unity.

Endnotes

1. Philoteus of Pskov, "Filofei's Epistle to Grand Prince Vasili III" (1515-1521), in *Medieval Russia: A Source Book, 850-1700*, ed. B. Dmytryshyn, Fort Worth, TX 1991, pp. 259–261.
2. See J.-F. Noël, *Le Saint-Empire*, Paris 1976.
3. R. Radłowska, "To było lustro. 25-lecie wystawy 'Polaków portret własny'" (That Was a Mirror. The 25th Anniversary of the Exhibition "The Poles: a Self-Portrait"). *Tygodnik Krakowski*, 22 October 2004, https://krakow.wyborcza.pl/krakow/1,42699,2351505.html (accessed 11.12.2019).
4. *Kronika Marcina Bielskiego* (The Chronicle of Marcin Bielski), Vol. 3, ed. K.J. Turowski, Sanok 1856, p. 1544.
5. An insult hurled by Bartosz Paprocki, also inimical toward Zamoyski. See W. Sobieski, "Żałobny hetman" (The Mournful Hetman) in his *Trybun ludu szlacheckiego. Pisma historyczne* (Tribune of the Noble Folk. Historical Writings), ed. S. Grzybowski, Warsaw 1978, p. 293.
6. Citation from S. Leśniewski, *Jan Zamoyski. Hetman i polityk* (Jan Zamoyski, Hetman and Politician), Warsaw 2008, p. 95.
7. *Relacye nuncyuszów apostolskich i innych osób o Polsce od roku 1548 do 1690* (Relations of the Apostolic Nuncios and Other Persons Concerning Poland from the Year 1548 to 1690), ed. E. Rykaczewski, Berlin 1864, vol. 1, p. 464.
8. For the Zborowski family, see Rymkiewicz, *Samuel Zborowski*, Warsaw 2010, pp. 15–24.
9. See W. Sobieski, "'Si non jurabis, non regnabis.' The Quarrel of the Royal Oath" in his *Trybun*..., op. cit., pp. 251–277.
10. Rymkiewicz, op. cit., p. 209.

11. J. Słowacki, *Samuel Zborowski*, in *Dzieła* (Works), red. M. Kridl, L. Piwiński, Warsaw 1930, Vol. 16, p. 278. See Rymkiewicz, op.cit., pp. 134–143.

12. Rymkiewicz, op. cit., p. 262.

13. Ibid., p. 260.

14. Ibid., p. 262.

15. Cited in W. Sobieski, *Żałobny...*, op. cit., p. 288.

16. In Latin: *Universa universis patavina libertas.*

17. Cited by S. Kot, *Polska złotego wieku a Europa* (Golden-Age Poland and Europe), Warsaw 1987, p. 310.

18. See S. Windakiewicz, *Padwa. Studium z dziejów cywilizacji polskiej* (Padua. A Study from the History of Polish Civilisation), Kraków 1891, cited by S. Grzybowski, *Jan Zamoyski*, Warsaw 1994, p. 19.

19. See J. Szujski, *Odrodzenie i reformacja w Polsce* (The Renaissance and Reformation in Poland), Sandomierz 2017, p. 19.

20. See Virgil, *Aeneid*, trans. R. Fitzgerald, New York 1983, Book I, lines 335–337.

21. See J. Kochanowski, *Dismissal of the Grecian Envoys*, trans. C.S. Kraszewski, Studio City, CA 1994.

22. See Livy, *The Early History of Rome*, Books I-V of *The History of Rome from its Foundation*, trans. A. de Sélincourt, Edinburgh 1960, Book I, p. 19.

23. F. Buonaccorsi, *Vita et mores Gregorii Sanocei*, ed. I. Lichońska, Varsovia 1963, chapter XVIII.

24. S. Orzechowski, *Rozmowa alby dyjalog około egzekucyjej polskiej korony* (A Conversation, or a Dialogue Concerning the Execution of the Polish Crown), ed. J. Łoś, S. Kot, Kraków 1919, p. 132: "Venice is a city that in its way of approaching all things is deserving of praise."

25. P. Skarga, *Kazania sejmowe* (Sermons at the Diet), ed. J. Tazbir, Kraków 1972, p. 132. Cited in S. Kot, op. cit., p. 314. *Translator's note*: in the original Polish: *Na Wenecję nie potrzeba patrzeć!*

26. "Zdanie sprawy JW. Pietro Duodo przed senatem weneckim za powrotem jego z poselstwa od Najjaśniejszego Króla JMci Polskiego w roku 1592" (The Report of His Excellency Pietro Duodo Before the Venetian Senate, Following his Return from his Embassy to HRH the King of Poland in the Year 1592) in J.U. Niemcewicz, *Zbiór pamiętników historycznych o dawnej Polszcze* (A Collection of Historical Memoirs of Ancient Poland), Leipzig 1830, Vol. IV, p. 69.

27. C. Backvis, *Comment les Polonais du XVI-e siecle voyaient l'Italie et les Italiens*, "L'Annuaire de l'Institut de Philologie et d'Histoire Orientales et Slaves" (Bruxelles), t. XV, 1960, pp. 195–288.

28. On Zamoyski's thesis, see M. Kuryłowicz, *Rozprawa Jana Zamoyskiego o senacie rzymskim* (Jan Zamoyski's Thesis on the Roman Senate), Lublin 1997.

29. S. Kot, op. cit., p. 312.

30. S. Grzybowski, *Jan Zamoyski*, op. cit., p. 23.

31. Ibid., p. 20.

32. F. Meinecke, *Die Idee der Staatsräson in der neueren Geschichte* (The Idea of State Interest in Modern History), Munich 1924.

33. H. Kissinger, *Diplomacy,* New York 1994, p. 59.

34. See S. Grzybowski, *Jan Zamoyski*, op. cit., pp. 41–42.

35. J. Bielski, *Dalszy ciąg Koniki Polskiej zawierającej dzieje od 1587 do 1598 roku* (Continuation of the Polish Chronicle from the Year 1587 to 1598), ed. F.M. Sobieszczański, Warsaw 1851, p. 25.

36. See W. Sobieski, *Żałobny...*, op.cit., p. 297.

37. E. Kantorowicz, *The King's Two Bodies: A Study in Mediaeval Political Theology*, Princeton 1957.

38. L. Stomma, *Wzloty i upadki królów Francji. Sposobem antropologicznym wyłożone* (The Ascents and Falls of the Kings of France. Arranged in Anthropological Fashion), Warsaw 1991, p. 77.

39. "Diariusz sejmowy z 1592 r." (Journal of the Diet from the Year 1592) in E. Barwiński, ed., *Diariusza i akta sejmowe r. 1591–1592* (Journals and Acts of the Diet for the Year 1591–1592), Kraków 1911, p. 208.

40. See E. Kantorowicz, op. cit., p. 400.

41. *Kronika Jana z Czarnkowa* (The Chronicle of Jan of Czarnków), trans. J. Zerbiłło, Kraków 2001, chapter 4, pp. 23–26.

42. J. Tazbir, *Myśl polska w nowożytnej kulturze europejskiej* (Polish Thought in the Context of Modern European Culture), Warsaw 1986, p. 76.

43. Cited by J. Orzeł: "Mityczni przodkowie—kim właściwie byli Sarmaci?" (Mythical Forebears—Who Really Were the Sarmatians?) *Pasaż wiedzy Muzeum Pałacu Króla Jana III w Wilanowie* (The Passage of Knowledge in the Palace of King Jan III in Wilanów), 23 April 2015, https://www.wilanow-palac.pl/mityczni_przodkowie_kim_wlasciwie_byli_sarmaci.html (accessed 14 December 2019).

44. Cited by W. Konopczyński, *Dzieje Polski nowożytnej* (The History of Modern Poland), Warsaw 1986, Vol. II, p. 20.

45. Cited by S. Łempicki, *Działalność Jana Zamoyskiego na polu szkolnictwa 1573–1605* (Jan Zamoyski's Activities in the Field of Education, 1573–1605), Kraków 1921, p. 259.

46. See S. Grzybowski, *Jan Zamoyski*, op. cit., p. 254.

47. See R. Abel, *The Gutenberg Revolution*, London 2012.

48. See S. Łempicki, op.cit., pp. 19–20.

49. Ibid., pp. 149–163. See also S. Grzybowski, *Dzieje Polski i Litwy (1506–1648)* (The History of Poland and Lithuania [1506–1648]), Kraków 1921, p. 259.

50. S. Grzybowski, *Henryk Walezy* (Henri Valois), Wrocław 1985, p. 128.

51. *Kronika Marcina Bielskiego* (The Chronicle of Marcin Bielski), op. cit., Vol. 3, p. 1371.

52. Cited in A. Malecki's introduction to his *Wybór mów staropolskich świeckich sejmowych i innych* (Selection of Old Polish Secular Speeches, Given in Parliament and Elsewhere), Kraków 1860, p. x.

53. Ibid., p. 72.

54. Ibid.

55. Ibid., p. 73.

56. Ibid.

57. Ibid., p. 49.

58. Ibid., p. 50.

59. Ibid., pp. 53–55.

60. Ibid., p. 55.

61. Ibid., p. 54.

62. Ibid., pp. 56–57.

63. Ibid., p. 61.

64. Ibid.

65. Ibid., p. 62.

66. Ibid., p. 57.

67. Ibid., pp. 75–77.

68. Ibid., p. 69.

69. S. Cat-Mackiewicz, *Klucz do Piłsudskiego* (A Key to Piłsudski), Kraków 2013, p. 228.

70. *Wybór mów staropolskich...*, op. cit., p. 57.

71. "Zdanie sprawy JW. Pietro Duodo...," op. cit., pp. 68–70.

72. J. Kochanowski, "Na most warszawski" (On the Warsaw Bridge), *Dzieła polskie* (Polish Works), ed. J. Lorentowicz, Warsaw 1919, p. 301.

73. Cited by B. Orłowski, *Nie tylko szablą i piórem* (Not Only By Sabre and Pen), Warsaw 1985, pp. 77–78.

74. Cited by S. Grzybowski, *Jan Zamoyski,* op.cit., p. 255.

75. J. Bielski, *Dalszy ciąg Kroniki...* (The Chronicles Continued...), op. cit., p. 11.

76. *Listy Annibala z Kapui, arcy-biskupa neapolitańskiego, nuncyusza w Polsce, o bezkrólewiu po Stefanie Batorym i pierwszych latach panowania Zygmunta IIIgo, do wyjścia arcy-xięcia Maxymiliana z niewoli* (The Letters of Annibale di Capua, Archbishop of Naples, Nuncio in Poland, Concerning the Interregnum Following the Death of Stefan Batory, and the First Years of the Reign of Zygmunt III, to the Liberation of the Archduke Maximilian from Captivity), ed. A. Przezdziecki, Warszawa 1852, p. 57.

77. J. Bielski, *Dalszy ciąg Kroniki...*, op. cit., p. 78.

78. S. Grzybowski, *Jan Zamoyski*, op. cit., p. 211.

79. *Diariusze sejmu koronacyjnego Zygmunta III Wazy 1587/1588 roku* (Diaries of the Coronation Diet of Zygmunt III Vasa, 1587/1588), ed. I. Kaniewska, Kraków 2016.

80. S. Grzybowski, *Jan Zamoyski*, op. cit., p. 213.

81. W. Sobieski, *Żałobny...*, op. cit., p. 303.

82. Gallus Anonymus, *Chronica et gesta ducum et principum Polonorum. Chronicles and Deeds of the Dukes and Princes of the Poles,* trans. P.W. Knoll, F. Schaer, Budapest 2003, Book I, 6, pp. 36–37.

83. A. Śliwiński, *Jan Zamoyski. Kanclerz i hetman wielki koronny* (Jan Zamoyski. Chancellor and Grand Crown Hetman), Warsaw 1947, p. 407.

84. S. Grzybowski, *Jan Zamoyski*, op. cit., pp. 223–225.

85. Ibid., p. 241.

SMOLENSK—A LAND ACCURSED

For many years I was afraid of the East, and it was a conscious choice never to wish to travel there. When I reached adulthood, I told myself that I would never go off in that direction. If I wanted to go anywhere, it was to the South, and when necessity demanded, then West. The East, on the other hand, remained for me something of a taboo, an exceptionally horrid story, which I preferred not to read. The foundational, historical significance of the South, of the Latin Mediterranean, to the Poles inhabiting the North was something obvious to me, requiring no explanation. But what of the East? I wouldn't want to give the mistaken impression that it doesn't count at all. The question of what the East is for Poles and for Polish identity—is an absolutely existential question, in the literal sense of the word. For us, as a nation, the Polish experience of the East is uncommonly important, and cannot be understood without reference to certain key events in history, on which I'd like to concentrate now. Without them we shall not grasp what the East is for Poland, or why the South became a counterbalance to it.

When this matter is broached, we often hear no more than the banal clichés so well known to us. Poland is spoken of as being situated between East and West or as a bridge between them; eventually, it might be called the *antemurale* of the West. The only goal of these sad little stereotypes seems to be to keep us from penetrating deeper into matters which are unutterably complicated, for delving into them might only destroy our sweet peace and the certainty that we know ourselves fairly well. What then is the East, for us? Something terribly important, for—to run the risk of oversimplifying things—at a certain moment in our history, it completely seduced us, probably because of its limitless spaces, only to destroy us later. It is in this, exactly, that the Polish experience of the East is contained: seductive power and horrid death. So we must come to know on what that great promise, that seduction, was based, and why it developed into a mortal trap.

From the very dawn of the Polish state, the East was, above all, a choice never made, a great geopolitical option which we cast aside, again, perhaps completely consciously. Parnicki's novel *Srebrne Orły* (Silver Eagles) speaks, to a great extent, of this very unrealized possibility: Byzantium instead of Rome. In the framework of this alternative, the East is, quite simply, the antithesis of Rome and the Latin world, and we, from our very first steps along our historical path, did not take advantage of this alternative option, but rather created our own paradoxical—incomprehensible for many, at times simply held in contempt—identity as the Latinized Slavs of the North. What is more, we confirmed this peculiar choice and in this way defined our permanent place in Europe, which we subsequently never abandoned.

Later, however, the East showed us its very threatening countenance. A certain ambivalence could continue for a while, a reciprocal permeation of the Piast state with the principalities of Rus existing in the East. For us these formed something of a geopolitical buffer. In his *Czerwone tarcze* (Red Shields) Iwaszkiewicz perfectly describes this on the basis of the concessions and interests of Kazimierz Sprawiedliwy (the Just) in Rus—something completely incomprehensible to his elder brother, that Hamletizing occidentalist, Henryk Sandomierski. However, at the turn of the thirteenth century that buffer broke down. The entire area of the princedoms of Rus was flooded by Mongols, barbarians of the steppe. This was a drama of tragic significance for the region. Perhaps then, for the first time in our experience, the East uncovered its gigantic, catastrophic nature to us, as a bloody shambles bringing horrid and violent death, a conflagration which we were entirely unable to restrain. The tortured head of poor Prince Henryk Pobożny (the Pious), separated from his body and spitted, with goggling eyes and extended tongue, on the point of a triumphant Tatar spear following the battle of Legnica, became for us the first, serious warning. If only we had heeded it! For from the East there came to us nothing but great forces which we were not to be capable of taming.

However, after a certain time, the situation improved. After the battle of Kulikovo, the Grand Duchy of Moscow got the upper hand of the Golden Horde, and thanks to our union with the Grand Duchy of Lithuania, the Republic garnered access to the wide-spreading terrain of the East to the Sea of Azov. Thanks to this new area, in the sixteenth and seventeenth centuries, the great masses of the lesser nobility—from Mazovia, Podlasie, and other places—set out for the East, for the Dnieper, for the Don, all the way to Crimea as if to a promised land. Some of them were setting out for adventure, others were eager for warring, and still others counted on new lands to bring under cultivation. The East became for us a thing of great promise—and it was then that we were seduced and disappointed. We thought to transform the East, while the East transformed us—but into what? With complete justice, in his *Samuel Zborowski* Rymkiewicz calls this Eastward orientation of the Poles a fatal decision, an evil direction to head in.[1] For it lured our attention away from Western Europe. However, at the time in question, things looked entirely different. The East gave the Poles a huge area upon which they could develop. It allowed them to settle broad terrains, building their homesteads and manors, erecting churches, founding monasteries and schools, building fortresses and implanting garrisons. The power of this civilizational impetus was truly amazing. Because even then, when the commonwealth of the Poles and Lithuanians, the First Republic, was defeated by the Russian Empire, with Catherine II committing the criminal catastrophe of the Partitions of Poland, which disappeared from the political map of Europe, that Polish style of life continued all the same to exist on the banks of the Dnieper and the Don, in Kyiv and Smolensk—enclosed in the capsules of the manors of magnates, in their libraries, their painting galleries, their porcelain services, their gardens, and their stables. It was, as someone once so beautifully put it, a beautiful flower which continued to bloom though deprived of root and stem: the Polish *Kresy* (Eastern Marches) without Poland.[2]

This idyllic Polish world of the Kresy came to a definitive end only with the First World War and the subsequent Bolshevik Revolution. Then the East showed us the historical end of Polish vitality, which as far as a sense of identity is concerned, weakened us mightily and deprived us of our self-confidence. And later—quite simply, it decided to kill us. Or at least reveal to our eyes just such an eventuality: the near possibility of our final extinction, as if it wanted to say through this: "you reckon that you're able to work me over into your image and likeness, but you are too weak; it didn't work; now I have total power over you and, if only I wish, I might slaughter you all with a shot to the back of the head in some forest near Smolensk; I can arrange a fine shambles for you in Katyń." I reckon that it was just there in Katyń that Poland and the East finally and forever parted ways. It was there that something irrevocable happened; something was overcome, split, crumbled into dust, and we bade a final farewell to our Eastern soul—to the hope it gave us, the panache—but also to the catastrophe that had fallen upon us thence.

From then on there was nothing left of the Polish East. There existed only the Soviet Union, *Realpolitik*, and the stupid, degrading ideology of Communism. The Polish experience of the East was transformed entirely into the sentimental recollections of a childhood spent in the Eastern Marches now lost for all time. In my mind I constantly have that characteristic perspective from the streets of Warsaw in the late PRL period: coming from Nowy Świat, from Złota, Wspólna—the hunched, pale figure of Tadeusz Konwicki, in oversized shoes and greatcoat, with his fists stuffed deep into his pockets, striding along the street with giant steps as he hurries as fast as he can to his café table at Czytelnik to have his cup. It always looked as if he were running away from someone. In the film *Dolina Issy* (The Issa Valley), in novels and screenplays, including *Matka Joanna od Aniołów* (Mother Joanna of the Angels), which I mention here not coincidentally, Konwicki strove to preserve the phantom of the Polish eastern borderlands (*Kresy*), which had been a real part of his childhood and youth. But he himself looked like a zombie from that Poland of the Eastern Marches, which had long vanished into oblivion. I felt that this very image of Konwicki on the streets of the PRL Warsaw would remain in me, forever, a symbol of the definitive end of the Polish experience of the East. Unfortunately, it turned out otherwise, and today, I have not a melancholic-nostalgic vision but one entirely different. That is the image of the horrible, nonsensical slaughter in a Smolensk wood in 2010.

Mother Joanna

One of the most fascinating literary treatments of the Polish experience of the East is, in my opinion, the masterpiece of narration by Jarosław Iwaszkiewicz titled *Matka Joanna od Aniołów* (Mother Joanna of the Angels), so rich in hidden meanings and symbols, and simultaneously touching upon the essence of the matter. This mysterious text contains within it certain content masked by the author. It is also a very interesting game played out with the historical facts dealing with the distant *Kresy*, the Eastern Marches of the Republic.

The work was written in 1943, and thus during the German occupation, but published by the author only in 1946. It is not entirely clear what went on with the manuscript in the meantime; above all it is unknown what sort of influence on its final shape might have been exerted by Ferdynand Goetel's visit of a few days in 1944 to Stawisko, amidst the glow sent up by Warsaw aflame, burning low. Was it the conversations that Iwaszkiewicz had with his guest that brought him to discover the basic sense of the story he'd written earlier? Or did they perhaps merely confirm the intuitions contained in the text? Was he terrified thereby? Did they cause him to hold back on his plans of publication? We know that the final manuscript version preserved in Stawisko is dated 23 March 1944. The story became well known much later, in 1961, thanks to its filming by Jerzy Kawalerowicz, who, along with Tadeusz Konwicki, composed a screenplay on the basis of *Mother Joanna of the Angels*. Perhaps the fact that both of these men, like the author of the story, were born in the Polish eastern borderlands has some significance. It was not a bad film, but from the get-go it became entangled in the ideological quarrel. The PRL critics wrote of it with approval, as an important work uncovering to our eyes the historical circumstances of the peasant's fight for freedom from corvée, the feudal lord, and the clergy. The picture fit the universal imagination of the seventeenth century as a time of the greatest darkness, lawlessness of the ruling classes, and obscurantism of the nobility. Kawalerowicz, already tightly entangled in the ideology of Marxist materialism, explained clumsily and not too convincingly or wisely, that the film was about, above all, the love of a man and a woman, only that they're wearing habits.[3] The Catholic Church, and primate Wyszyński himself, recognized—not without taking into consideration the strained relations at the time between the government of the Polish Communist state and the Church hierarchy and faithful—that the picture was in service to Communist propaganda, anti-clerical, and thus appealed to the faithful to boycott it.

Iwaszkiewicz's story about Mother Joanna presents a dark history of possessed Ursuline nuns in the monastery of Ludyń, located by the author in the distant Eastern Marches of the Republic, near Smolensk, and the unsuccessful attempts at exorcising the same by the Jesuit exorcist Suryn, from Wilno (Vilnius), whose efforts were to end tragically for him. It is also obvious that the basis for this fictional account were some historical events from the seventeenth century which took place in Loudun, a little town in the Poitou-Charentes region, in west-central France. A case of collective satanic possession took place in the Ursuline convent there, seemingly on account of spells cast upon it by a young rector named Urban Grandier. These happenings echoed far and wide throughout France. For Grandier was condemned to be burnt at the stake—which sentence was carried out, although, most likely, black magic and spells weren't behind his death, but rather a conflict between the priest and the royal court. The story of the collective possession at Loudun was mysterious and infamous enough so that later on, the case fascinated many physicians, psychiatrists, and historians, as well as writers. It was the inspiration, among others, for Aldous Huxley's *Devils of Loudun* (1952), a novel in which he presents the story in detail; the play *The Devils* by John Whiting (1960) was also based on it. Krzysztof Penderecki made use of both these texts for his opera *Diabły z Loudun* (The Devils of Loudun), which was performed for the first time in Hamburg in 1969. Ken Russell's film *The Devils* (1971) was also inspired by the works of Huxley and Whiting. As can be seen, the history of the possessions in Loudun had a strong artistic motive power. Iwaszkiewicz had taken note of it earlier, but the fact of his being first in his story of Mother Joanna is not what interests us. Rather, it is how the writer linked the problem of evil and possession with the Polish experience of the East, consistently dressing everything in well-defined historical costume.

Iwaszkiewicz interweaves some important historical information into the very first sentence of his story. We learn that the Ludyń nunnery of Ursulines, the one that would later be taken over by demons, was founded in 1611 by the wife of Zygmunt III Waza (Vasa), Queen Konstancja Habsburżanka (Constance of Austria). This seemingly trivial information cannot be overlooked, as, truly, 1611, and the year preceding it as well, was a completely unique time for both the Republic and the state of Muscovy. I believe that this also may have had some key significance for Iwaszkiewicz's story. For it was a time of great events, which are very tightly bound to the Smolensk land and thus with the location described in *Mother Joanna of the Angels*.

July 1610 was a turning point in the Polish-Russian war, which had been going on for more than a year. Crown Field Hetman Stanisław Żółkiewski completely shattered the Russian army of Prince Dmitri Shuyski at the battle of Klushino, a village located some 250 kilometers beyond Smolensk, which Zygmunt III Waza had been besieging unsuccessfully since September 1609. On account of this victory, not only the Russian army began to disintegrate. The power of Dmitri's elder brother, Tsar Vasili Shuyski, also began to crumble, and, along with his family, he was to be imprisoned in Moscow by the boyars, who were now inclined to transfer government over Russia into the hands of the young Polish prince Władysław. After a quick march, Żółkiewski approached the no longer distant walls of Moscow, and after a few weeks of negotiation, entered the city. According to the agreement, Władysław, aged fifteen, was to ascend the throne of Muscovy as the new Tsar—but only after he guaranteed the preservation of the Orthodox faith in Russia. The Shuyskis found themselves in the power of Żółkiewski in the character of prisoners of war, and a Polish garrison was established in the Kremlin under the command of Aleksander Korwin Gosiewski, later the voivode of Smolensk. However, despite the taking of Moscow, the war went on. Smolensk held out until June 1611. The fortress walls, erected under Godunov, were six meters thick and nineteen meters tall; they resisted the Poles for nearly two years. The taking of the fortress and the city brought the military campaign of Zygmunt III to a conclusion, which allowed the recognition of the main aims of the war as having been attained. Above all, the Smolensk land was recouped for the Republic, after having been lost in 1514, whereas in Moscow (as it seemed) some promising ground had been broken for a personal dynastic union linking Poland and Russia.

Many historians have shown that the war with Moscow, officially begun by Zygmunt III in 1609, was dissimilar to all others waged against the Russian Tsars by Zygmunt Stary (the Old) or Stefan Batory. Indeed, this war was something completely different. Earlier, it had been about conquest: the Courland, the Vitebsk and Smolensk lands, the Ukraine; wars aimed at gaining a better strategic position in the face of the growing strength of Poland's neighbor to the east; wars aimed at securing the eastern flank of the Republic. This time, the stakes were Moscow and Russia. It was the culminating moment of an extraordinary Polish experience of the East, when Poles believed that they might, at last, change the East. There was no single program, no common idea, no plan for any one great task. There was a lot of chaos, conflicting interests, colliding forces and personalities. The king and his camarilla saw things one way; Żółkiewski another, and the magnates from the eastern lands: the Potockis, the Wiśniowieckis, the Sapiehas, the Ostrogskis, still another. The great majority of the lesser nobility were skeptically oriented to these far-reaching intentions. Despite the fact that the nobles were generally realists, especially as far as foreign affairs were concerned, in moments of sudden, short-lived triumph, it was rather easy to enflame their enthusiasm. The recouping of Smolensk and the settling of Prince Władysław on the Tsarist throne could indeed look like a moment of great triumph for the Republic, for she had not only succeeded in winning a victory over her enemy but also in bringing about a situation in which there was a chance for the final transformation of the East in a Polish manner. However—and this was no good harbinger for the whole politically and culturally farsighted idea—the Moscow campaign of Zygmunt III was preceded by the rather shameful and loud international row elicited by, among others, the Wiśniowieckis, the Mniszechs and the False Dmitri.

In 1611 it could still seem that the great wheel of geopolitical fortune was turning the Republic's way. On 29 October, Warsaw prepared a triumphal greeting for Żółkiewski such as no Polish military leader ever experienced before or after: a triumphal entry into the city organized according to the ancient Roman pattern. With this in mind, the place at which the Krakowskie Przedmieście enters the Plac Zamkowy—there, where today the Column of Zygmunt stands, a triumphal arch was erected especially for the occasion. Żółkiewski rode down the Krakowskie Przedmieście to the castle in a true victory parade, as various accounts relate: "riding in a sumptuous chariot drawn by six white Turkish horses [...] before him, in rich garments, colonels and captains of cavalry, while behind him came the royal carriage with Tsar Vasili Shuyski and two of his younger brothers. The queen and other ladies looked down upon the celebratory parade from the windows of the palace, while great crowds of people pressed in from all sides, raising great cries of joy."[4] Different descriptions, indeed, relate the numerous crowds present for this occasion, so one may well give credit to the accounts speaking of the gigantic swarm of people descending on Krakowskie Przedmieście and the common euphoria accompanying the triumphal entry of Żółkiewski into Warsaw. The mood of those gathered must certainly have been extraordinary and vehement, since—as we read in another description—"Vasili Shuyski, the Tsar of Russia," riding behind Żółkiewski in an open leather royal carriage, "dressed in a garment of white cloth of gold and a tall fur cap (*szłyk*), gazed out with his gloomy, savage eyes upon the great concourse of people in the street." It seems to me that the gloomy stare of the Tsar being carted down Krakowskie Przedmieście must have been prompted by the fear aroused at the sight of those crowds.

From the time when he was imprisoned by the boyars in Moscow and delivered into Żółkiewski's hands, a whole year and more had passed. And so, he had had more than enough time to think over what had just happened: his catastrophic fall from the throne—his entire sad situation. Riding down Krakowskie Przedmieście, he gazed out upon the crowd gloomily and savagely, for he wasn't quite certain what would be his fate as the moments ticked away. Prisoners of war were treated cruelly, savagely, in his country, so he might well suspect that he would be treated in a similar manner now—torn apart by the crowd or publicly humiliated and executed. This seemed quite probable, considering memories of how, just a few years earlier, the Poles who had arrived in Moscow along with the False Dmitri were treacherously murdered at the Kremlin, with only the smallest number escaping the butchery.

As some eyewitness accounts report, a whole sixty carriages passed down Krakowskie Przedmieście on that historical day. They were carrying not only the victorious hetman and the defeated Szuyskis. There was also Mikhail Shein, who had defended Smolensk for two years from the Polish siege, as well as Patriarch Filaret, the father of the first Romanov to ascend the tsarist throne. When the column arrived at Palace Square, the first through the triumphal arch was the conquering hero, the hetman, and after him, the officers under his command. Only then did Vasili pass through, escorted by Polish dragoons and led thereafter into the Senate chamber of the palace, where king and senators were awaiting him. Zygmunt was expecting the prisoner, surrounded by his closest advisors, sitting on the throne in his coronation robes. Vasili, along with his younger brothers Dmitri and Prince Ivan, had to prostrate themselves before the king in tribute, in the presence of all assembled: "Bowing his head deeply before HRH, he touched the floor with his right hand and then kissed it. The tsar's brother, the hetman [Dmitri], struck the floor with his very forehead, while the third brother, the youngest

(Ivan) struck his brow thrice, and wept." The most important Russian standards taken in the battle were also lain at the king's feet. Then Żółkiewski delivered a speech before the king in which he stated that "it is a beautiful thing, Your Royal Highness, to defeat one's enemy; it is an even more beautiful thing—to show mercy to the defeated." Feliks Kryski spoke as well—that great supporter and propagator of the Russian expedition; a man who, most probably, thought up and organized Żółkiewski's Warsaw triumph as well as the prostration of the tsar at the palace, as an essential political spectacle. In his speech, he praised the moment of the Republic's great triumph over the tsar. As one of the witnesses noted, the scene in the senate hall was "a strange spectacle, wonderfully exciting one's pity as well." I reckon that it aroused wonder not only because it made all present strongly aware of the various meanderings of fate in the Polish-Russian wars, which had been going on for so long, but also for this reason that all those gathered at the celebrations at the palace—at least a portion of them—knew perfectly well the great differences and tensions that had driven a wedge between Zygmunt III and Żółkiewski in the matter of the conquest of Moscow. Żółkiewski believed that the war was a mistake, that it diverted the Republic from the real threat of Turkey. And after he negotiated in Moscow with the boyars their agreement for the Polish-Russian personal union and the Russian crown for Prince Władysław, the rug was simply pulled out from under him by Zygmunt. For the king imprisoned the boyars and declared that he himself was to become the Tsar of Russia. Żółkiewski's memoirs are full of bitterness and rancor toward the king, which was held in check only by the exceptional loyalty of the hetman to the Crown.[5] This rancor was rather widespread amongst the nobility, who suspected from the very start of the Moscow campaign that the king wished, with Polish blood, to arrange his own—Swedish and dynastic—matters.

At the Very Edge of the Latin World

We first needed to remind ourselves of all these happenings in order to approach, at last, Iwaszkiewicz's story and understand the historical issues it touches. The author himself invites us to consider them, as in the first few lines he reminds us of Queen Konstancja, the foundress of the Ludyń nunnery, who in 1611, along with other women of the court, watched from the palace windows in Warsaw Żółkiewski's triumphal procession leading Tsar Vasili Shuyski. It is proper to begin with these events because, as I see it, without recalling them we cannot fully understand the sense of the strange possession of the Ursulines in the Ludyń cloister, which, in Iwaszkiewicz's story, took place a few dozen years later, in the second half of the seventeenth century. I wish to say by this that the possession of Mother Joanna of the Angels, the daughter of one of the influential princely houses of Smolensk, along with the rest of the nuns (who were also maidens born of rich Smolensk families), as well as the stubborn activities of the devils in the Ludyń cloister, are facts that in a certain way link up with what was taking place at the start of the seventeenth century.

Usually, interpretations of the story pass over this historical question and relate the whole problem of possession, devils, and evil to, for example, the author's experiences of the occupation lasting from 1939 until 1945, during which Iwaszkiewicz wrote the story, or to his wife's mental illness. It is true that in Iwaszkiewicz's memoirs and correspondence with various persons one can find fitting testimony to these theories. However, it seems to me that, for the author, a question no less important than possession and evil demons entering into human beings is that concerning the place in which these things were happening, namely: in the East, and precisely in this specific historical region. In this way, the possessions in *Mother Joanna of the Angels,* the location of the root of the evil, and the East, to speak more precisely: the Polish experience of the East, were consciously linked by the author. Iwaszkiewicz was not merely writing the next version of events taking place in seventeenth century Loudun, a typical little town in France, in which—one may assume—on account of its prosaic life, there is no great evil to be looked for. Instead, he transferred the story into the late years of the seventeenth century and to the Eastern Marches (*Kresy*) of the Republic, somewhere on the very edge of the Latin world and, concretely, on the border dividing two worlds, two different kingdoms—the Smolensk region. The writer recognized, quite properly, that the influence of evil would be quite potent here, and human beings would experience it most strongly. In his notes we can find such a comment: "elements of Russianness—there are many elements of the East, Buddhism, Lamaism, the religion of Siva—which penetrated to us to a weak degree without influencing our life. For this reason our life—even our religious life—was always surface-oriented and nervous, and thus I had to locate Mother Joanna near Smolensk, because if I placed her in Częstochowa, the story wouldn't get off the ground"[6] (11 September 68). And so, only on the border between two kingdoms, two worlds, the question of the struggle of good and evil—in other words, the most important problem both from the point of view of human life and from the perspective of human history—may come into its clearest focus.

All right then, but why not—let's say—near Kyiv or even further, in the Chernihiv Region, or—even better—past the Dnieper, in Poltava? Why exactly near Smolensk? Perhaps the Ursulines in Ludyń were used, quite simply, to figure forth one of the regions of true Catholic presence located as far to the east as possible? A place where Latin was used in the liturgy of the Christian faith, in other words, that which vaccinated us against those Buddhisms, Lamaisms and Sivas beckoning from the East ("Ludyń, after all, lay to the side, far from all highways, amidst forests and muddy roads; there weren't all that many Catholic families in the area"[7]—as we read in the story). The farthest of such points, though, was probably Smolensk.

A reading of the story reveals that Iwaszkiewicz set his Ludyń somewhere between Polotsk and Smolensk, but decidedly before Smolensk, since Stefan Batory was to station his forces in Ludyń during his military campaign, most likely in 1580, when he withdrew from his intention of attacking Smolensk and turned instead to Velikiye Luki. Smolensk, Smolensk, and once again Smolensk... For some reason it is very important to Iwaszkiewicz that the history of the satanic possession take place precisely in the lands around Smolensk, and nowhere else in the Eastern Marches. This matter is constantly underscored in the story. At each step on the way we read about the land around Smolensk: wasteland, empty, accursed—the Smolensk mire, the Smolensk woods. Even in the fragment describing the self-flagellation of Fr. Suryn there appears the note of blood on the "Smolensk canvas."[8] Why Smolensk? Iwaszkiewicz so desires to interweave his story with the Smolensk region representing the Eastern Marches of the Republic, the Kresy, that he is even prepared to play fast and loose with historical facts. The events described by him took place, supposedly, in the Smolensk voivodeship of the Republic—he says this directly—but the few bits of evidence that would allow us to precisely identify the time when the action were to have taken place prove this to be impossible.

One of the crucial moments in the story is the great scene of public exorcism, which the priest performs upon the nuns in the Ludyń parish church. All this is happening on the feast day of the Exaltation of the Cross, so, despite the fact that Ludyń is located in a wasteland and—as we know—there aren't many Catholic families in the area, the church is filled with a curious crowd of people arrived there from neighboring lands for the feast. The possessed nuns, who perform the strangest feats with the aid of the devils—they pirouette like tightrope walkers, they scream, they sing, they dance, they speak in uncanny voices—constitute a loud local attraction, which has also tempted to Ludyń a very important guest from Warsaw. For no less a personage than Prince Jakub, sometimes known as "Fanfonik," the Frenchified son of the Sarmatian King Jan III Sobieski, *nota bene*—the grandson of Hetman Żółkiewski on his mother's side—is present at the spectacle. Prince Jakub had just arrived at Smolensk with his court when the strange rumors concerning Ludyń and the possessed Ursulines attracted him to the place. All of this is beautifully imagined, but in reality, impossible. During the days of Prince Jakub there was no longer any Smolensk voivodeship in the borders of the Republic—to speak more precisely, there was, but only on paper, *de nomine*, whereas in reality no more, and Prince Jakub couldn't simply go visit Smolensk (even if he did, it would have to be incognito, at the risk of his very life) because for a long while already Smolensk had found itself in the hands of the tsars.

Iwaszkiewicz realized that his conception of locating the happenings near Smolensk was in disaccord with historical chronology and geography. The author's interior struggle can be seen, after all, in the manuscript of the story preserved in Stawisko. It is neat, clean, almost devoid of corrections. Only in a few places is Smolensk crossed out in pencil and changed to Połock (Polotsk), which is a nod in the direction of geographical realities of the First Republic in the second half of the seventeenth century, but introduces a still greater orientational confusion in the reader's mind. "These events," Iwaszkiewicz writes in his short introduction, "took place under different skies and in a different climate [...] and this had no other aim but to make the author himself aware of their uncanny nature."[9]

The Burst Necklace of Orthodox Rus

In order to untangle Iwaszkiewicz's historical riddle, we must once again reach into the past. Once more, the year 1611, mentioned at the start of the story, will be crucial. The Smolensk region lay within the borders of the Grand Duchy of Lithuania, and the city of

Smolensk was, from a strategic perspective, absolutely the most important fortress of the entire Republic, set as it was virtually on the suburban fields of Moscow. Thanks to Smolensk, the Republic was secured from attack by the tsar from the East, and at the same time, offered the possibility of conducting quick blows in response. It was for this reason that at the turn of the sixteenth century unending wars were waged between the Grand Duchy of Lithuania, the Polish king, and the Russians, chiefly over the Smolensk region, but in particular, over the fortress of Smolensk itself.

The autonomous voivodeship of Smolensk was first established in 1508, in the second year of the reign of Zygmunt Stary (the Old), two years into the war between the Grand Duchy of Lithuania and the Rurikoviches over Smolensk and the middle course of the Dnieper. The establishment of the voivodeship can be understood as an attempt at administrative consolidation of the eastern borderlands of the Republic by the King and the Senate under the pressure of growing Muscovite expansion. It did not last very long, however, since as early as 1514, Smolensk had submitted to the armies of Vasili III Rurikovich, and the Smolensk region was lost to the Grand Duchy of Moscow. It is significant that Vasili immediately and methodically carried out a program of expropriation in Smolensk and the surrounding region, transporting a significant number of its inhabitants into the depths of Russia and introducing Russian colonists into the area to take their place, with the intention of eliminating once and for all a Polish presence in the region so important to him. These lands were thus lost to the Republic for nearly one hundred years.

The Smolensk voivodeship was only to be re-established by Zygmunt III Waza (Vasa) thanks to Żółkiewski's Moscow campaign, the defeat and imprisonment of Vasili IV Shuyski, and the taking of Smolensk by the king after a long and exhaustive siege of the fortress. The breaking of the resistance of the Russian defenders of the Smolensk kremlin had a huge strategic significance, but a symbolic one as well. Tsar Godunov, who had effected the construction of the fortifications, was supposed to have said that "the walls of Smolensk constitute the necklace of our orthodox Rus, and there is no other such in the entirety of the holy Russian land."[10] And now that necklace had been burst—the city returned to the Republic after nearly a century of Russian subjection. Along with the establishment of a new ordination of the Smolensk voivodeship there commenced the reconstruction of the old administrative structures and the return of the properties that the Russians had expropriated. Smolensk became the capital of the new voivodeship; officials were appointed along with a titular voivode at their head (a position later to be held by Gosiewski, who had earlier commanded the Polish garrison at the Moscow kremlin in 1610); two counties were erected: Smolensk and Starodub, and in 1621, for the first time, the voivodeship sent representatives to a plenary diet. The Smolensk region was represented in the Republic's government by two lay senators—the voivode and the castellan—as well as one man of the cloth—the Bishop of Smolensk. The revindication of land and estates usurped by the Russians in 1514 began immediately as well. However, noble manors in the Smolensk region were primarily distributed by the King amongst those who distinguished themselves in the battles with the Muscovites, and so: professional soldiers from the enlisted army. Thus, one might say that the social structure of the Smolensk voivodeship in the seventeenth century was quite militarized. It had the character of a front-line outpost and depended on the military—it was a war voivodeship. The expression of this was the levée en masse which—otherwise than in other regions of the Republic—was incumbent upon all nobles regardless of their landed property. Shirking this responsibility might lead to the loss of the properties granted by the King. For all intents and purposes, this meant that the voivodeship found itself under the direct administration of the King, or, more precisely, of Prince Władysław. For his part, the voivode filled an additional function as sub-administrator. The Lithuanians, mindful of the fact that the Smolensk region had once been torn from the Grand Duchy of Lithuania by Moscow, nursed a great rancor toward the King on account of this arrangement of his. Actually, however, in 1654, and *de iure* following the Andruszów Treaty, the lion's share of the Smolensk region was lost, once and for all, to the Russians, never again to return to the Republic. Only its western portion remained, with Orsza County (Orsza nad Dnieprem being the county seat) conjoined to the Witebsk (Vitebsk) voivodeship, forming part of the Republic up until the first partition in 1772. The authorities of the Republic never acknowledged the loss of Smolensk and the surrounding region. For this reason the Smolensk voivodeship remained, nominally, until the final downfall of the Republic. The king continued to appoint a voivode and castellan as senators, and the regional diets of the nobles continued to meet in Wilno (Vilnius) with a division into two counties (*poviats*).

These stormy twists of fate experienced by the Smolensk region indicate not only its character as a town on the "front" as well as its crucial significance for the relations of the Republic with Moscow. They also make us clearly aware of the fact that Iwaszkiewicz was constrained to bend the truth a bit, in bringing Prince Jakub to the feast day celebrations in Ludyń, after which he sent him and his court on to Smolensk. In the days represented in his story, Smolensk had no longer belonged to Poland for some thirty years already, and the Smolensk voivodeship as such no longer existed.

It was very important to Iwaszkiewicz to locate his story in that very nonexistent Smolensk voivodeship, although the place, as he constantly underscores, was deprived of all attractiveness and charm. "Weak soil, bearing nothing but flax and barley... that's it. Sour apples, knotty flax, and barley like barley... Good for beer, nothing else"[11]—as one of the protagonists of the story puts it. Mud everywhere, especially in spring and fall. As Iwaszkiewicz tells us, the main square of Ludyń was one huge mud puddle that never dried. And at last, the emphatic summing up: "They say that the land is cursed, and refuses to bring forth anything good from its womb..."[12] And it is exactly there, in the Ursuline nunnery founded after the Moscow triumph, somewhere in the muddy eastern borderlands of the Republic, on the borderline of two realms, where the struggle between man and evil, man and the devils who wish to govern him, takes place. In this way, the locality of Smolensk in the Eastern Marches becomes an arena of the eternal battle between good and evil, salvation and damnation, light and darkness.

Young Father Suryn travels to Ludyń at the command of the Jesuit provincial in Połock. He is tasked with performing exorcisms in the cloister, to lay the demons who have possessed the nuns there. The mother superior, known as Mother Joanna of the Angels, has become the special object of horrid persecution at the hands of the dark forces who have entered into her. We know nothing of the causes of this possession except for the short tale concerning Father Garniec, who was to have been a sorcerer. It was he, supposedly, who brought this evil upon the nuns. Later, he was condemned for his alleged spell-casting and burnt at the stake. However, the possession of the nuns did not abate—on the contrary, it grew in severity. It was the exorcisms performed by Fr. Suryn that were supposed to take care of that. Nor do we know why it was he, exactly, whom the father provincial chose for such a serious and dangerous task. It was known, however, that before his arrival, four other priests had tried, unsuccessfully, to exorcise the demons. So the case had been going on for quite a while. It was widely known and at the center of the Catholic Church's attention. Fr. Suryn was well prepared for his mission. He had spoken in depth about the case with the father provincial and other pious, influential persons. For the possessed mother superior was, after all, the daughter of a prince, the descendant of an illustrious aristocratic clan. So the matter also had, shall we say, a powerful social context for the surrounding region. It seems that the choice of Fr. Suryn cannot have been a coincidence; rather, he was acknowledged as the best man for the task. We learn a few things about the priest from Iwaszkiewicz that make our hypothesis a probable one. His mother had entered a cloister herself—after the death of her husband, one supposes—and his sisters had become nuns too. Suryn himself joined the Jesuit order in Wilno at the age of sixteen. As he said of himself, he had never come to know an "ordinary" life. Later, he was transferred to Połock. We also know that Fr. Suryn's cell was stocked with many learned theological tomes, which bears witness to his intellectual ambitions. And one more thing: several times, Iwaszkiewicz refers to an unsettling, fundamental character trait of the priest: emotional instability, a constant balancing act between spiritual euphoria, outright elevation and exaltation on the one hand, and complete despair, dread, and doubt on the other. At any event, Suryn was deeply sensitive to questions of good and evil, salvation and damnation; deeply, directly, and personally sensitive. However, it would be difficult to say whether the provincial took this into account when he made his decision, or whether he was completely ignorant of this trait of Suryn's, merely seeing in his candidate a young priest either completely submerged in prayer or poring over his books.

On the other hand, Iwaszkiewicz says nothing at all about the Jesuits, as if it were something obvious that his hero should elect to enter this particular order. So it is important to note that in the times in which his story is set, the Jesuits had already been active on Polish soil for over one hundred years. They fostered the Catholic faith, did battle with heretics and the idea of a national Polish Church independent of Rome. They also enjoyed a growing influence on the politics of the realm. Their rising significance was taken by the nobility, especially the Protestants among them, as nothing positive. They were often suspected of being, quite simply, the agents of Rome, the Habsburgs, and the Pope. Naturally, the most well-known representative of the order was Piotr Skarga, a man of tireless missionary and organizational energy, a close confidant of King Stefan Batory and court preacher to King Zygmunt III Waza. Skarga played a gigantic role in the missionary activity of the order and the development of its power and influence, especially in the Grand Duchy of Lithuania. He was active for many years in Wilno, where with the aid of Bishop Protasiewicz, a Jesuit college had been established, which a few years later was raised to the rank of an academy by Stefan Batory. Wilno became the most important place for the activity and influence of the Jesuits in the eastern and northern territories of the Republic, something that was in complete accord with the politics of Batory—indeed, an integral element thereof. To this very day the central significance of Wilno for the counterreformation activity of the Jesuits in the Republic, and their missionary activity in the east, can be seen in the architecture of the city. We also need to remember that it was Batory's energetic support for the Jesuits' activities, expressed, among other ways, in his personal engagement in the affairs of the Wilno college, and later Academy, that had a key significance for the order and for Skarga himself. Neither Wilno nor the Grand Duchy of Lithuania were facile terrain for re-Catholicizing. The Lithuanian nobility, especially the magnate clans like the Radziwiłłs, had eagerly adopted Calvinism in the sixteenth century, seeing in the new Christian religion a confirmation of their independence from royal power. The strong influences of the Protestantism of northern Courland also played a significant role here. On the other hand, other Lithuanian clans such as the Ostrogskis, for example, underscored their role as the defenders of Orthodoxy in the East. For these reasons Wilno was, for Skarga and the Jesuits, an arena of real confessional conflict, which had to be won with the help of the academy, with the aid of the king, and finally, with their own missionary zeal. The city constituted the central nexus for missions stretching far to the east and the north. And so, Skarga supported Batory in his strivings, which were crowned by the establishment of a Jesuit school in Dorpat, as well as his ideas for the erection of a Jesuit college in Riga. Now, after the king had acknowledged as necessary the establishment of a Jesuit college in Połock, far to the east of Wilno, following his successful military expedition against Moscow, it was Skarga he sent to found it and lead it as its first rector. He also became, simultaneously, the first superior of the order's community in that city. The king explained to the Wilno Jesuits his reasons for the establishment of their new post in the East in these words: "Be not jealous of your Portuguese and Spaniards for the strange worlds of Asia and America, which they strive to convert: here nearby there are Indias and Japans in the Ruthenian region of Połock, a city ignorant of things Divine."[13] Such a royal idea and such events accompanied the foundation of the college and the Jesuit order in Połock, to which Father Suryn travelled at a certain moment from Wilno. Living in the Połock Jesuit community for several dozen years, he certainly prayed in his cell, read theological works, and perhaps taught at the college, sharing with his other brethren respect and wonder for the great founder of the Połock Jesuit community, Piotr Skarga.

The Boundaries of Two Realms

Mother Joanna of the Angels was possessed by as many as nine different devils: Behemoth, Balaam, Isacaron, Gressil, Aman, Asmodeus, Begerit, Leviathan, and Zapaliczka—at least so she maintained. And it was these nine demons as well as a whole herd of lesser hell-sprites that infested the souls of the other Ursulines which, as Father Suryn himself said, he was to exorcise according to the *Rituale Romanum*. But was there anyone to drive out in the first place? The priest was bothered from the first by such questions: what is evil, what is the nature of evil, why do devils torment people? Is it enough to simply open oneself entirely to the grace of God, for the eternal light of God's love to pour into the soul of man and fill it to brimming, as if it were a vessel empty up till then?—"Lord I am not worthy of Thee, but say the word only, and my soul shall be healed!" Or perhaps something stands in the way of that, something or someone, some perverse power, which pulls us in the other direction?

These questions grew in intensity the further Father Suryn pressed toward the eastern border of the realm, to Ludyń, which lay on the accursed soil of Smolensk. Simultaneously, that disturbing trait of his character: that inner vacillation between exaltation and downfall, grew in intensity as well. The Jesuit's expedition to the East becomes, then, also an expedition to meet with evil and to gaze deeply into his own inner self. His questions and doubts become quite evident, displaying their full, terrifying extent during the very first night he spends in the Ludyń inn, even before he goes off to the nunnery infested with devils. In reference to himself, Father Suryn is tormented by an explicit sense of evil, which at times leads him to despair. "I sense him constantly. The evil one. I sense constantly his horrid work"[14]—he would say in his torment. He also stubbornly held to the idea that the soul of man is more similar to a walnut than to a vessel to be filled by the grace of God. "There are so many pieces there, portions, corners tucked away, and hollows."[15] All that is needed, then, is for the evil one to leave behind some small shard of devilry tucked away in one of those corners, and that person will never have peace again. Sensing so clearly the work of evil as well as—concurrently—his own efforts to fight against it, Father Suryn had a strangely large amount of doubts concerning the very nature of the devil, whom he was commanded to expel from the souls of others. On the above-mentioned night, during his prayers, he had a vision of the evil one as an all-too-well-defined, giant black body, mighty and horrible, seen through the window against the background of the dark starry night—against the entire cosmos. "I see you, I see you!" he cried out at the sight: "I see how you bristle against me, who have come to do battle with you. This is your kingdom, here, but I am sent by other people in the name of God. I am from another realm, I am from the light, as you are from the darkness; I am from the good, as you are from evil..."[16] And so, already on that first night it is clear that in Ludyń Suryn is standing on the borderline of two realms—those of good and evil, salvation and damnation. However, on the next day, when, for a better orientation of the situation he first goes off to meet with the local parish priest and has a long conversation with him about the situation in the nunnery, he is seized with panic at the thought that there might be no devils there at all. In quite an Augustinian fashion the suggestion occurs during the conversation that, perhaps, evil has no being of itself; it is no being at all, no force that enters into a man and exits from him, but is rather a lack, a void in man himself: his very own unfettered inclination. That would mean that the nuns in Ludyń, not excepting the mother superior, are performing all of those horrid things of their own free will, not at the urging of some exterior power. This thought will never abandon Suryn. With all its power it returns, among other times, in his discussion with the zaddik of Ludyń, when the horrid sentence, piercing him through with dread, falls: "I am thou—thou art I,"[17] which suggests that perhaps there is no difference between the devil and man; that demons are not working their will upon men, but that men begin to desire evil, choosing it for the lack of good in themselves.

Of course, in the question of possession and struggle with evil powers, the culminating scene of the story is the collective exorcism of the nuns in the Ludyń parish church. The Magnificat is sung, there are Latin psalms, organs... a crowd is gathered in the nave, the stalls are occupied by the officials of Prince Jakub, and four priests seeking to expel the devils from the frantic nuns. These exorcisms are intended not so much to free the poor Ursulines from the evil one, as much as they are to fill the assembled crowds with dread and draw them closer to God. If, however, we are to speak of the question of evil as well as the borderline character of this place in the Smolensk region where the essence of evil most clearly became exteriorized, visible, then the key scene is to be found only in the final fragments, in the final meeting between Mother Joanna of the Angels and Father Suryn. This is the moment in which the devils pass from the mother superior to the Jesuit—the scene of his final, despairing attempt at conquering evil by his own sacrifice and, ultimately, the irrevocable defeat of the priest in the battle. The priest thought that he could free Mother Joanna of evil if he offered himself in sacrifice. He recognized that, if he should offer his own soul, he would indicate to the Ursuline the path to salvation, to a renewed discovery of the God of love. However, it turns out that this act of limitless and unconditional love on the part of the priest for the tormented soul of the nun simply confirms all the very worst fears of Suryn touching upon the nature of evil. Of course, the mother superior does not want to open herself to God and accept the offered sacrifice, while at the same time she does this not out of concern for the fate of the priest, but rather because—as she says—"I have a relish for Satan. This possession has brought me joy. I am proud of having met with this fate, and I find a certain satisfaction in the fact that the devils are torturing me more than anyone else... What would become of me, if not even a single devil remained in me?"[18] Father Suryn understands this as a typical expression of pride, that sin of which Leviathan is especially fond, but Mother Joanna's declaration is something entirely more serious, as it uncovers the essence of the problem which, on the historical and spiritual level, played out and was concentrated in the land of Smolensk. Mother Joanna of the Angels is not concerned in the least with the fate of the priest; she is concerned with herself, in love with evil, which provides her life with meaning. The Jesuit priest wants for her to follow him along the path he indicates, which would lead her out of the darkness. But with contempt, the nun throws the horrid truth into his face: "What sort of a road is it, Father, that you are showing me? Where does that road lead? Where are you leading me, you old monk you? All you want is for me to calm down, to get control of myself, to grow grey, to grow small, so that I would be just the same as all other nuns. [...] You want to make me similar to thousands, thousands of people who stumble about the world without any purpose! You want to see me at prayer, morning, noon, and night; you want me to eat lentils in oil, every day, every day! And for all that, what do you promise me? Salvation? I don't want that sort of salvation."[19] Mother Joanna desires sanctity—the true, absolute sanctity that apotheoses man—theosis—she wants to melt into the everlasting light—and since such a thing is impossible, she prefers to be damned.

How thoroughly Russian, how utterly, totally Holy-Mother-Russia Orthodox reasoning that is—a thought process completely foreign to Latin spirituality, according to which each soul can become a saint by striving for sanctity! The entire attitude of Russia to the West is contained in these words. Control, humility, discipline, a quieting down, a patient expectation, trust—all of these values of Western Christian life are cast aside in the name of this one, violent, and completely unattainable dream—the ideal of holiness. For me, Mother Joanna of the Angels—after all, the daughter of the Smolensk Kniaz Bielski, whose antecedents were certainly archly Orthodox, expresses the very essence of the spirituality of Orthodoxy and of Russia in this casting away of normal, quiet life, in her ecstatic thirst after a holy greatness, which leads her to complete and conscious subjection to absolute evil. Some will speak of this essence as the dictatorship of the idea, which will later allow for the formation of the historic triad: Orthodoxy—Russia—Communism. In this story, the idea of holiness, the theosis of man, sets such a high threshold that any attempt to cross it must result in catastrophe. It will remain the chief idea in Orthodoxy, its most important indicator, but its absolute character, which tolerates no compromise, makes it for mortals of real flesh and blood practically unattainable. This dramatic trait of Orthodoxy determines, to a great degree, Russian spirituality, its understanding of reality and its negative status. Holiness, or, more broadly: the main idea (for after all, we are speaking here of the same phenomenon expressed in Orthodoxy and Russian Communism), destroys the sense of human existence. According to it, actual human reality has no intrinsic value, for it is not holy. Man is torn between the idea of unattainable holiness and the reality of daily life deprived of all value. For this very reason then, in the name of holiness, in the name of the idea, man may, in a reality deprived of sense, struggle as he will, kicking others about, lying, spitting, cursing, tearing his hair out; he can curse and dishonor others as he will, his eyes fixed all the time upon the bright ray of holiness, which shines down upon him from eternity.

I think that in this very phenomenon the entire difference between Orthodox, Russian spirituality, on which Communism later battened itself, and Latin Europe is contained. And it seems to me something archly interesting that Iwaszkiewicz not only took up the challenge of describing this problem in his story, but also stubbornly insisted that the struggle between these two worlds, between salvation and damnation, good and evil, should play out exactly there, on the soil of Smolensk. Let us remember that Suryn—a Jesuit and a Latin—was in the end overcome by the devils of Smolensk, and on account of the horrid crime that he committed, his soul was finally damned. Suryn lost his soul. Poles can never transform the East, however many times that thought should return and provoke them to the boldest deeds, such as those which Stefan Żółkiewski accomplished. For all that, the East transformed their life very frequently and sometimes very harshly, until at one moment it determined to show them that it could quite simply slaughter them. One must be, however, very careful with the relations that link Poles with the East. Without a doubt, they are cut through by the border between two realms, which in result divides us from the East. However, on the other hand, this bond reminds us somewhat of Father Suryn's walnut, with all its pieces, portions, corners tucked away, and hollows. In the head of the Jesuit possessed by the devils of Smolensk, one thought constantly revolves: "I am thou, thou art I."

The memory of the great victory over the armies of Tsar Shuyski and the taking of Moscow had an enormous significance for Zygmunt III Waza (Vasa), as it did for the inhabitants of the Republic. It underscored the authority and the meaning of the monarch as well as the might of his state. But the memory of these events had still more weight for Moscow. The state took as its sacred obligation the preservation of the consciousness of the great catastrophe and humbling of Holy Rus, persecuted, as it was said in Russia, by the "vulpine Lechites," the "dirty Jews," and the "pagan Lithuanians."[20] This is a good illustration of how deep the roots of Russian political mythology are, as well as the historical policy of that region. But those events also had a practical dimension. This very unimaginable humiliation of Holy Rus occurred at the same time as the establishment of the new ruling dynasty in Russia, that of the Romanovs. Is it, then, that the humiliation of Holy Rus had to take place for the foundation of the new dynasty to be laid? That looks bad, especially as the idea of Holy Rus, radiant Russia, the beloved of Christ, had a key significance for Russians. As Alain Besançon has noted: "No other country in the world—outside of the Holy Land—has ever dared to describe itself as "holy." The term *Holy Russia* bestows an aura of sanctity, simultaneously, upon the land, the people, and the Russian state."[21] But the Latins, in other words, Rome, always wanted to deprive Russia of that holiness, at least since 1439. From the Union of Florence and the fall of Constantinople on, they strove doggedly toward her subjection. The erasure from Russian memory of the catastrophe of 1610 and 1611, or at the very least the presentation of the same in the best possible light, was always the highest priority for the new government of the Romanovs. And the same thing is true for each subsequent government at the Kremlin, up until today. Certainly Putin spared no expenses for the creation of a film treating the liberation of Moscow from Polish occupation in 1612, and the employment of Polish actors for the same, renting them for roubles, must have been a source of great satisfaction to him. After all, he made the date the official state holiday of the Russian Federation: the Day of National Unity.

Still, this history sits in the minds of many Russians who concern themselves with Russia and Russianness, although not necessarily supporting the régime of Putin. Solzhenitsyn, for example, was of the opinion that the "Polish aggression, which could effect *genetic changes*, was much more of a threat than the Mongol invasions, which left the religious structures of the country untouched."[22] Also, not all that long ago the Russian writer Victor Yerofieyev, the son of Molotov's personal translator and author, among others, of the *Encyclopedia of the Russian Soul*, immediately referred to our matter when queried in an interview for the French press about the relations between Russia and Europe, between Russian and European values: "It's about the dark seventeenth century. That was the time when the Poles occupied Moscow, and our state was ruled by their king. Formally then, at this time, we became Europeans. But then the Poles were expelled and the tsar recouped his throne. It seemed then that Russian values triumphed, those ancient, Orthodox values, but only a few dozen years passed and Peter I overturned everything. As Pushkin put it, he opened the window wide to Europe."[23]

The events that interest us here have their own interesting iconography, closely aligned to the political priorities whereby the Romanovs directed their steps from the early years of their rule. It is, therefore, an iconography of immense political significance. In order to crown his great victory, Zygmunt III Waza commissioned the Italian painter Tommaso Dolabella to create two canvases: the "Reception of the Shuyskis in the Senate Hall in 1611" as well as the "Conquest of Smolensk." Both of these canvases along with a series of other historical paintings by the Italian artist decorated the Royal

Palace all throughout the seventeenth century. Supposedly, they were to have ornamented the ceiling of the Senate Chamber, on two plafonds. Another important relic of these times, material testimony to the victorious Moscow expedition, was the Orthodox church known as the Muscovy Chapel, which was built at the very beginning of the Krakowskie Przedmieście, near the place where the Staszic Palace was later to be constructed. This formed one element of the gigantic architectonic foundation of the Wazas, the so-called *Forum Vasorum*, of which only the Column of Zygmunt was realized. In this chapel, the remains of Tsar Vasili Shuyski, his brother Dmitri and the Grand Duchess Yekaterina Grigorievna were laid to rest. Zygmunt had a tablet affixed above the entrance to the chapel bearing a Latin text, which read: "Zygmunt III, King of Poland and Sweden, having conquered the Muscovite armies at Klushino, accepted the capitulation of the capital Moscow, returning Smolensk to the Republic. Vasili Shuyski, the Grand Duke of Moscow, and his brother Dmitri, a military leader, were captured and held according to military law. Kept under guard at the Castle of Gostynin, it was there that their lives came to an end. With the fate of humans in mind, he deposits their mortal remains here. And although as our enemies they ruled lawlessly and wielded a lawless scepter, they were not deprived of a funeral."[24] Indeed, some two months after the Warsaw triumph and the tribute paid at the Royal Palace, the Shuyskis were transported to the castle in Gostynin, a locality in Mazovia to the north of Warsaw, on the left bank of the Wisła.

Now, a brief digression: literally a few kilometers to the east lies the village of Lucień, with its presidential retreat set on a lakeside. Here, between 2006 and 2009 Lech Kaczyński organized gatherings of Polish intellectuals. The nearness of Gostynin and the history of its highly-born captives from the seventeenth century had for the President—as I can personally testify—a certain significance for the choice of Lucień as the center for such meetings.

However, the Szuyskis were not to live long in the castle at Gostynin. The mention on the tablet of the guard that watched over them has an ambivalent ring to it. The tsar was in fact the prisoner of the king, but he did have contact with the outside world and could receive guests. Now, Vasili died in September 1612, and shortly thereafter Dmitri, and Ivan's wife Yekaterina, also passed away. The official version lays the blame at the feet of "pestilential air." However, the presence of the tsar and his family on the soil of the Republic seemed at least so politically problematic, that it would be difficult if other hypotheses were not put forward. And so, it cannot be ruled out that death came to them from Moscow, from the hands of Mikhail Romanov. When Zygmunt III Waza hesitated too long with sending his son, Prince Władysław, to accept the throne of Moscow, the Polish faction in the ranks of the Russian boyars began to melt, and the Romanov family began to seem more attractive to the proponents of the reconstruction of Holy Rus and its liberation from foreign rule.

Zygmunt III set out for Moscow very belatedly: in July 1612, in order to fulfill his promise of setting his son on the throne of Russia. He got as far as Volokolamsk, some one hundred twenty kilometers from Moscow. However, the situation in the capital had changed diametrically. At the beginning of November, the Polish garrison at the Kremlin perished, taken by hunger. It is said that, out of despair, some of the defenders even resorted to cannibalism. Zygmunt's expedition to Moscow ended in complete failure. His envoys were not even let into the city, and Mikhail Romanov grew into a natural candidate for the new ruler. Despite that fact, in accord with the principle of unitary rule, he could not be chosen tsar as long as Vasili were alive. And so, the death of the latter, as well as that of his brother, occurred at the very right moment, opening the path to the throne to Mikhail—which indeed took place when the Zemsky Sobor met in March 1613 to elect him as the Tsar of All Russia.

Immediately, Mikhail I Romanov took up the task of bringing the history of the eight years of the "Time of Troubles" or *smuta* to a definitive end, sweeping away all traces of that period. In this we can find much personal umbrage on the part of the new tsar. For after all, it was his father, Filaret, that the Poles trundled down Krakowskie Przedmieście in a wagon during that triumphal parade. All documents touching upon the Shuyskis, even Godunov, as well as the whole unfortunate episode of the False Dmitri were destroyed. The son of False Dmitri, Ivan, was hanged. His mother, Maryna Mniszchówna, was throttled. At the cost of a considerable amount of money and gifts, Mikhail negotiated the transferal of the remains of the tsarist family with King Władysław IV. In 1635, they were sent to Moscow from Warsaw and reburied with pomp in the Cathedral of the Archangel. Mikhail's son, Tsar Alexei, continued the labor of washing clean the memory of the humiliation of Holy Rus, liquidating all evidence associated therewith. It was he who demanded that the Poles demolish the Moscow Chapel standing at the entrance to the Krakowskie Przedmieście, and one of the Russian points in the negotiations during the Andruszów Treaty was the removal of Dolabella's paintings from the Senate Chamber of the Royal Palace. The brashness of this request infuriated the Poles to such a degree that the Crown Field Hetman Stanisław Jabłonowski could not restrain himself from addressing the following words to the Russian envoys: that the paintings would be removed only then, when a new victory over Muscovy required the painting of new ones. The next tsar, Fyodor, straightforwardly demanded the paintings from Jan III Sobieski. Yet Dolabella's works continued to hang in the Royal Palace, most likely until 1707, when they were stolen, or acquired from August II, by Peter I, the grandson of the first tsar of the Romanov dynasty. They disappeared without a trace. Doubtlessly, they were destroyed.

The only image of one of the lost canvases, the one representing the tribute of the Shuyskis in Warsaw in 1611, is contained in an engraving by the cartographer Tomasz Makowski, created on the basis of the painting itself as well as, most probably, its copy in the collections of the castle in Podhorce. In the eighteenth century, the Moscow Chapel was also devastated, shorn of Zygmunt's memorial tablets at the command of Repnin. And thus all memory of the grand, never to be fulfilled, Polish dream of transforming the East came to a final end.

The Immensity of Eastern Issues

The matter of the seductive charms of the East as well as its sweet, poisonous aroma of corruption, capable of befuddling even the soberest minds, is a constant motif in European culture. These are those Sivas, Lamaisms, and Buddhisms, of which Iwaszkiewicz writes. Beginning with Herodotus and his grand history of the wars between Greece and Persia, it is always the same story, though developed in different manners, of the seductive force of Eastern splendor, of the irresistible fascination that always ends badly—with enslavement or death. It is also interesting that fascination with the East is usually linked to the necessity of denying one's own self.

It is worthwhile to mention in this place a fragment of an interview with Zygmunt Kubiak, which bears the title—so strange at first sight—of "Cleopatra and the Polish Issue."[25] If we take Latin Rome into consideration—still that Rome in which the last bits of the republican ethos were burning down, yet it might still seem, at least to some, that Roman Republicanism might still be saved from extinction—the history of Cleopatra, or rather, of her violent relationships with Roman leaders, is perhaps the most interesting and well-known example of the destructive charms of the East. For Cleopatra seduced Pompey, Julius Caesar (with whom she had a child), Mark Antony (perhaps the most well-known of the stories concerning her), and finally—she tried to seduce Octavian. We must remember that for the Romans of the Mediterranean world Egypt was an eastern culture, no less than the Parthians, the Assyrians, the Scythians, and other nations of Asia Minor and the Near East. It was for this reason that the inhabitants of Rome took Cleopatra, quite simply, as the ruler of just one more exotic state in the East conquered by the Roman legions. However, it is thought-provoking how quickly the delight of the Roman crowd at her entrance into Rome along with Caesar turned to vibrant hatred. Cleopatra became the object of the authentic hostility of the Romans—from the very start they noticed her dangerous foreignness, which, under the guise of seductive charm, was capable of penetrating the hearts of Roman leaders and transforming their souls. Simply put: Cleopatra was in possession of that most dangerous of weapons: the ability to slay the Latin world, the Latin soul. The list of complaints against the eastern powers of decay is a long one: cruelty, violence, indiscipline, a tendency to a vulgar love of wealth and luxury, deceit, mendacity, effeminacy or, indeed, excessive power in the hands of women. In some way, for the inhabitants of Rome, Cleopatra personified all of these horrid and repulsive traits of the Orient.

The most well-known victim of the eastern weapon of seduction used by Cleopatra was, of course, Mark Antony, the circumstances of whose strange transformation under the influence of this woman is recorded in Shakespeare's *Antony and Cleopatra*.[26] The action develops from the politician's incipient romantic fascination with Cleopatra during her tenure in Rome, and follows the slow transformation of his tastes and growing distaste for Roman obligations, into symptoms of complete insanity of power typical for an eastern satrap, up until the final downfall of his personality.

Octavian, on the other hand, remained completely resistant to the charms of Cleopatra, to seductive eastern beauty—which Shakespeare also records. His dry, Latin practicality won the day here. He wanted to reign over the East, not submit to exotic emotions. The greatness of Octavian depends not only on the fact that he was victorious over Mark Antony at Actium and led to the fall of Cleopatra. Rather, proof of his genius and extraordinariness—of which Kubiak speaks in the above-cited interview—lies in the fact that he understood perfectly that Latin Rome would never dominate the East unless it was transformed itself.[27] As long as Roman republicanism did not find a new political formula for itself, a new way of organizing order, it would not be capable of defending its own values against the ruinous influence of exterior forces from the East. Even if the Roman legions should, for a certain time, bring the East under their military occupation, sooner or later the East would spiritually destroy Rome. It is for this reason that Octavian's work of the ages was not the seizure of power, the elimination of all his rivals: Brutus, Cassius, Pompey, and Mark Antony, but rather his providing the Romans with the new political form of the Empire, a type of unity grounded, after all, on the old republican values, thanks to which Rome could rule the East and the entire Mediterranean world through the ages, and not only militarily, but spiritually and politically as well.

As I see it—and this is my fundamental thesis—it was just such a work of transformation that we Poles lacked. And for this reason, our experience of the East ended in catastrophe. Quite simply, it always seemed to the Poles—each and every time, whenever in history they set themselves to grapple with the East—that it would be sufficient for them to remain who they are, with all of their straightforwardness, their piety, their love of freedom, in order to transform the East and tame it. And it was this fatal error, only avoided, perhaps, by Piłsudski in the first half of the twentieth century, that is made again and again to this very moment. Meanwhile, in order to transform the East, what is needed is not only military courage as during the days of Batory or Zygmunt III but also a fundamental reconstruction of our own political life so as to make our own values resistant to the influences of the forces of decay that waft in from the East. Whereas in the fifteenth and sixteenth century Poles pushed toward the East with enthusiasm, they were poorly prepared for it. As Jarosław Marek Rymkiewicz writes, they took this direction to expand as a result of some mistaken decision, fatal in its outcome; a decision quite in disaccord with the laws of nature, which indicate a movement from east to west, rather—which is the most frequent path of civilization. Expansion was necessary, for when something swells, it must find a release.[28]

Indeed, those two centuries are a period of great demographic development in the Republic, for which the colonization of Ukrainian Rus was the easiest option. All one need do is cast one's eye on the map of the Republic in the times of its greatest territorial reach. The tiny voivodeships in the western regions of the realm: Łęczyca, Płock, Brześć Kujawski, look like risible dwarfs in comparison to the gigantic territories of such immensities as the voivodeship of Kyiv, Minsk, or Lwów (Lviv). This expansion toward the east was, of course, the result of the above-mentioned societal and economical necessity, but there was a certain enchantment that accompanied these practicalities as well. Rymkiewicz describes this Polish fascination with the East beginning at this time, with examples, among others, of the Oleśnicki clan, who in the fifteenth century wandered east, as a result of which one of the Oleśnickis became the voivode of the Lwów region, the other an archbishop, and yet another the castellan of Halicz.[29] Many noble Polish families followed the same path. Immense careers, possibilities, and hopes! It was from these that the Moscow expeditions of Batory arose, followed by the insane Dmitriad of Jerzy Mniszech, the voivode of Sandomierz, and Prince Wiśniowiecki, the conquest of Smolensk and Moscow; but here too one finds the source of the insanity of Mother Joanna of the Angels and Father Suryn. That was a warning: for these activities turned out to be in disaccord with the age-old direction of expansion—as Rymkiewicz stresses—from east to west, and since the opposite direction was so carelessly taken, Poland was to be punished cruelly at the hands of fate.[30]

I don't know whether or not Iwaszkiewicz would agree with such a diagnosis. In works devoted to him we can frequently come across the opinion that two fundamental things played a significant role in his formation: the Polish manor house in Ukrainian Rus, and Mediterranean culture. It is true that he blossomed, just like his neighbor and friend Karol Szymanowski, from that extraordinary root of Polish culture of the Kresy, the strange remnants of the colonizing élan of that Republic which by then had ceased to exist for many years. The future writer grew up in Kalnik, not far from Elizavetgrad, to the south of Kyiv. The Szymanowskis lived in neighboring Tymoszówka. And so, Iwaszkiewicz grew up in the very heart of Ukraine, on the western edges of the ancient Pontic Steppe, which thanks to Polish colonists and Ukrainian peasants, as well as on account of the rich black earth there, was transformed over the course of several generations into a highly developed area of agriculture on a large scale. This production, with the significant participation of Polish landlords and the so-called "officialists," was based primarily on the cultivation of grains and the sugar industry. For this region, Odessa was a window on the world. Through that port passed goods from and to Ukraine. Kyiv played not only a central administrative role, but also rose to the significance of a main educational-cultural center, especially following the closing of the Krzemieniec Lyceum.

In the images of that world, the old Kresy at the turn of the twentieth century, which we find in Iwaszkiewicz's writing—especially in his *Książka moich wspomnień* (Book of My Memories),[31] but also in the memoirs of August Iwański senior and junior, edited by him,[32] as well as in many others—we find ever-repeating descriptions of the absolutely fantastic cultural aura that pervaded these places. The manors of the Polish magnates, the splendid palaces of the old magnate clans, neighboring upon the Russian landholdings, the Ukrainian villages with their new churches in vibrant colors raised following the suppression of the Uniate Church and the establishment of the hierarchy of the Moscow patriarchate over them, the little towns with their large Jewish populations—all this, sprinkled over the immense areas of black earth and sparse woods, created a space for a wanton and chaotic, and yet, for all that, fascinating culture. With its exotica, the region attracted restless souls from Western Europe—not only such men of grand format as Balzac and Liszt, but also whole legions of Germans, Frenchmen, and Englishmen, who worked as tutors in the manor houses or teachers in the schools, or tried their luck at business and service. One read Goethe, Nietzsche, Chesterton, and Wilde in Polish manor houses and by more modest hearths too; one played Brahms and Mahler, while also frequently singing Ukrainian songs. There was a vibrant interest in the world, about which one read in the magazines and newspapers delivered there. In winter, one took oneself off to Warsaw, while in the summer one made frequent trips all around the world: Vienna, Rome, Sicily. All of this gave rise to an extraordinary mixture, which began the great ferment from which such extraordinary personalities as Iwaszkiewicz and Szymanowski grew.

There was one other essential circumstance that endowed central Ukraine with a completely unique specific—the Greeks. I'm not speaking of Byzantium here, but of the real, ancient Greeks. Due to the long channel of the Dnieper, all of that vast area, all of central Ukraine, "Dnieper" Ukraine, was united to the Black Sea in a natural way. Here led, of course, the road to Constantinople, the fundamental point of reference for Russian Orthodoxy through the ages—until the very fall of the city in the fifteenth century. However, alongside Byzantium, the capital of the Greek-speaking world, the actual Greeks, the classical ones, were also important, as much earlier on, indeed, from the eighth century before Christ, they had colonized and kept a stable presence on the coasts of the Black Sea—above all, its Western and Northern portions, in Thrace and Scythia. In comparison with the tame, warm, and island-sprinkled Aegean Sea, the Black Sea must have been no small challenge for the Greeks. And yet they pushed deep into the North, struggling with this immense and deep body of water, its violent storms, its icy winds in winter, in search of places convenable to promising colonization. And so, in the relatively short space of two centuries, the shores of the Black Sea became the granary of the classical Greek world, first and above all, of the Ionian cities, and later, in the fifth century, of the entire Athenian Empire. Pericles dreamed up some bold plans concerning these territories, sensing that if Athens were to succeed in subjecting the entire colonized area to herself, an inexhaustible reservoir of foodstuffs would thus be guaranteed. For the *poleis*, crowded since time immemorial on the rocky Hellenic peninsula, this matter was absolutely crucial. In Greece per se there were always too few people, too little space, too little food. The shores of the Black Sea opened wide completely new, unlimited possibilities of development.

One of the largest port cities built by the Greeks on the Black Sea was Olbia, which they founded in the Dnieper delta. It is said that in its heyday, the city had a population of some thirty thousand. The famous Greek historian Herodotus was sent there for a time on a secret mission from Pericles. In Olbia, the Greeks dealt mostly with the grain cultivated in the nearby steppes, along with animal skins and fish. The region thus became one of the most interesting examples in the whole of European history of the coexistence of two completely different civilizations: that of the settled Greeks and the nomadic Scythians. These two peoples were united by common interest as well as the memory of military glory and a timeless victory. For both the Greeks and the Scythians had been able to restrain the might of the Persian Empire and rescue their own, unique manner of life. Both of these peoples valued freedom above all.

Now, by the time that Iwaszkiewicz and Szymanowski were growing up in central Ukraine, Greek Olbia was nothing more than an archeological site, scrupulously studied by the Imperial Russian Archeological Society. And yet the warm winds wafting up from the Dnieper delta, from Crimea and the Black Sea, gave one the sense of a direct proximity to the ancient Mediterranean classical culture, to Hellas. And this proximity had left some real, substantial traces on the Ukrainian coast of the Black Sea. This is something absolutely unique. It is as if—let's imagine—the ruins of an ancient Greek city in which Plato once spent some time, working on his newest dialogue, the *Symposium*, were to be found somewhere between Sandomierz and Kraków. In the twelfth century, Master Wincenty had to concoct some links between us and the ancient Greeks. In Ukraine, on the other hand, nothing had to be invented, for they had actually been there. That is why, when Iwaszkiewicz is describing the atmosphere that reigned in the circles of the young enthusiasts of art in Kyiv, where he went to school and university, there returns, again and again, the motif of strongly felt bonds with Mediterranean culture, with Hellas. It is significant that his first attempts at collaboration with Szymanowski—on the composition of the opera *King Roger* in which, after all, such thick Greek, Apollonian and Dionysian strands interweave, took place still in the Ukrainian phase of their biographies, before the outbreak of the First World War.

All of this leads me to the following conclusion. Even if the experience of the East constituted a complex issue for Iwaszkiewicz, personally it was for him, first and foremost, an experience of central Ukraine. I would also like to underscore that this was a unique world, exceptional and self-extant in the face of the voracious and unhealthy designs of Moscow. At any rate, this was something completely different from the mire of Smolensk. The soil here was neither empty nor waste, and even if the Poles had lost that world, irrevocably, along with the Bolshevik Revolution when manors, estates, sugar factories, and palaces were lost, still and all, the people from that region continued to constitute an awesome injection of vitality in the worlds of culture and politics of the Second Republic. It was their variousness, their breadth, their fantastic Ukrainian mix that gave Poles and Polishness its extraordinary verve in the interwar years. Iwaszkiewicz understood this perfectly, especially later on, in the cramped and musty spaces that made up homogenized People's Poland. "Polish culture derived its strength from sucking the juices of Russia, Ukraine, the Ural regions and the Caucasus. Now, those roots have nothing to drink, and for this reason the tree has grown dwarf-like,"[33] he was to write on 4 February 1966.

I imagine the scene which brings my meditations on Smolensk and *Mother Joanna of the Angels* to an end in this way. Another October day. Autumn in all its glory begins—the dusk falls early, and the first frosts grip the soil at night, coating the grasses here and there with white in the morning. The exodus of the population of Warsaw lasts several days, as they traipse through Pruszków, Podkowa Leśna, and Grodzisk; the pressure of the monstrous events that has been growing causes time to shrink to the present moment, the moment of life and death, and no one pays any attention any more to the seasons changing around them. It is already completely dark in Stawisko when the vigilant dogs begin barking and howling in warning. The inhabitants of the house look through the windows, peering with anxiety at the figure nearing them along the walkway. Although a whole mass of acquaintances or people recommended by friends had been passing through the manor, they also know that, especially lately, the region was full of incensed Germans, unaccountable Russians from Vlasov's fascist forces, bands of run-of-the-mill robbers, as well as simply desperate refugees, ready for anything. Fortunately, it turned out that there was nothing to be worried about, as at the threshold there arrives an expected guest: Ferdynand Goetel.

That's how I imagine the scene. I reckon that, on account of the current circumstances, Iwaszkiewicz greeted his guest cordially, even though it might just as well have been quite different. Judging from the sparse comments sprinkled about their writings—to put it lightly, the two gentlemen did not enjoy each other's affection. Even before the war Iwaszkiewicz wrote of Goetel as being a "horrible type."[34] Goetel didn't leave the debt unpaid long, referring to Jarosław as a prevaricator, a person interested in no one but himself, the "carefree ephebe of the occupied country," a "taxi dancer of appeasement."[35]

Despite their undisguised, reciprocal antipathy, Goetel spent several days in Stawisko with Iwaszkiewicz. Why so long, why there, and why together? What could they have talked about during his stay? Goetel, an avid mountaineer and controversial man of letters, had been the president of the Polish PEN Club and the Union of Polish Writers (Związek Literatów Polskich) before the war. Iwaszkiewicz's dislike of him, to the extent that it was authentic, was no exception to any rule. Goetel won himself a lot of enemies and fierce critics with his 1938 book *Pod znakiem faszyzmu* (Under the Banner of Fascism)[36] in which the author defended the fascist idea by contrasting it strongly to Communism (which he had experienced first hand, having been deported after the First World War to Turkestan by the Soviets). Iwaszkiewicz was certainly to be counted among these enemies and critics, as he had left his own period of admiration for the idea of Greater Germany long behind him. Later, Goetel abandoned his opinions on Fascism, and during the occupation, which he spent in Warsaw, he worked on behalf of the underground state. He experienced the catastrophe of the Warsaw Uprising and at the beginning of October set out in that exodus of the inhabitants of Żoliborz and Marymont to the west: through Pruszków, Podkowa, and Milanówek to Grodzisk. However, along the way, he showed up at Iwaszkiewicz's manor in Stawisko.

I suppose that the natural theme of their conversations over those several days was Warsaw: the events that took place during the Uprising, all of that monstrous agony of the city, which was all the more horrible, since if the two gentlemen went out onto the porch after dark during those conversations, they could probably see against the dark sky the red glow of the capital as it was being systematically burnt to ash by the Germans. They probably debated over whether it all had to end that way, whether the disaster was avoidable, and also—a universal topic of conversation amongst the intelligentsia at the time—whether the Russians might have put an end to that suffering by coming to the aid of the Poles. Goetel was categorical in his opinion that such hopes were unreal, since it would have required a magnanimity of which the Russians are simply incapable. He knew what he was talking about.

I reckon that the conversation must have inexorably turned to Russia. A few months earlier, Iwaszkiewicz had finished his narrative of Smolensk—did he boast of it to his guest? In the spring of 1943, when the text was just underway, Goetel had himself been in Smolensk. This unexpected expedition of his was to weigh on him all throughout his subsequent life. One might even say that it destroyed him. In April of that year, the Germans organized a trip to Smolensk for a Polish delegation that was to inspect on site the mass graves of the Polish officers murdered by the NKVD, which had just been discovered. The Germans stated that the numbers of the murdered might well reach ten thousand. It looked as if the horrid truth of the fate of thousands of Polish army officers who had vanished in Kozielsk and Starobielsk had been unearthed. The immensity of the crime committed by Stalin was not yet known, and no one yet knew of the other Golgothas: near Minsk, Kharkiv, or Mednoye. The forest known as Kozyi Gory (Goat Mountains), located some thirty kilometers from Smolensk, was the first. Goetel, who informed the underground Home Army (Armia Krajowa, AK) about it all, flew off from the Okęcie airfield near Warsaw along with the delegation on a special flight to Smolensk. There, he was led around the terrain of the uncovered graves; he observed the exhumations carried out there by the Germans, and could confirm both the scale of the crime as well as the fact that they were Polish officers lying there, among whom were Generals Bohatyrewicz and Smorawiński, and that all of the victims had perished from a shot to the back of the head. The shell casings discovered there pointed to handguns. "What an immensity of questions is covered over by the forest of Katyń!"[37] Goetel was later to write. It was an immensity that exceeds man's widest reach, an immensity that overwhelms and oppresses. For this reason, before their return, when the members of the Polish delegation wished to show their respects to the victims, when one of them, Dr Seyfried, standing at the edge of the trench serving as a mass grave full of mummified, uniformed bodies, exclaimed: "My dear countrymen! Let us honor with a moment of silence the Poles fallen here, who perished so that Poland might exist," Goetel began to understand that following what he had just witnessed, nothing would ever be as it had been in the past: "I stand there, gazing into the black earth that yawns beneath my feet. And I don't know if Poland, which shall exist and must exist, will ever be capable of forgetting this burial mound."[38]

Personally, this trip to Smolensk became a curse for Goetel. I reckon that, to some extent, as early as the second half of 1943, knowledge of the Katyń massacre and who committed it was already widespread in Warsaw thanks to Goetel's report and those of the other members of the delegation. Certainly, the news also arrived at nearby Stawisko. Rumours and innuendos began to swirl around Goetel, and finally, accusations concerning his trip to Smoleńsk. Goetel was, of course, accused of collaboration with the Germans. As one of the chief witnesses to the Katyń massacre, he found himself later on the black list of the Communists, who never let up on him until the day he died. I also think that, after what he'd seen in Kozyi Gory, he himself never regained his balance. The Katyń forest indeed covered over too great an immensity of questions. It was just too much—the knowledge that the East had determined to show that it could well kill us, turned out to be too strong an experience to be digested by the soul—whether that of an individual or that of the nation. It would be present in memories and hearts for decades on end, fixed there like stigmata following the touch of evil, poisoning emotions and thoughts.

When, many years later, Andrzej Wajda determined upon creating his film about Katyń, he explained it as a personal and national necessity of throwing its horrid weight off the shoulders, throwing off the curse of that accursed land. I remember well the gala première of the film in the Teatr Wielki, in September 2007. The famous director was not free of petty-mindedness, even here. Standing on the stage, in front of the great screen, he did not even direct a single word of greeting to Maria and Lech Kaczyński, sitting directly across from him in the presidential box—he simply ignored them. At the time, aversion to them was too great. The film itself did not seem much of a success to me; it was too shallow, as if lacking in historical imagination to bear the weight of the questions. In the last scene—a sequence lasting twenty minutes, portraying the methodical murder of the Polish officers, the figure of an NKVD functionary in leather apron and leather gloves, who appears again and again in the scene, shooting victim after victim in the nape of the neck—is the incarnation of all the horrible demons of the East. That scene overwhelmed the public. When the credits began to roll over the black screen, instead of applause a deathly silence filled the great hall. And then someone, in that absolute quiet began, in a resonant voice, the words of the prayer: "Our Father, who art in heaven..." No one present at the time had even the slightest inkling that the horrible immensity of the Smolensk questions would have its sequel.

Endnotes

1. J.M. Rymkiewicz, *Samuel Zborowski,* op. cit., pp. 95–96.
2. A. Iwański senior, *Pamiętniki 1832–1876* (Memoirs 1832–1876), A. Iwański junior, *Wspomnienia 1881–1939* (Recollections 1881–1939), introduced by J. Iwaszkiewicz, ed. W. Zawadzki, Warsaw 1968.

3. Fr. A. Luter, "Księża na ekranie" (Priests on the Screen). *Tygodnik Powszechny*, 20 February 2007, https://www.tygodnik-powszechny.pl/ksieza-na-ekranie-138895 (accessed 16 January 2020).

4. There are various versions of the events, which differ amongst themselves in details. I have especially made use of J.U. Niemcewicz's *Dzieje panowania Zygmunta III, króla polskiego, wielkiego księcia litewskiego, itd.* (The History of the Reign of Zygmunt III, King of Poland, Grand Duke of Lithuania, etc.), Kraków 1860, vol. 3, pp. 301–303. See also A. Kraushar, *Z dziejów Warszawy. Grobowiec carów Szujskich* (From the History of Warsaw. The Tomb of the Shuyski Tsars), Kraków 1894.

5. See S. Żółkiewski, *Początek i progres wojny moskiewskiej* (The Beginnings and Progress of the War with Muscovy), Warsaw 1966.

6. J. Iwaszkiewicz, *Dzienniki 1964–1980* (Memoirs 1964–1980), Warsaw 2011, Vol. 3, p. 186.

7. J. Iwaszkiewicz, *Opowiadania wybrane* (Selected Stories), ed. A. Zawada, Wrocław 2001, p. 304 (French translation see J. Iwaszkiewicz, *Mère Jeanne des Anges*, trans. G. Lisowski, Paris 1959).

8. Ibid., p. 320.

9. The manuscript may be found in the Anna and Jarosław Iwaszkiewicz Museum in Stawisko.

10. G. Łoś, "Naszyjnik na złość wrogom Rusi" (A Necklace to Spite the Enemies of Rus), *Rzeczpospolita*, 13 May 2010, https://archiwum.rip.pl/artykul/946946-Naszyjnik-na-zlosc-wrogom-Rusi.html (accessed 17 December 2019).

11. J. Iwaszkiewicz, *Opowiadania wybrane...*, op. cit., p. 255.

12. Ibid., p. 297.

13. Cited by K. Koehler, *Boży podżegacz. Opowieść o Piotrze Skardze* (Divine Rabble--Rouser. An Account of Piotr Skarga), Warsaw 2012, p. 58.

14. J. Iwaszkiewicz, *Opowiadania wybrane...*, op. cit., p. 282.

15. Ibid., p. 280.

16. Ibid., p. 263.

17. Ibid., p. 345.

18. Ibid., p. 352.

19. Ibid., p. 353.

20. J.H. Billington, *The Icon and the Axe. An Interpretative History of Russian Culture*, New York 1970.

21. A. Besançon, *Sainte Russie*, Paris 2012.

22. Ibid., p. 37.

23. V. Erofeiev, "Dans la maison européenne La Russie est une grande chambre sale" (In the House of Europe Russia is a Large Dirty Room), *Boulevard Extérieur*, 27 February 2015, https://www.boulevard-exterieur.com/Dans-la-maison-europeenne-la-Russie-est-une-grande-chambre-sale.html, accessed 16 January 2020.

24. For the Latin text of the inscription see A. Kraushar, *Z dziejów Warszawy...*, op. cit., p. 20.

25. Z. Kubiak, "Kleopatra a sprawa polska," in *Klasyczne miary i świat współczesny. Z Zygmuntem Kubiakiem rozmawia Paweł Czapczyk* (Classical Measure and the Contemporary World. Zygmunt Kubiak in Conversation with Paweł Czapczyk), Warsaw 2009, pp. 118–123.

26. The Polish translation referred to by the author is that of Roman Brandstaetter, printed in Warsaw, 1958.

27. Z. Kubiak, *Kleopatra a sprawa polska*, op. cit., pp. 118–119.

28. J.M. Rymkiewicz, *Samuel Zborowski*, op. cit., p. 96.

29. Ibid., 94–95.

30. Ibid., 95–96.

31. J. Iwaszkiewicz, *Książka moich wspomnień,* Kraków 1957.

32. A. Iwański sr., *Pamiętniki...,* op. cit.

33. J. Iwaszkiewicz, *Dzienniki*, op. cit., vol. 3: 1964–1980, p. 105.

34. Ibid., Warsaw 1980, vol. 1: 1911–1955, p. 127.

35. F. Goetel, *Czasy wojny* (War Times), London 1955, p. 166.

36. F. Goetel, *Pod znakiem faszyzmu*, Warsaw 1938.

37. F. Goetel, *Czasy wojny,* op. cit., p. 128.

38. Ibid., p. 132.

THE GERMAN HEGEMONS

The life of Julian Klaczko commenced in 1825, on ulica Niemiecka, that is, German St., in Wilno (Vilnius). It will come to an end in 1906 in Kraków on ulica Smoleńsk, in a neo-Renaissance villa giving out onto the Planty, the green park that encircles the Old Town. Can there be anything more symbolically significant for a great nineteenth-century Polish political thinker? An entire life stretching from German St. to Smoleńsk St.? I say that Klaczko was a great Polish political thinker. I also need to add that he was a cultural thinker who inspires to this very day. By birth, Klaczko was a Lithuanian and a Jew; only later did he become, by choice, a Pole and a Catholic. His Jewishness sometimes constituted a certain obstacle in his relations with other Poles—with Zygmunt Krasiński, for example. He himself was rather sensitive on this point, since he declared that it was his custom always to inform his Polish interlocutors of his Semitic background. However, I feel that this also gave him a broad, and in consequence, a more independent perspective on Polishness and European culture. When he left Wilno in 1842 for the none-too-distant Königsberg to attend the university there, he was taking an essential, though none too surprising cultural decision in favor of the German, classical *Bildung*. It was Germany at that time, not Prussia, that constituted a mature culture, already shaped to a particular form, and an important point of reference—a place of special cultural renaissance and that, furthermore, in the spirit of bourgeois liberalism. Having cast aside the obsolete, odiferous costume of the age-old Roman Empire, and having acquired a patriotic self-confidence in its self-defense against the imperialism of Napoléon, this is the Germany of Winckelmann, Schiller, Goethe, Kant, and Hegel—Germany reborn in a new spirit. At any rate, they certainly had an attraction for the intellectually curious, young, talented people from all over Europe, people like Klaczko, who was to acquire a splendid knowledge of history, classical literature, and philosophy from his German professors in Königsberg. Outfitted with such solid knowledge, he would take himself next to Heidelberg, that most Romantic of all the cities of Germany, which pulsed at the time with the new ideals of German liberalism espoused by its wealthy, solid bourgeois. I think that young Klaczko must have seen a great hope in these German ideas, a hope for the ability to achieve a fundamental reconstruction of old, reactionary Europe as well as the rebirth of Poland in a new guise. This is not an absurd thought at all. For since the 1780s, it would occur to the minds of Poles again and again that it was the King in Berlin who would stand up in defense of the Polish state, at the very least in order to avoid an over-close proximity to the greedy tsars, seeking ever new territories in the west, ever new European conquests. And now, since the Hohenzollerns proved themselves just as worthy friends as the Habsburgs and Romanovs, there arose a real hope that bourgeois Germany—not reactionary Prussia—reborn in that new liberal spirit, caught up in classical ideas as well as the romantic faith of the heroism of nations; that these very nationalist Germans should stand up in defense of the rights of the Poles, in the name of freedom, of the principles of reciprocal respect, common decency, and, of course, the obvious necessity of protection from the imperial despotism of Nicholas I in the East. For after all, was it not the units of defeated Polish insurrectionists in November 1831, marching with head held high, that aroused such stirring and sincere enthusiasm among the liberal burghers of the German cities through which they passed? Was it not in their honor that those sublime *Polenlieder* were composed? That enthusiasm of the German liberals for the independence struggles of the Poles basically was a harbinger of an inevitable breakthrough. In any event, those hopes couldn't have been baseless. It was for this reason that Klaczko accepted with ardor his first job in the national newspaper of the German liberals, the *Deutsche Zeitung*, published by Georg Gervinus—a newspaper that was to become an important intellectual source—and source of cadres—for the 1848 national parliament in Frankfurt. Klaczko edited in the paper his own column titled "Russland und Polen" in which he printed a series of articles on the theme of Polish-Russian relations, which was of great interest to the German reader. He also composed popular reports from the Berlin trials of the Polish leaders of the unsuccessful 1846 Poznań Uprising—Mierosławski and Libelt. Nonetheless, in 1848, that year of unrest in Europe, also known as the European "Spring of the Peoples," Klaczko himself underwent a breakthrough in his sentiments and violently broke with the German liberals. Summing up this sudden about-face, and totting up a balance sheet of the illusions that had heretofore beset him, he wrote and published in Berlin a German brochure titled *Die deutschen Hegemonen, Offenes Sendschreiben an Herrn Georg Gervinus.*

Sigurd and his *aqua tofana*

The German Hegemons, Klaczko's open letter to Gervinus, is without a doubt the best and most profound text on the subject of Germans and Germanness as ever was written by a Polish author. Full of passion and a familiarity with the subject it takes up, it is an attack on German politics and the German spirit. And yet for certain reasons which Klaczko will make clear later on, it is this very text, along with his youthful verse written in Wilno (Vilnius), that he demanded never be published again. The author had a sense of having been very mistaken in his evaluation of the Germans. In 1848 it seemed that he had caught sight of the true face of German liberals or, rather, their vacuity and the real reasons behind their unconquerable weakness. He felt that they had become not only a source of great disappointment, but perhaps even deserved a just contempt, and their strivings to construct a new, powerful, German state in the middle of Europe must in the end turn against them and end up in total catastrophe. Obviously, years later, especially looking back from the perspective of the later Germany of Bismarck and Wilhelm, these decided judgements and Cassandra-like prophecies of Klaczko must have seemed entirely mistaken, and worse—completely frivolous. However, when one reads the *Hegemons* today—not only from the perspective of what happened with the Germans and our part of Europe in the twentieth century, but from that of the present moment—it is obvious that Klaczko had been able to see to the very depths of the problem of Germanness. What is more, he was able to compare it to the question of Polishness in such a manner that allows the reader to understand the huge difference between the Polish approach to form and that of the Germans, and so: he explains the entire difference between them in their position in European culture. And so I wish to pose the following thesis: in my opinion, Klaczko, a Jew and Lithuanian by birth, became a Pole by choice after arriving at his own understanding of Polishness because of his experience with German liberalism, the German approach to form, and it is his *Hegemons* that documents the course of that transformation.

"Here we have the essence of Germanness," Klaczko writes with bitter irony in this work, "the striving toward the endless and boundless. To us, poor Poles, barbarians, unenlightened by the rays of philosophy, who continue to live with our poet in the impractical conviction that the greatest wisdom is virtue, it seems that this *Drang nach Osten*, as Herr von Gagern puts it, this drive for the sake of having a drive, this all-possessing feeling, is something we have always lacked. Even our first king, Bolesław Wielki (the Great), was impaired to such an extent that he ordered the borders of his realm to be marked by having gunmetal posts driven into the stream beds of rivers."[1]

The von Gagern, or more precisely, Heinrich von Gagern, to whom Klaczko refers, was one of the leaders of the moderate wing of the German liberals. He began his career by being chosen presiding officer of the German National Assembly in Frankfurt, that famous parliament that constituted the German Republic, holding its debates in the Church of St. Paul. Later, at the turn of 1849, he held the position of Prime Minister of new Germany. It is to him that Klaczko attributed the articulation of the idea of the "drive to the East" as an expression of the German strivings to the endless and boundless. In essence, it was not just about a geographical or territorial dimension, although, on account of the direct proximity of the German lands to their own, this drive had an obvious ominousness for the Poles. Really, what he had in mind was rather German universalism in general, which always constituted a strong motive force in traditional German politics—whether in the search for its concrete expression in the idea of the Roman Empire and the Roman Emperor of the first Reich, or in the conception of the loftiness of German culture and *Bildung*, created by the German renaissance of the eighteenth century, or at that moment, when it found expression in German, bourgeois liberalism and its vision of a German state—and thus when it took on the guise of national German politics. And this politics once more placed the Germans at the very top of all nations in Europe, or rather, because of that very universalism, it placed them above them. However much in Goethe's writings (perhaps with the exception of Part II of *Faust*) or, in particular, in those of Schiller, this universalism in reference to culture might still give one the impression of something truly noble, sublime, and exceptional, in its political guise of the German liberalism of Frankfurt, Klaczko suspects it to be something vital, firm, and practically aggressive. Certainly, to a great extent, the Germans owed this progress from the noble universalism of the spirit to the inexorable universalism of politics to their greatest philosopher of those times—Hegel, who injected them with that horrible gene of historical dialectics. In this way, he made it come about that the "striving for the endless and boundless" became an indispensable, firm task, the historical vocation of the German nation. In his *Hegemons*, Klaczko attempts in his peculiar, often quite emotional manner (because he is really furious at the German liberals who, he feels, deceived him) to describe what he saw in the German Parliament in Frankfurt in the years 1848 and 1849, namely: that on the basis of the national interests of Germans and Poles, conflict between German universalism and Polish particularism of being is inevitable. For the Germans make use of national politics in order to create a total form, searching desperately for a possible rationalization therefor (for which reason they are ever doomed to failure, something that Thomas Mann came to understand only in 1945), whereas the Poles are always satisfied with their particularity, making use of politics for the creation of their own place in the sun. But it is for this very reason, as Klaczko notes in the fragment cited above, that in German political culture rule over everything—whether literally, in a physical sense, or indirectly, normatively, for example—will always be an obvious vocation, even if it is preserved only for themselves somewhere deep inside, but nonetheless as a profound inner conviction, whereas in the Polish tradition this will always be seen as an absurd, not to say insane, idea (*furor teutonicus*). What is more: according to Klaczko, sooner or later, but inevitably, such an indispensable German universalism, solidly founded upon Hegelian dialectics, has to see in the particularism of its close neighbor a misunderstanding—a mistake which must quickly be corrected. And should the mistaken party stubbornly insist on remaining where it is, that party must be treated just as a historically speaking "bastard race" deserves.

As we have noted, this sublime universalism of spirit, progressing into the political universalism of German firmness (the source of that peculiarly German mixture of sentimentalism and brutality), will appeal to the most various rationalizations in order to explain its own iron necessity. Primarily, Klaczko sees, in a long historical perspective, three of these: Christianity, civilization, and freedom. At bottom, however, it is above all a basic hunger for power, which will be symbolized by the mythical Nordic hero Sigurd. He, in the *Song of the Nibelungen* becomes Siegfried—the great conqueror of lands and treasures, and slayer of dragons. Somewhere at the basis of this transformation from the noble universalism of the Winckelmanns, Schillers, and Kants to the universalism of iron necessity may be found that figure of Sigurd or Siegfried, this *animus dominandi.* Klaczko, who in the 1840s permitted himself to be seduced by the noble values of German liberalism, now clearly senses in it the presence of the warrior-German. After all, this was also the time when on account of Romanticism, many Germans were searching out their roots not only in mediaeval figures such as, for example, Faust but also, by reaching even farther backward into the misty past, in ancient and mythological Germanic heroes. It is from such that just a little later on Wagner—who as a young man took part in the revolutionary events of 1848 (as did Bismarck)—was to mold his monstrous operas which, to this very day, constitute for many Germans the highest expression of their German, national spirit. And yet Klaczko most clearly understood that this grand, endless, and boundless might of the Germanic heroes, the Sigurds and Siegfrieds, was an empty and blind force. In this context, he adduces the truly interesting story of Olaf, a mediaeval king of Norway, who once asked one of his German knights: Who do you believe in? I believe in myself, the knight responded. The Germans believe only in themselves and in nothing more—Klaczko states, and it is for this reason that they search out universal rationalizations for their otherwise empty power. Just such a function will be played in support of the imperialism of the German Empire by Christianity. It will be nothing but a form for that blind force, and the beautiful idea of "one flock and one shepherd" will serve to rationalize conquest after conquest; in the first place, the pacification of the Slavs. And this will continue up until the Reformation, which will uncover the vacuity of the political Christianity of the emperors and, as Klaczko sees it, turn the iron sword of Germany into one of wood. The *animus dominandi* will need a new rationale, and for this reason it will reach for the idea of civilization—German civilization. And this will turn out to be just such a rationalization for conquest and partition as Christianity had been before. Here we must introduce a few longer fragments from Klaczko's work in order to better realize what exactly, according to him, is that German civilization: "If one were to search for a term, which in the world of morality would express that, which *aqua tofana* expresses in the physical world, that is: a state of eternal morbidity and hemorrhages lasting whole hours, the struggle against the toils of the serpent as in the case of Laocoon, or the self-combustion of Hercules, enlightened lunacy, or rays of light as sharp as a stiletto, situations in which the sacrificial victim shivers eternally under the blows of the bloody axe and knows no other comfort than the words *Vae Victis!*, and where the horrid statement of our poet who *would die, but cannot* becomes a quotidian fact [...] such a term, in the world of the Slavs, is German civilization. To slice through the last artery of Slavic life, to deprive them of the desire of rebirth, to sever with the scalpel of criticism the nerves of their national and religious traditions, and with the aid of history, deformed and distorted by the art of alexandrine reflection, to teach them to look at their own past with disgust, and through constant tutelage to deprive them entirely of their voice, to twist their tongue from their mouth thanks to foreign and dull people, and through perniciously arranged "education" to transform them into children babbling nonsensical imprecations against their own parents, and thanks to a philosophy that rationalizes everything, to cause them to take delight in the injustices committed against them, cursing the day, like some Richard III, of their ever being born as they were, and through unstinting oppression, which allows them not a moment's rest, to lash them on to a place where nothing remains for them but the choice between physical and moral suicide, so that they should take themselves off along with the bones of their forebears, and thanks to industrious efforts diligently lead them to starvation and complete ruination [...] such, indeed, has been the driving motivation of German civilization in the lands of the Slavs."[2]

However, 1848, along with the striking of the great hour of German liberalism, brought with it a new rationalization for the universalism of iron necessity—the idea of freedom. In the name of universal freedom it became necessary to liberate the Poles and other Slavs from themselves.

All right then, but what exactly was Klaczko getting at with those German liberals, at whose feet he first sat as a student in Königsberg, and for whose *Deutsche Zeitung* he wrote later in Heidelberg, supporting their efforts toward the creation of a new German constitution and republic? What was it that made him feel so deceived that, in the end, he saw nothing but the empty might of Sigurd in the firm universalism of the Frankfurt liberals, the might which, throughout the centuries, remains the same, changing nothing but its outward garments of Christianity, civilization, and freedom? In order to understand this properly, we must first explain what exactly were those events of 1848. For it seems to me that there is not only a lot of shallowness in the manner in which generally received public opinion considers them but also a certain unsubstantiated dismissiveness, too, of that year, which saw the great swelling of so many nationalist and liberal movements in Europe—and their complete, subsequent flop. For it seems that the significance of the so-called Spring of the Peoples was much more profound, and constituted a turning point for the political thought of many regions of Europe. Many proponents of freedom, who had the most noble intentions in mind, but also did not shun political radicalism and the slogans of democratization, quite properly understood that the political system of police-like surveillance constructed in Europe by the monarchs after the fall of Napoléon and the Congress of Vienna, the symbol of which became the idea of "restoration" and the government of Metternich, was unacceptable, even though it endured without interruption, despite various upheavals, for more than thirty years. Many of them gazed with hope toward England where, along with the reform of the voting laws, liberal political rights were developing; others, like Tocqueville, sought inspiration and answers across the Atlantic, studying the evolution of the new democratic society of America. In an exalted inspiration, Mazzini was circling about Europe—the lion of liberal salons and societies, who would cast off the yoke of evil monarchies and establish an ideal order throughout the entire continent. From the point of view of many European nations: Serbs, Greeks, Croatians, Belgians, Irishmen, Italians, and Magyars, this reactionary and anti-liberation order of Europe was understood as a truly onerous injustice imposed upon them from above. Poles especially might have felt aggrieved at their treatment at the hands of the monarchs' European order, on account of their decades-long sanctioning of the partitioning of their state. The 1830 uprising failed, but to a certain degree it enabled the Belgians to establish their own state, by deflecting from them the eventual intervention of Petersburg. The Poles enjoyed some advantage of their reputation in Europe, which saw them as a heroic nation—a particularly strong sentiment among the German liberals, who greeted the insurgents marching westward through their cities as the apostles of new nationalist freedom on the continent. However, eighteen years later, the situation of the Poles was completely different. When the next uprisings and revolts broke out in 1848 in Sicily, Paris, Vienna, Berlin, Budapest, and Rome, the

Poles had already suffered the gloomy experiences of 1846—an unsuccessful uprising in Poznań, which concluded with the arrest of the leaders, the trial of whom in Berlin Klaczko reported for the *Deutsche Zeitung*. Above all, however, there was the disastrous Kraków Uprising and Galician Massacre (the *Rabacja*) inspired by the Austrians, which led to bloody pogroms of landholders in the western part of the province. For the Poles, these events had a traumatic dimension. And thus, two years later, many of them—including Klaczko—believed that now, the western liberals, who stood at the head of the democratic movements of national liberation, would take some real steps toward the liberation of their sorely tried nation. However, this turned out to be a complete illusion.

The Polish Debate in Frankfurt

Word of the March events in Berlin: the street fighting, the formation of a national guard, the declaration of basic republican rights, the abolition of censorship, and the freeing of political prisoners (including Mierosławski and Libelt) immediately resonated in Poznań, leading to the establishment of the National Committee (Komitet Narodowy). At this, Klaczko quit his job in the Heidelberg *Deutsche Zeitung* and set out for Poznań. The Committee was just about to declare the independence of Poland and call for the creation of a Polish Army. However, the situation that Klaczko meets with upon arriving in Poznań is none too promising. Actually, it is miserable. Stanisław Tarnowski has preserved for us Klaczko's detailed report in which he mentions coming across a National Committee entirely divided between proponents of a decided, popular revolution and those who wished to negotiate new conditions of broader autonomy with the King of Prussia. The radicals, including Libelt, were of the opinion that the peasants needed to be armed and, following the pattern of an insurrection, would carry out a decided social and political revolution. Certainly not without significance for this calculation, besides the radicalism of his ideas themselves, was the recent experience of the Galician Massacre. However, the more conservative members of the Committee were horrified at the very idea. "For God's sake!" Potworowski was supposed to have cried, "Why should we send these poor peasants, who have nothing to hand except scythes, off to certain massacre? We promised them Poland, then we disappointed them, and now here comes a storm of shrapnel right at them, defenseless..." But Libelt would not be moved. With the halo of the Berlin trial and his sentence of twenty-five years' imprisonment hovering over his head, he shouted back: "This is our testament! We must perish, for such the honor of Polish arms demands!" At this point, according to Klaczko, a tall, dark-haired man with swarthy face and fiery eyes entered the room. It was Słowacki. Libelt repeated his project for the uprising. "At this, Słowacki rises—I can see him now as if he were standing in front of me—and standing there with his arms crossed on his bosom, in a loud voice, he pronounces these words: 'What are you thinking? Does it seem to you that we still need, today, as before, cannons, regiments, officers? I tell you: today the epoch of sacred anarchy has arrived...' He wanted to say something more, but Stefański suddenly interrupted him. Having heard the two words pronounced in connection with one another: sacredness and anarchy, he threw himself at the poet's feet in delight and, stretching out his hands, cried, 'O Master! What great words thou hast pronounced...'"[3] Klaczko sums up the whole scene of the meeting of the Committee with but one word—COMEDY.

In this chaotic situation it's hard to be surprised that Friedrich Wilhelm IV realized that he might make perfect use of the question of the Grand Duchy of Poznań to come to his own terms with the Frankfurt liberals who sought to transform the German Union into a new, constitutional German Republic. He announced magnanimously that the Prussian provinces belonging to the Reich, including the Poznań region, should decide for themselves, according to the principle of ethnic nationality, whether they wished to form part of the new Germany or not. On 21 March, the National Committee in Poznań submitted a significant appeal to the German inhabitants of the Duchy, which well illustrates the credo of the democratic Polish Romantics: "The history of Poland bears witness to the fact that we have always defended the principles of Christianity at the cost of our own blood. We have been conquered by an absolutism, which at the same time stemmed the liberty of the neighboring peoples as well." Further: "That is what placed the yoke on our necks, that deprived us of our political life. At the time, the peoples did not yet understand the gravity of the issue and applauded the governments that divided our country. The monarchs progressed in their activities and committed the final act of their nefarious politics by abolishing the Republic of Kraków. But now the peoples no longer applauded them; numerous voices were raised on all hands in protest of this new political crime—the seventh partition. We found then many friends among various nations. Our cause became the cause of Europe as a whole, and today, when the peoples have reacquired their independence, they sense that their liberty will have no firm guarantee until Poland also comes to enjoy her own rights again."[4] The revolution of the nations in Europe, which was to cast off the old order of the Holy Alliance, was therefore also to lead to the reconstruction of the Polish state—as the members of the Committee and doubtlessly Klaczko himself saw it. The German liberals ought not only to feel morally obliged to support this imperative arising from solidarity in support of free peoples but also to see in it their own practical geopolitical interest. For it was the Polish state, waging "war against Asia since the dawn of our history," that constituted the only bastion capable of restraining Nicholas I, that defender of absolutist thrones, from intervening, inevitably, in revolutionary Europe. And so, the Committee's proposal was based on the conviction that the German liberals in Frankfurt as well as the German inhabitants of the Poznań region, taking advantage of the possibility offered by the King of Prussia, ought to restrain their nationalistic appetites, recognize the autonomy of the Duchy of Poznań, and treat it as the beginnings of a reborn Polish state, which would be for the new Germany a natural geo-strategic partner in common defense against the despotism looming from the East. However, the problem lay in the fact that such calculations could not count on any understanding amongst the German liberals, nor upon the loyalty of the German inhabitants of the Duchy of Poznań, nor upon the favor of the Prussian King in Berlin. And so, when in April the Duchy's parliament, in accord with Friedrich Wilhelm's desire, expressed by a vote of twenty-seven to seventeen that the Grand Duchy of Poznań does not wish to be part of the German Union, the German minority of the Duchy organized a separate meeting at which they appointed their own representatives to the National Assembly in Frankfurt. And it was their arrival at the Church of St. Paul in that city that became the direct cause of the debate concerning the future of the Grand Duchy as well as the need to partition it according to a line of demarcation separating territories inhabited by the German and Polish peoples. From the Polish perspective—if we choose to employ the chronology contained in the appeal of the National Committee—this would amount to nothing less than the eighth partition of Poland.

The July debates of the Frankfurt Assembly were therefore concentrated on the Polish question, which meant, in practice, on the future of the Grand Duchy of Poznań as established on the basis of the 1815 Vienna treaties. For many liberal and democratically-inclined Poles such as Klaczko, who continued to consider German liberalism the splendid fruit of a spiritual renaissance cultivated by the geniuses of Goethe and Schiller, the language they heard concerning themselves at the Frankfurt Parliament was tantamount to a huge culture shock. The Poles certainly had no illusions concerning the manner in which they were spoken of at the absolutist courts in Berlin, St. Petersburg, or Vienna; it was the language used by the generals of the imperial forces occupying the Polish territories and by other officials of the partitioning powers. Yet to hear this language of contempt and hatred from the mouths of German liberals in Frankfurt—amidst turmoil, earthy jokes and guffaws—must have been a shock never to be forgotten by people such as Klaczko: "The words that you pronounced at the time cannot be erased. They will never pass away, but will remain forever in the heart of every Pole," Klaczko was later to write. "The fact that the German hegemons, in the manner of those Italian bandits who kiss the medal of the Most Holy Virgin while sharpening their stilettos, wish to destroy us with slogans of justice on their lips, enslave us in the name of their own freedom, deprive us of our culture in the name of their own culture, and divide us once more on behalf of their own unity, making of us a race of bastards on behalf of the purity of their own noble generation—this shook us to the core, certainly; it horrified our hearts and undermined our faith in humanity."[5]

The only thing Poles know how to do is dance the mazurka! That image of the Polish nation deprived of culture and civilization was especially savored by the German liberal historians, the so-called "Reich-professors"—Stenzel, Droysen, and others, whom Bismarck was later to mock—during the July debates in the Frankfurt Assembly. It is the image of an ignorant, fallen nation, which over the ages brought nothing to Europe except chaos, anarchy, and cruelty. A nation that owes its civilization entirely to German influences, incapable of self-government or of taking advantage of political freedom. For this reason, it had been obliterated once and for all by the civilized European powers. This horrid image of Poland would characterize the official narrative of German historians on the topic of all of Central Europe, which would dominate the nineteenth and twentieth centuries, and which can still be heard every now and then today. On the other hand, according to Klaczko, another delegate to the assembly, this time an Austrian, purportedly suggested in all seriousness that Poland today is the Germans' California in Europe. However, the general tone of the debate concerning Poland and the Poles was set mainly by the leftist Hegelian Wilhelm Jordan, a man sympathetic to the views of von Gagern, but also—and this is perhaps worth remembering—the translator of Lelewel's *History of Poland*. In his speech he mocked the sentimentalism of those who defended Poland as an eternally oppressed nation, and called for the Germans, at last, to wake up from that sentimental dream of freedom for all nations and consider such issues from the perspective of their own, healthy national egoism. And it was just this healthy national egoism of the Germans that, according to Jordan, obliged them to cast aside all dreams of an independent Poland standing as if a bastion against threats from Russia. To the contrary: "Should Poland succeed in regaining its independence, it would go along hand in hand with Russia. The first day of Poland's independence would be the first day of Germany's struggle for existence. In our day and age, no nation can exist without a seaboard, so Poland would be obliged to press toward the Baltic shore—all the way to Königsberg. On the other hand, despite all that, should we bestow freedom upon Poland, would it be capable of defending its autonomy from Russia? Absolutely not. The liberation of Polish lands would be a gift presented to Russia. Were we not to wish to permit this, we would become entangled in a war with Russia."[6] And from this, according to Jordan, there flows the obvious deduction that the new German state should accept the Duchy of Poznań as a buffer zone under its entire control and simultaneously work to avoid conflicts with Russia that might lead to war. Not only did geopolitical calculations argue in support of this, but also powerful cultural considerations. "The superiority of Germans to Slavs is a natural historical fact,"[7] he cried from the podium. The Polish Republic showed clearly that it was not capable of enduring, and for that reason other nations had the right to deprive the Poles of the state which they could not support on their own: "The spirit of history has spoken in the history of Poland with sublime tragic irony: the same Holy Alliance which later joined hands in common monarchical defense against revolution, earlier divided Poland, which was already seething with a revolution yet unborn. It executed a death sentence upon the nation which itself never found enough strength to pulverize its feudal system, the downfall of which was demanded by culture, since it had in its bosom no vanquishers of aristocracy—no middle class, and for that reason, the vanquisher had to come from without [...] Who will deny that it was necessity itself, which had spoken through the lips of Jacobins, declaring: peace to the cottage, war to the palace, that was speaking here through the lips of the crowned heads who decreed the partition of Poland? Here we have the revolutionary, humanitarian sense of the division of Poland."[8] I reckon that no one could have formulated that better than Jordan, the leftist Hegelian and German liberal—the "progressive." His words were met with thunderous applause from the delegates gathered at Parliament. The Frankfurt liberals had decided: Poland had lost its right to exist—in the name of liberty, political and social progress, and modern culture, and the resurrection of that "corpse" of backwardness, ignorance, exploitation, and superstition was highly improbable.

The Faust Complex

These days, Frankfurt, the place in which the German liberals debated the fate of Poland in 1848—the debate which, for the young Klaczko and many other Poles of the time, became a true turning point in their appreciation of Germany and the West—today, that Frankfurt, the center of German commerce and bourgeoisie as it has been for ages, the home city of radiant Goethe, is not the political center of Germany, nor has it been for many years now. The German genius no longer lives there. It is the largest airport, communication hub, in Europe; it is where the European Central Bank is located—the real sovereign of the current European Union—and, of course, the location of a famous book fair. It is, thus, a part of the great infrastructure of a German state of which the hegemons, the German liberals, could only dream back in 1848. For that reason, if someone should wish to behold the firmness of German universalism in full bloom today, he'd have to take the trouble of travelling elsewhere—to the old capital of Prussia, to Berlin, which is the true political center of today's united Germany, in consequence of which all other German cities have been reduced to their actual provincial dimensions. I had the opportunity of looking upon that strange city in its various stages over the course of an entire half century. In history, fifty years is no especially long period, but those fifty years were a peculiar era during which the firm, German universalism was reborn in Europe in a new character. As we recall, Klaczko saw the various incarnations of the iron universal necessity of Germans first in Christianity, then in civilization, and finally in his own day and age in that peculiar version of liberalism and the idea of freedom (understood of course according to Hegel, and not some Mill or other). Today the new imperial clothes of that universalism, which robe the nakedness of the restless Sigurd, is Europe. So, over those fifty years I've beheld Berlin, which at first had been a front-line city, something on the order of a firing range for a probable Third World War, divided by a wall and barbed wire, where everyone in his own part of the city built—according to his own tastes and understanding—monuments to the victorious modernity of his times: to the east in the style of Stalinist Baroque, and later from prefab, and to the west from concrete, glass, and aluminum. Later, when that polarized world had disappeared, the fall discovered to the eyes of all in Berlin huge swathes of no man's land, overgrown with high grass and bushes, in the very center of a great, dysfunctional city, which seemed like a fallen region. But I must admit that it was then that Berlin seemed to me to be the most human city in Germany because everything all around, those great swathes of no man's land, the cobbled streets that often led nowhere, the stone buildings of Wilhelm's time stretching up here and there as black as tar, the great buildings that remained behind after the fall of the Berlin Wall: pre-fab orphans of Communism, and those office buildings covered with glass and aluminum in imitation of America, that is, the West, all of that gave the impression of a salutary German standstill. As if history had suddenly stopped in its tracks (which, as we know, is something unimaginable to Hegel). This state—so strange for Germany—did not last long, however, for categorical universalism hates nothing as much as it does states of blessed repose. Quickly enough the necessary tasks were undertaken: with methodical and stubborn élan whole fragments of the city fabric were recreated, an incessant transformation was begun, which continues to this very day, over thirty years later, and which will never pause unless perhaps something else stops it violently, brutally, in its tracks. In this way, Berlin has become what it is today: a great, ever bustling construction site, an area on which human reality is being transformed in the direction of the realization of a never completely specified perfection. The German Genius has woken up for good, in order to busy itself with its favorite pastime—the construction of a still better, more splendid, and new Europe with its splendid, new capital of Berlin.

Indeed, it is these very fifty years of peculiar German metamorphosis that lead inexorably to a grappling with the problem which, for today's Europe, has a fundamental significance, and for us Poles also has its weight; which in 1848 Klaczko noticed with such insight, and which he strove to explain in his text on the German hegemons. That is the German approach to form. To grasp the absolute, or rather, to become the center of the absolute and to fill it with one's never ending, tireless activity, one's drive—that, of course, became the chief task with which Hegel confronted the Germans in his *Phenomenology of Spirit*.[9] He enclosed in the parentheses of his monumental work, his philosophical summa, the conception of what constitutes form for the German, and what should be his relationship thereto. It is the idea of form as an endless task. Just such a discovery of form we can find among the creators of that noble German universalism, which initiated the classical renaissance of the second half of the eighteenth century. Enthused with this newly discovered idea, Schiller explained that "one needs to strive on, always, without ever being satisfied, without ever growing tired," to which thought Goethe would add, with the characteristic precision of a wise man: "our incapacity to pause is what makes us great." And so, if I am not mistaken, the German attitude to form is a certain type of peculiar disposition, set in motion by the logic of categorical universalism, because form is understood here otherwise than in the meditations of St. Augustine, who, in making use of the term, has in mind a well-defined, positive, and peaceful manner of life, an expression of himself and his conversion. The particular German idea of form as task expresses itself above all in opposition to the world. It is in basic disagreement with it, and sets in motion the imperative of endless transformation and permutation of reality, a reality with which there is no truce, nor can there ever be. In this manner, form becomes a way to constantly impose one's will, expressing simultaneously a fundamental and paramount discord toward the world. And conversely, an understanding of form as the practice and experience of one's own form of life posits some sort of acceptance of the world as it exists, as something given us, human beings, in good faith.

And yet what does this mean, and how are we to understand it, if the world is not a wonder, not a gift bestowed upon us in love, but some horrid, difficult task that we must endlessly undertake? In 1945, Thomas Mann published an extraordinarily eloquent text, "Germany and the Germans,"[10] to which reference must necessarily be made here. Independent of his explosive inclinations to polemical opposition toward the German liberals, Klaczko might always be accused of partisanship on account of his Polish, national point of view. It would be difficult to address such a charge at Mann, and it is he, exactly, who declaring himself as someone who consciously cast off his German citizenship to become an American by choice, undertakes a decided reckoning with the German understanding of form, which leads him to terrifying conclusions. In so doing, he makes reference to the syndrome of Faust—that figure who became the hero of the greatest work of German literature, created by Goethe. Mann recognized that it is indeed Faust who best expresses the essence of the peculiar German understanding of the world through the prism of the idea of form as a never-ending task. As he sees it, the drive to the world is the basic motive force of the German soul: the Germans possess a simply unbelievable thirst to turn their attention toward the world, coupled with a simultaneous, panicky dread of the same. This makes of them on the one hand natural cosmopolitans, people who don't much like to dwell on themselves, while feeling a strong vocation to take humanity as a whole in hand. As we have said, their dread arises from the fact that German universalism and cosmopolitanism have their source, above all, in a disaccord with the world; in a conviction that the world as it is is somehow fundamentally not the way it ought to be. The German cosmopolitans, who desire to face up to the task of setting the world in proper order are therefore not only condemned to loneliness but also, as Mann notes, to an inner provincialism. Their lack of accord toward the world impoverishes them, makes them lonely, and deprives them of their freedom. If we are to give credit to this perception, it turns out that the Germans train all of their attention on what is exterior, on what surrounds them, on what is "task"—and in this they are indeed mighty, powerful, rich, and inexhaustible: they are themselves. On the other hand, within themselves they haven't much to say: they are in a certain manner shockingly impoverished, lonely, and fettered. Mann calls this the "unworldly, provincial, German cosmopolitanism."[11] In a stubborn way, and yet one that is simultaneously in complete accord with the choice of Faust as the best guide to the backstreets of the German soul, he unites this with demonism. He returns to this theme several times in his text. In a certain place he states it plainly, without any circumlocution, that Germans are by nature evil, directed by an immense demonic force that through them makes its appearance in the world around them. It is only on account of this power that something which is weak and impoverished inwardly, brittle and finite, may so fundamentally negate the world, and later take advantage of all that power in order to will the imposition of its own form upon it, and change it. It is on this that the story of Faust is founded—Faust, who sells his soul to the devil.

In Goethe, we find a statement concerning Faust, which essentially, as Mann sees it, concerns Germany, and which we should always keep in mind. It speaks of the mysterious force that moves Faust toward his inexhaustible efforts—it is a force "that always wishes to do evil, but always works the good." In essence, here we have to deal with a perfect inversion of what Augustine wrote of form from the Christian perspective, as a manner of expressing his own conversion to the good. In Faust's understanding of form there is no longer any place for conversion, for form is all about a peculiar type of accomplishment (a magical one, the German word: *Leistung*), which has a demiurgical character, and in the final summing is demonic sleight of hand, attainable only at the price of one's soul. Can good be worked while intending evil? Faust acknowledges that this is the only path that permits action and knowledge, and in consequence, power as well. There is of course something tragic in all this, when it is necessary to offer oneself, to sell oneself on behalf of the carrying out of all these splendid possibilities for the good of mankind, to make the world something other than it is.

But still and all, one way or the other, it is the selling of oneself to the devil.

In just such a way, as Mann sees it, the Germans understand form, and thus do they understand politics. The source of the latter is, for them, a negation of the world and of life, which, ultimately, can only be overcome by "Satanic might" at the cost of one's own soul. "The peoples born and qualified for politics," he states, "instinctively know how to guard the unity of conscience and action, of spirit and power, at least subjectively. They pursue politics as an art of life and of power that cannot be entirely freed from a strain of vitally useful evil, but that never quite loses sight of the higher, the idea, human decency, and morality: in this regard they feel politically, and they get along with themselves and with the world in this fashion. Such getting-along with life, founded on compromise, the German regards as hypocrisy. He was not born to get along with life and he proves his lack of qualification for politics by misunderstanding it in a clumsily sincere manner. Not at all wicked by nature but with a flair for the spiritual and the ideal, he regards politics as nothing but falsehood, murder, deceit, and violence, as something completely one-sidedly filthy, and if worldly ambition prompts him to take up politics, he pursues it in the light of this philosophy. When the German takes up politics he thinks he has to act in a fashion to dumbfound humanity, that's what he regards as politics. Since he thinks it is unalloyed evil, he believes he has to be a devil to pursue it."[12]

There can be no doubt of the fact that in expressing these words in 1945, Mann was under the direct impression of the horrifying deeds that had been worked on behalf of his nation, with which he had earlier consciously parted ways. I don't wish to judge. That does not belong to me. Usually, the problem of Germany in Europe is confirmed by the statement, popularized by Kissinger, that Germany is too small to rule the entire continent, and too large to be a normal European country. This statement, repeated ad infinitum, has become so banal it no longer means anything. The matter is much more profound than any graceful *bon mot* of political realists. What I am getting at is this: that German approach to form, which is a type of escape from oneself and an imposition of one's will upon the world, is in Europe something very peculiar and becomes again and again the source of great problems. For us, Poles, it constitutes an essential experience of alienation, or dread. And although we may be fascinated by that exterior force and efficiency—especially in moments of our own weakness—still and all, what terrifies is that incapability of accepting the world as it is, the categorical concentration on the exterior, which becomes an area of endless tasks and accomplishments, which in essence aspires, after all, to some sort of immortal, inexhaustible power, and that is something which can never be at peace with itself and enjoy the blessedness of rest.

Glory

We return in the end to Klaczko and to his *Hegemons*, which is not just an immense polemic, though. The text arose from the author's profound disappointment with German liberalism, which proved itself to be empty, void. Not only in the sense that Bismarck would affirm it to be later—the future Iron Chancellor, who had once been a participant in those events in Frankfurt. German liberalism proved itself to be an empty force not because it was unsuccessful in its efforts at creating a German state, but above all because it failed to inspire Germans with any vital strengths that could fill them with positive content such as would be important for them and for Europe at the time. For they first had to overcome their own vacuity, to learn to turn toward themselves and effect a conversion of sorts. This, however, did not happen in Frankfurt, which thus became for Klaczko, who had arrived in Heidelberg right after university certainly full of faith in the positive motive power of the German soul, a turning point that would define the rest of his life. However, *Hegemons* is not, as we have just said, merely a polemic with German liberalism. It is also a text with an unambiguous conclusion, a clearly formulated hope, a certain, clear conviction, which motivates the author and his readers in the direction of another city: Prague. At the exact time when the German hegemons were meeting in Frankfurt, Prague was experiencing an exaltation, full of pathos, connected with the idea of Slavic unity and brotherhood. The first Slavic Congress, inspired by the Spring of the Peoples, was taking place in open opposition to the Frankfurt debates as well as the idea of a new German state, but also in answer to Magyar nationalism and the autonomy of Hungary in the bounds of the Habsburg Empire. The idea was the evocation of a separate federation of independent Slavic nations in the ambit of the Austrian monarchy, capable of achieving similar rights as those enjoyed by the German and Magyar populations. Amongst the hundred and some delegates of the congress that was meeting on the Zofinský Ostrov (Island of St. Sophia) in the Vltava river, there were thirty Polish representatives, including Karol Libelt, Jerzy Lubomirski, and Konstanty Zalewski. Seweryn Celarski has left a report concerning the mood of universal enthusiasm that reigned in the city at the time, writing, among others: "It is difficult to describe the ardor with which the waiting crowds greeted us—women waved kerchiefs, men their hats [...] Directly from our carriages we stepped into the embrace of the Czechs and greeted one another with such sincerity, love, and exaltation like brothers coming together again after a long period of separation."[13] The crowd sang the patriotic song "Hey, Slavs," and Pavel Šafařík made a fiery speech in which he stated that, gathering in Prague, the Slavs must prove themselves "capable of freedom and a higher political life." "For it's either victory and a free people, or an honorable death, and after death, Sláva"[14]—with such words he brought his address to an end. To this Slavic Sláva, in other words, Glory and thus to some sort of Slavic greatness, Klaczko will allude several times in his polemic against the German hegemons, making of it the main conclusion of his own text.

He too was caught up in the enthusiasm of the Prague events. They took upon a special meaning, after all, in the context of all those horrid words that were hurled at the Poles from the rostrum of St. Paul's in Frankfurt. For Klaczko, Slavic greatness, opposed to German liberalism, had a particular significance not only as the capacity for some higher and independent political life, some sort of formula of political unity of the Slavic nations, which they wished to win for themselves in opposition to their non-Slavic neighbors. Here the matter had nothing to do with rebelliousness or disobedience, as Berlin and Vienna saw it, but something truly fundamental and important. It was all about the Slavic idea of freedom, the Slavic model of civilization, and the right to their actual existence. When in his *Hegemons* Klaczko develops his Slavic conclusion, derived as a lesson learnt at the debate in Frankfurt, the first Slavic Congress in Prague had been dispersed long before. On 12 June 1848, the delegates succeeded in ratifying the "Manifesto to the European Nations" before a few hours later, literally, the Austrian artillery under the command of Feldmarschall Windischgrätz commenced its bombardment of the city. In haste, the Polish delegation evacuated from Prague. However, the question remained, and it could not be stifled by the fire of Austrian cannon—for it concerned Slavic freedom and civilization, which Klaczko now began speaking of in opposition both to German liberalism as well as another immense danger—the Russian idea of Pan-Slavism.

In the final fragments of his text on hegemony, he writes: "O no! *Sława* is not at all a spirit that is merely contrarian; she wishes to confirm many great things. Her destiny is not only to overthrow, but to build as well. She is to be a new principle introduced to the world, and it is for this reason that the future belongs to her."[15] According to Klaczko, German universalism, whether in the costume of

Christian faith, or under the aegis of modern liberalism, brings with it the immense threat of natural radicalism and possessiveness, which characterize every cosmopolitan idea. For this reason, the Slavs will always be better democrats than the German liberals, and it is their understanding of freedom that is more authentic. For they are free from all temptation to universalism, which inclines one to treat form not as a manner of expressing oneself in communion with others, not as the art of life, but rather as a means for imposing one's own will on others. They also understand perfectly that freedom can only be expressed through the equality of all nations, and by respect for the reciprocal principles of sovereignty and self-determination. "Only cosmopolitanism is radical, whereas patriotism is conservative."[16] Love for one's own fatherland and the freedom of its expression by all is the path to conserving, fostering, and developing real, varied life, without the perversion of self-salvation, casting aside, overcoming, and executing dialectical leaps. On the other hand, the idea of universal freedom must lead inexorably to centralization and some form of despotism of the imposed will, which in this manner is transformed into empty and blind force. The Poles and the other Slavic nations understand this difference, and it is for this reason that their comprehension of freedom, democracy, civilization, and Christianity is distinct. German universalism considers this other approach as treason to universal values, and it is for that reason that it will continually fall into ever new types of radicalism and aggression, as it seeks to bend other forms of life to its unreal imaginings. As Goethe wrote, this force of transformation will never pause. Otherwise, the Germans would have to accomplish some profound transformation of themselves—perhaps they would simply have to cease being themselves. One can, on the other hand, attempt to counteract it. "Poland must become a counterbalance (*korekta*) to cosmopolitan progress, founded upon the national conservatism of the Slavs,"[17] Klaczko states in his conclusion. National conservatism has the potential to resist the radicalism of the cosmopolitans, establishing a relation of fundamental significance for the reciprocal dealings of Poles and Germans, but also for the entirety of European culture and the relation of the forces upon which Europe is built. These thoughts, written down in 1849 by Klaczko, seem to be viscerally relevant today.

Conclusion

Analyses of *The German Hegemons* and the conclusions contained at its end are indeed striking in their aptness today, even if some ideas and notions, such as that Prague idea of Slavdom, have completely evaporated since those days. National conservatism as a counterbalance to cosmopolitan radicalness—this thought remains absolutely timely as a description of our present situation in Europe. Klaczko hadn't thought this matter through to the end in 1849. He wrote under the influence of strong emotion, sometimes striking out blindly, but in this way, he was successful in touching the very central nerve of the situation of the Poles, which is still our case today. But what exactly is to constitute that national conservatism of the Poles and other Slavs? In what is it to be manifest? Klaczko himself did not quite know yet, and so wrote about it somewhat mysteriously (though only seemingly so) that to the extent that the southern Slavs have a greater tendency to the natural world, which makes them more Oriental, so the Poles always tend toward culture, which in the end makes them more occidental. All of these statements are merely tropes, hazy traces, but in the end, intuitions of genius.

Klaczko was aware of the dangers threatening the Poles should they become disillusioned with the West. To gaze at Latin Europe solely through the prism of the iron German logic of universalism is a misunderstanding, and simultaneously a horrid trap for them. On the other side of deadly Hegelian dialectics there waits only the Russian knout. The Slavic Sláva, of whom they sang in Prague, may exist as a cultural and historical allegory, but not as any concrete political program. For in its concretized form it would always lead the Poles where their Latinism and Catholicism—and so, just that which makes them Europeans—will be something profoundly alien, constituting a fatal threat, for which reason it must in the end either submit to a complete *pieriekovka* (reforging) of the soul, or be physically annihilated somewhere in some muddy wood. We are speaking here of the so-called Pan-Russian anathema cast upon "treasonous" Poland, which in 1863 Yuri Samarin expressed in this way: "Poland is a sharp wedge driven by Latinity into the very heart of the Slavic world, in order to split it apart [...] Like two souls enclosed in one body, Slavicness and Latinity have waged, and continue to wage an implacable war in Poland, the stakes of which are life and death [...] Her future, if Poland has any sort of future, is in the Slavic world [...] not in some queue of Latinity."[18] Exactly for this reason Sergei Solovyov, Slavophile and messianist, was of the opinion that the partitioning of the Republic was nothing else than a just punishment for Poland's betrayal of Slavdom.[19] In the light of this, the Slavic Sláva could only have a significance to Klaczko as a counterbalance to German liberalism and Protestantism, when organized within the framework of the Catholic Habsburg Empire, and in no way as a scaffolding for Russian imperialism, Orthodoxy and Pan-Slavism, which was the open intention of the Russians at the Slavic Congress of 1867 in Moscow.

Polish culture contains within it the inseparable gene of Occidentalism, which cannot be removed. Our national conservatism cannot be torn away from Europe. Klaczko understood this perfectly, already as a young man during the events of the Spring of the Peoples, which transformed his attitude to Germany. The source of Europe, and thus also of the Occidentalism of our Polish culture, was never and never will be German universalism. And it is indifferent whether it speaks to us in the language of the Christian empire,

Enlightenment civilization, or liberalism. For the roots of our incurable Occidentalism are planted elsewhere: in the Latin, classical, and Christian South, to which Klaczko was to return in the 1880s in his two most splendid books: *Wieczory florenckie* (Florentine Evenings) and *Juliusz II* (Julius II).

Today, we need to read Klaczko's works again. Not because, as we stated at the beginning of this chapter, he was a renowned Polish political thinker of the nineteenth century, and thus an important part of our national, intellectual heritage, who demands to be treated in proper proportion to his historical rank. Above all, I suggest that Klaczko indicates a question which again today faces us as our greatest problem. We have become jaded with the West in its present character; above all, the West has disappointed us after thirty years of our nursing the hope of becoming an inseparable part of the same, the West, our natural home. That was an illusion, and not just only our illusion after all, which arose from the vast majority in Europe recognizing that an escape from ourselves, a running away from our very selves, was the only way to ensure that never again we should have to face what, following the long history of the nineteenth and twentieth centuries, constitutes our differentiation, our unique essences—and which is difficult, sometimes dangerous, but without which there is no real life. But all the same, it was a dream, an illusion. And so Europe dreamed on, and we dreamed along with her in these last few decades. What else but an escape into dreams was the idea of constructing a Europe without any borders, and so without its varied forms of life; what else was our aspiration to be the West—exactly that, an aspiring to it, and not "being" it? Now, however, because of what we call the European crisis or the crises of Europe, some phase of a general awakening is underway, which, for the sleepers, might seem a bitter experience. And so *être* and not *paraître*, which demands, however, a turning inward. "Whoever gazes outward, dreams. Whoever gazes inward, awakens," wrote Carl Jung, and this statement seems ever so apt to me today in reference to the situation currently reigning in Europe, and reigning among us as well. Today, just as then, in 1848, the same problem of the categorical universalism of the German liberals, and those from other parts of Europe and from the world at large, has become manifest—and those liberals wish still to gaze outward and dream. On the other hand, there is the problem of the national conservatives, who have ceased harboring the hope that freedom is there to build one's own place in the sun. The problem is profound, as such attitudes have begun to course throughout the entire continent. As I have striven to show in this book, they contain within them an entirely different understanding of form, a different approach to the world and to life, which expresses itself in the choice between a turning toward the good, a conversion to the good, and the idolatry of one void's own void. There is nothing wrong in turning inward in our search for the good—let us not allow anyone to shame us for it. But the thing is not to allow ourselves to be seduced, either. Let us not gaze at the West through the prism of German, radical universalism, for the West is something different, and it is constantly present in our culture. Poland will be Latin, or it will be nothing at all.

Endnotes

1. J. Klaczko, *Die deutschen Hegemonen* (The German Hegemons), Berlin 1849. See also the following text for Polish translations: J. Klaczko, "Niemieccy hegemoni. List otwarty do Georga Gerviniusa" (The German Hegemons. An Open Letter to Georg Gervinius), trans. Z. Baran, *Archiwum Historii Filozofii i Myśli Społecznej*, 1987, vol. 32, pp. 285–331.
2. Ibid.
3. S. Tarnowski, *Julian Klaczko*, Kraków 1909, pp. 29–30.
4. Citation from J. Kucharzewski, *Sprawa polska w parlamencie frankfurckim 1848 roku* (The Polish Question at the Frankfurt Parliament of 1848), Warsaw, undated, p. 20.
5. J. Klaczko, *Die deutschen...*, op. cit.
6. Cited by J. Kucharzewski, op. cit., p. 44.
7. Ibid., p. 45.
8. Ibid., p. 46.

9. G.W.F. Hegel, *Phenomenology of Spirit*, trans. A.V. Miller, ed. J.N. Findley, Oxford 1977.

10. T. Mann, *Germany and the Germans*, Washington 1945.

11. Ibid., p. 3.

12. Ibid., p. 13.

13. "List Seweryna Celarskiego do Rady Narodowej 2 VI 1848 r." (Letter of Seweryn Celarski to the National Council, 2 June 1848): *Slovanský sjezd...* (The Slavic Congress), pp. 238–239; cited by M. Chamczyk, "Zjazd słowiański w Pradze, 2–12 czerwca 1848 roku" (The Slavic Congress in Prague, 2–12 June 1848), *Młodsza Europa. Portal Europy Środkowo–Wschodniej*, 17.12.2010, http://www.mlodszaeuropa.eu/news/37/104/ Zjazd-slowianski-w-Pradze-2-12-czerwca-1848.html (accessed 17 December 2019).

14. As reported in the *Gazeta Polska*, ed. H. Cegielski, nr 69 (14 June), Poznań 1848, pp. 3–4. *Translator's note*: The word "Sláva" (Czech or Slovak, Polish spelling *Sława*) means "glory"; some nineteenth-century Slavs, especially those associated with Pan-Slavic or Austro-Slavic movements, derived the name "Slav" from this word. Czecho-Slovak poet Ján Kollár uses the term in reference to a mythical mother-goddess, partially of his own invention, in his extensive epic sonnet-cycle *Slávy dcera* (The Daughter of Sláva) 1824, 1852.

15. J. Klaczko, *Die deutschen...*, op. cit.

16. Ibid.

17. Ibid.

18. See K. Zernack, *Polen und Rußland. Zwei Wege in der europäischen Geschichte* (Poland and Russia. Two Paths in the History of Europe), Berlin 1994.

19. For more on this see K. Błachowska, *Wiele historii jednego państwa. Obraz dziejów Wielkiego Księstwa Litewskiego do 1569 r. w ujęciu historyków polskich, rosyjskich, ukraińskich, litewskich i białoruskich w XIX w.* (Many Histories of One State. An Image of the History of the Grand Duchy of Lithuania to the Year 1569 as Comprehended by Polish, Russian, Ukrainian, Lithuanian, and Belarusian Historians in the Nineteenth Century), Warszawa 2009.

ACKNOWLEDGEMENTS

This book arose as the result of my own thoughts and readings over the space of several years, but it would not have been possible without the support of some special people: those closest to me as well as friends and acquaintances. First of all, I would like to thank Ania Słota for our many conversations, which are reflected in the book as important inspirations. Ania, to a great extent, it is to your credit that this book was written!

I would also like to thank Dariusz Gawin and Dariusz Karłowicz for their Political Theology seminars, particularly those centered on the Piasts, which drew my attention to Wincenty Kadłubek's *Chronicle* and the novels of Iwaszkiewicz and Parnicki.

I also thank Mateusz Matyszkowicz for making me aware of the enormity of Eastern issues contained in *Mother Joanna of the Angels*.

SELECTED BIBLIOGRAPHY

Abel R., *The Gutenberg Revolution*, London 2012.

Aeschylos, *Oresteia*, trans. S. Goldhill, Cambridge 2004.

Augustine, *Confessions*, trans. T. Williams, Indianapolis/Cambridge 2019.

Backvis C., *Comment les Polonais du XVI-e siecle voyaient l'Italie et les Italiens*, "L'Annuaire de l'Institut de Philologie et d'Histoire Orientales et Slaves" (Bruxelles), vol. XV, 1960, pp. 195–288.

Balzer O., *Studyum o Kadłubku*, vol. 1–2, Lwów 1934.

Besançon A., *Sainte Russie*, Paris 2012.

Brague R., *Europe, la voie romaine*, Paris 1992.

Buonaccorsi F., *Vita et mores Gregorii Sanocei*, ed. I. Lichońska, Varsovia 1963.

Cat-Mackiewicz S., *Klucz do Piłsudskiego*, Kraków 2013.

Czapczyk P., Kubiak Z., *Klasyczne miary i świat współczesny*, Warszawa 2009.

Dobosz J., *Kazimierz II Sprawiedliwy*, Poznań 2011.

Eliot T.S., *Notes Toward the Definition of Culture*, New York 1949.

Erofeiev V., "Dans la maison européenne La Russie est une grande chambre sale" (In the House of Europe Russia is a Large Dirty Room), Boulevard Extérieur, 27 February 2015.

Gałczyński K.I., *Dzieła. Poezje*, vol. 1, Warszawa 1979.

Geoffrey of Monmouth, *History of the Kings of Britain*, trans. L. Thorpe, London 1977.

Gibbon E., *History of the Decline and Fall of the Roman Empire*, Basil 1789.

Goetel F., *Czasy wojny*, London 1955.

Goetel F., *Pod znakiem faszyzmu*, Warszawa 1938.

Gombrowicz W., *Diary*, trans. L. Vallee, Yale 2007.

Grzybowski S., *Jan Zamoyski*, Warszawa 1994.

Hegel G.W.F., *Phenomenology of Spirit*, trans. A.V. Miller, ed. J.N. Findley, Oxford 1977.

Heidenstein R., *Pamiętniki wojny moskiewskiej w 6 księgach*, trans. by J. Czubek, Warszawa 2017 (Latin text: *De bello Moscovitico commentariorum, libri VI*, Cracoviae 1584; German translation: H. Rätel, *Warhafte, gründliche und eigentliche Beschreibung des Krieges welchen... Stephan Batori... geführet*, Görlitz 1590).

Herodotus, *The Histories*, trans. T. Holland, London 2015.

Huxley A., *The Devils of Loudun*, London 1952.

Ilski K., *Idea jedności politycznej, społecznej i religijnej w świetle pism Ambrożego z Mediolanu*, Poznań 2001.

Iwaszkiewicz J., *Czerwone tarcze*, Warszawa 1994.

Iwaszkiewicz J., *Dzienniki*, vol. 3: 1964–1980, Warszawa 2011.

Iwaszkiewicz J., *Książka moich wspomnień*, Kraków 1957.

Iwaszkiewicz J., *Matka Joanna od Aniołów*, Warszawa 1975 (French translation: J. Iwaszkiewicz, *Mère Jeanne des Anges*, trans. G. Lisowski, Paris 1959).

John of Salisbury, *Policraticus: Of the Frivolities of Courtiers and the Footprints of Philosophers*, trans. Cary J. Nederman, Cambridge 2007.

Jasienica P., *Trzej kronikarze*, Warszawa 2008.

Kantorowicz E., *The King's Two Bodies: A Study in Mediaeval Political Theology*, Princeton 1957.

Kissinger H., *Diplomacy*, New York 1994.

Klaczko J., *Die deutschen Hegemonen, Offenes Schreiben an Herrn Georg Gervinus*, Berlin 1849.

Klaczko J., *Wieczory florenckie; Juliusz II*, Warszawa 1965.

Kochanowski J., *Dismissal of the Grecian Envoys*, trans. C.S. Kraszewski, Studio City, CA 1994.

Koehler K., *Boży podżegacz. Opowieść o Piotrze Skardze*, Warszawa 2012.

Kot S., *Polska złotego wieku i Europa*, Warszawa 1987.

Krasicki I., *Myszeidos: Canto X*, Wrocław 1986.

Kubiak Z., *Brewiarz Europejczyka*, Warszawa 1998.

Kucharzewski J., *Sprawa polska w parlamencie frankfurckim 1848 roku*, Warszawa 1908.

Kuryłowicz M., Witkowski W., *Rozprawa Jana Zamoyskiego o senacie rzymskim*, Lublin 1997.

Łempicki S., *Mecenat wielkiego kanclerza*, Warszawa 1980.

Mann T., *Germany and the Germans*, Washington 1945.

Memoriały polityczno-ustrojowe XV–XVI w. Monumentum *Jana Ostroroga i* Rady Kallimachowe, ed. A. Talarowski, Kraków 2024.

Modrzewski A.F., *Commentariorum de republica emendanda*, ed. C. Kumaniecki, Varsovia 1953.

Niemcewicz J.U., *Dzieje panowania Zygmunta III, króla polskiego, wielkiego księcia litewskiego itd.*, vol. 1–3, Kraków 1860.

Ostroróg J., *Monumentum pro Comitiis Generalibus Regni sub rege Casimiro pro reipublicae ordinatione congestum* in J. Domański, *Łacina w Polsce*, Kraków 2020, pp. 495–512.

Parnicki T., *Aecjusz, ostatni Rzymianin*, Warszawa 1957 (German translation: *Aetius, der letzte Römer*, trans. F. Griese, Frankfurt am Main 1989).

Parnicki T., *Historia w literaturę przekuwana*, Warszawa 1980.

Parnicki T., *Rodowód literacki*, Warszawa 1974.

Parnicki T., *Srebrne orły*, Warszawa 2004.

Pietras Z.S., *Bolesław Krzywousty*, Katowice 1978.

Pietrzyk-Reeves D., *Polish Republican Discourse in the Sixteenth Century*, Cambridge 2020.

Polska stanisławowska w oczach cudzoziemców, ed. W. Zawadzki, Warszawa 1963.

Rymkiewicz J.M., *Samuel Zborowski*, Warszawa 2010.

Shakespeare W., *Antony and Cleopatra*, London 1994.

Sobieski W., *Trybun ludu szlacheckiego*, Warszawa 1978.

Spengler O., *The Decline of the West*, trans. Ch.F. Atkinson, Oxford 1991.

Spieralski Z., *Jan Zamoyski*, Warszawa 1989.

Starowolski S., *De claris oratoribus sarmatiae. O znakomitych mówcach Sarmacji*, trans. E.J. Głębicka, Warszawa 2002.

Szwejkowska H., *Książka drukowana XV–XVIII wieku. Zarys historyczny*, Wrocław 1980.

Śliwiński A., *Jan Zamoyski. Kanclerz i hetman wielki koronny*, Warszawa 1947.

Tarnowski S., *Julian Klaczko*, Kraków 1909.

Thucydides, *The Peloponnesian War*, trans. M. Hammond, Oxford 2009.

Tuchman B., *A Distant Mirror: the Calamitous 14th Century*, New York 2011.

Wat A., *My Century. The Odyssey of a Polish Intellectual*, trans. R. Lourie, Berkeley and Los Angeles 1988.

Wincenty (called) Kadłubek, *Kronika polska*, trans. B. Kürbis, Wrocław 2003 (Latin text: *Magistri Vincentii dicti Kadłubek Chronica Polonorum*, ed. M. Plezia, Kraków 1994).

Windakiewicz S., *Polacy w Padwie*, Kraków 1922.

Wojciechowski T., *Szkice historyczne jedynastego wieku*, Kraków 1904.

Wybór mów staropolskich świeckich sejmowych i innych, collected by A. Małecki, Kraków 1860.

Wybór mów staropolskich, choice and edition by B. Nadolski, Wrocław 1961.

Zaborowski S., *Traktat w czterech częściach o naturze praw i dóbr królewskich oraz o naprawie królestwa i o kierowaniu państwem*, trans. H. Litwin, J. Staniszewski, Kraków 2005.

Zernack K., *Polen und Rußland. Zwei Wege in der europäischen Geschichte*, Berlin 1994.

Żółkiewski S., *Początek i progres wojny moskiewskiej*, Warszawa 1966.

INDEX

A

B

C

R

S

Š/Ś

T

U

V